THE COLONIAL OFFICE AND NIGERIA, 1898–1914

THE COLONIAL OFFICE AND NIGERIA, 1898–1914

John M. Carland

Hoover Institution Press
Stanford University
Stanford, California

The Hoover Institution on War, Revolution and Peace, founded at Stanford University in 1919 by the late President Herbert Hoover, is an interdisciplinary research center for advanced study on domestic and international affairs in the twentieth century. The views expressed in its publications are entirely those of the authors and do not necessarily reflect the views of the staff, officers, or Board of Overseers of the Hoover Institution.

Hoover Press Publication 314
First printing, 1985
Printed in Hong Kong
89 88 87 86 85   9 8 7 6 5 4 3 2 1

Library of Congress Cataloging in Publication Data
Carland, John M., 1942–
    The Colonial Office and Nigeria, 1898–1914.

    Bibliography: p.
    Includes index.
    1. Nigeria--Politics and government--To 1960.
2. Nigeria--Economic conditions--To 1960.   3. Great
Britain.   Colonial Office.   I. Title.
DT515.75.C37 1985   325'.341'09669   84–15712
ISBN 0–8179–8141–1

To
Kathryn Allen Carland
and
Harold Maxwell Carland (1915–84)
who by their example
taught me that reading was fun

Contents

Acknowledgements

I would like to acknowledge the following individuals and institutions in whose debt, after writing this book, I find myself.

Professor A. P. Thornton of the University of Toronto became my mentor in 1970 and, later on, my friend. I went to Toronto to study with him after reading *The Imperial Idea and its Enemies*. Throughout the years at Toronto Professor Thornton, as major field adviser and dissertation director, was always available but never intrusive. He was always ready, willing, and able to provide what I, as a graduate student, needed in the way of academic and intellectual assistance. He suffered through more than one revision of my thesis (an early version of this book) giving valuable conceptual and editorial advice. In all this I can recall only one Thorntonian dictum on how to organise one's written work ('watch the number of chapters, keep it to a maximum of eight, if humanly possible'), which, as anyone can plainly see, he himself follows. Professor Thornton greatly contributed to making my graduate student years – intellectually and personally – both enjoyable and productive.

The planning, research, and writing of the thesis was generously supported by an Open Fellowship from the University of Toronto, a grant from the University of Toronto's International Studies Programme, and two Province of Ontario Graduate Fellowships. Since the foundation of the book is in the thesis it is fitting that these sources of financial assistance be acknowledged. In a period of declining support for graduate studies in the United States and elsewhere I am extremely grateful to Canadian institutions for making my doctoral research and degree possible.

The turning-point in the process by which the thesis was transformed into a book came in 1979. By that time I had returned to the United States and had been teaching at the University of Kentucky for two years. Part of the summer of 1979 had been spent in England doing further research, mostly in Treasury files, on the Colonial Office and Nigerian policy. This research was funded by the

University of Kentucky Research Foundation. During late 1979 and throughout 1980 I reflected on this new material and integrated it with material gathered in England during 1972–3. I gradually began to understand the possibilities inherent in the research. Out of this understanding came the argument and conclusions which justify this book.

While writing this book (1980–3) I incurred other debts. Raymond Betts of the University of Kentucky gave one chapter, while it was in article form, a critical reading and made constructive suggestions. Ralph Austin of the University of Chicago did the same. Lewis Gann of the Hoover Institution on War, Revolution and Peace read the entire rewritten manuscript. I might add that Dr Gann additionally gave advice, encouragement, and assistance when all three were very much needed.

I would also like to thank the editors of *Albion, The Historian,* and *The International History Review* for their kind permission to reproduce, in slightly different form, the following material: 'Public Expenditure and Development in a Crown Colony: The Colonial Office, Sir Walter Egerton, and Southern Nigeria, 1900–1912,' in *Albion,* 12(1980), which appears as Chapter 3 here; 'Budgetary Conflict and the Northern Nigerian Revenue Estimates, 1899–1913', in *The Historian,* 45(1984), which appears as Chapter 4 here; and 'Enterprise and Empire: Officials, Entrepreneurs, and the Search for Petroleum in Southern Nigeria, 1906–1914', in *The International History Review,* 4(1982), which appears as Chapter 7 here.

I am indebted to the following for permission to publish material of which they have copyright: the Controller of Her Majesty's Stationery Office for use of Crown copyright material in the Public Record Office; the Bodleian Library, Oxford University, for use of the Harcourt Papers; the British Library for use of the Campbell-Bannerman Papers and the Strachey Papers; Churchill College, Cambridge University, for use of the Lyttelton Papers; Rhodes House Library, Oxford University, for use of the Holt Papers and the Lugard Papers; the third Lord Southborough for the use of the first Lord Southborough's (Sir Francis Hopwood's) private papers; and University Library, Cambridge University, for use of the Crewe Papers.

I would additionally like to thank Barbara Bentley and Dorothy Leathers for typing an early draft and Sharon Hamilton for typing the final draft of this manuscript. It was no easy task.

Finally I would like to acknowledge a debt to Maria Pinto Carland too great to be discharged by mere admission of its existence. She has been thesis and manuscript editor of the first and sometimes last resort. She has helped me to understand that research has to be moulded and shaped and, most importantly, thought about. I also owe her greatly for moral support given across the years. In as much as these things can be done with words, I acknowledge, with love and gratitude, what she has given me.

Lexington, Kentucky   JOHN M. CARLAND

List of Tables

List of Maps

Cast of Characters

*Anderson, John** (1882–1958). Entered Colonial Office, 1905; Secretary, Northern Nigerian Lands Committee (1908) and West African Currency Committee (1910–11); transferred to National Insurance Commission, 1912; Secretary to Minister of Shipping, 1917; Chairman, Board of Inland Revenue, 1919; Joint Under Secretary, Irish Office, 1920; Permanent Under Secretary, Home Office, 1922; Governor of Bengal, 1932; Member of Parliament (Independent), 1938–50; Member of War Cabinet, 1940; Chancellor of the Exchequer, 1943–5; knighted, 1919; created first Viscount Waverley, 1952.

Anderson, John (1858–1918). Entered Colonial Office, 1879; Joint editor, *Colonial Office List*, 1885–91, and Editor, 1892–7; Senior Clerk, 1896; Principal Clerk, 1897; Governor, Straits Settlements, and High Commissioner, Federated Malay States, 1904–11; Permanent Under Secretary, 1911–15; Governor of Ceylon, 1916–18; knighted, 1911.

Antrobus, Reginald (1853–1942). Entered Colonial Office, 1877; Private Secretary to various Secretaries of State for the Colonies, 1880–9, and to the Permanent Under Secretary and the Parliamentary Under Secretary, 1892; Acting Governor, St Helena, 1889–90; Senior Clerk, 1894; Principal Clerk, 1896; Assistant Under Secretary, 1898–1909; Senior Crown Agent, 1909–18; knighted, 1911.

Baynes, Denman (1885–1918). Entered Colonial Office, 1908; Secretary, West African Currency Board, 1912; on leave to serve in Army, 1915; awarded Military Cross and died in action, 1918.

Bell, Hesketh (1864–1952). Clerk in Governors' offices, Barbados and the Windward Islands, 1882; Official, Gold Coast, 1890;

* In the text the elder Anderson is 'Sir John Anderson' and the younger is 'John Anderson' or plain 'Anderson'.

xiii

Administrator, Dominica, 1899; Commissioner (and later Governor), Uganda, 1906; Governor, Northern Nigeria, 1909; Governor, Leeward Islands, 1912; Governor, Mauritius, 1916–24, knighted, 1908.

Butler, Frederick (1873–1961). Entered Admiralty, 1896; transferred to Colonial Office, 1897; Secretary, West African Currency Committee, 1899; Private Secretary to Parliamentary Under Secretaries (the Duke of Marlborough, 1904, and Winston Churchill, 1905); Senior Clerk, 1907; Private Secretary to the Secretaries of State for the Colonies (Lewis Harcourt, 1912, and Bonar Law, 1917); Principal Clerk, 1916; transferred to Foreign Office; 1917; Assistant Under Secretary, Foreign Office, 1933–40; knighted, 1920.

Chamberlain, Joseph (1836–1914). In business until 1873; Mayor of Birmingham, 1873–5; Member of Parliament (Liberal), 1876–86; Member of Parliament (Liberal Unionist), 1886–1914; President, Board of Trade, 1880–5; President, Local Government Board, 1886; Secretary of State for the Colonies, 1895–1903; resigned from Cabinet and led Tariff Reform campaign, 1903–6.

Churchill, Winston Spencer (1874–1965). Son of Lord Randolph Churchill; entered Parliament as Conservative, 1901; changed to Liberal Party, 1904; Parliamentary Under Secretary for the Colonies, 1905–8; President, Board of Trade, 1908–10; Secretary of State for the Home Office, 1910–11; First Lord of the Admiralty, 1911–15; Minister of Munitions, 1917–19; Secretary of State of the War Office and Air Office, 1919–21; Secretary of State for the Colonies, 1921–2; changed to Conservative Party, 1924; Chancellor of the Exchequer, 1924–9; First Lord of the Admiralty, 1939–40; Prime Minister, 1940–5, and 1951–5; knighted, 1953.

Crew, first Earl of (1858–1945). Robert Offley Ashburton Crewe-Milnes; Assistant Private Secretary to Lord Granville, Foreign Office, 1883; 2nd Baron Houghton, 1885; Lord-Lieutenant of Ireland, 1892–5; Earl of Crewe, 1895; Secretary of State for the Colonies, 1908–10; Secretary of State for India, 1910–15; Marquess of Crewe, 1911; British Ambassador in Paris, 1922–8.

Egerton, Walter (1858–1947). Cadet, Straits Settlements, 1880; Magistrate, Singapore, 1881; Collector, Penang, 1883; Acting Resident, Penang, 1894; 1st Magistrate, Penang, 1897; British Resident,

Negri Sembilan, Malay Peninsula, 1902; High Commissioner, Southern Nigeria, 1903–6; Governor, Lagos, 1904–6; Governor, Southern Nigeria, 1906; Governor, British Guiana, 1912–17; knighted, 1905.

Elgin, ninth Earl of (1849–1917). Victor Alexander Bruce; Commissioner of Works, 1886; Viceroy of India, 1894–9; Chairman, Royal Commission on the War in South Africa, 1902–3; Chairman, Royal Commission on Free Churches Controversy in Scotland, 1904; Chairman, Royal Commission on the Administration of the Scottish Churches Act, 1905; Secretary of State for the Colonies, 1905–8; Chancellor, University of Aberdeen, 1914–17.

Ezechiel, Percy H. (1875–1950). Entered Colonial Office, 1898; called to Bar, Middle Temple, 1903; Secretary to Crown Agents, 1905–20; 3rd Crown Agent for the Colonies, 1920–37; knighted, 1935.

Fiddes, George V. (1858–1936). Entered Colonial Office, 1881; Senior Clerk, 1896; Imperial Secretary to Lord Milner in South Africa, 1897–1902; Principal Clerk, Colonial Office, 1902; Accounting Officer, Colonial Office, 1907; Assistant Under Secretary, 1909; Permanent Under Secretary, 1916–21; knighted, 1912.

Geikie, Roderick (1874–1910). Entered Local Government Board, 1897; transferred to Colonial Office, 1899; Secretary, Railways and Concessions Committee, Colonial Office, 1907.

Girouard, Percy (1867–1932). Engineer, Canadian Pacific Railway, 1886–8; Railway Traffic Manager, Royal Arsenal, Woolwich, 1890–5; Director, Sudan Railway, 1896–8; Director of Railways, South African Field Force, 1899–1902; Commissioner of Railways, Transvaal and Orange River Colonies, 1902–4; High Commissioner and Governor, Northern Nigeria, 1907; Governor, East African Protectorate, 1909–12; knighted, 1900.

Grindle, Gilbert (1869–1934). Entered Local Government Board, 1893; called to Bar, Lincoln's Inn, 1895; transferred to Colonial Office, 1896; Senior Clerk, 1900; Principal Clerk, 1909; Assistant Under Secretary, 1916; Deputy Permanent Under Secretary, 1925–31; knighted, 1922.

Hamilton, William Baillie (1844–1920). Entered Colonial Office, 1864; Secret Service mission in British North America, 1867; called to Bar, 1872; Principal Clerk, 1894, Chief Clerk, 1896–1908; knighted, 1897.

Harcourt, Lewis (1863–1922). Private Secretary to his father, 1881–1904; entered Parliament, 1904; Secretary of State for the Colonies, 1910–15; First Commissioner of Works, 1915–16; created first Viscount Harcourt, 1917.

Harding, Alfred (1878–1953). Entered Colonial Office, 1901; Private Secretary to Lords Crewe and Harcourt; Senior Clerk, 1912; Assistant Secretary, 1920; Director of Colonial Audit, 1928–41; knighted, 1935.

Hopwood, Francis (1860–1947). Solicitor, Board of Trade, 1885–92; Private Secretary to President of the Board of Trade, 1892–3; Secretary, Railway Department, Board of Trade, 1893–1901; Permanent Secretary, Board of Trade, 1901–7; Permanent Under Secretary, Colonial Office, 1907–11; Additional Civil Lord, Admiralty, 1912–17; Secretary, Irish Convention, 1917–18; knighted, 1901; created first Baron Southborough, 1917.

Lugard, Frederick (1858–1945). Entered Royal Military College, Sandhurst, 1878; commissioned in the 9th Foot (Norfolk Regiment), 1878; on active duty in India until 1887; served on Gordon Relief Mission, 1885; received DSO for work as transport officer in Burmese War, 1885–6; raised and commanded West African Frontier Force, 1897–9; High Commissioner, Northern Nigeria, 1900; Governor, Hong Kong, 1907; Governor, Northern and Southern Nigeria, 1912–13; Governor-General, Nigeria, 1914–19; knighted, 1901; created first Baron Lugard, 1928.

Lyttelton, Alfred (1857–1913). Called to Bar, 1881; entered Parliament, 1895; Secretary of State for the Colonies, 1903–5.

McCallum, Henry (1852–1919). Served as military and colonial administrator in British Far East, 1874–97; Governor, Lagos, 1897; Governor, Newfoundland, 1899; Governor, Natal, 1901; Governor, Ceylon, 1907–13; knighted, 1898.

MacGregor, William (1848–1919). Assistant Medical Officer, Seychelles, 1873; Surgeon, Civil Hospital, Mauritius, 1874; Chief Medical Officer, Fiji, 1875; Administrator, Acting High Commissioner, and Consul-General, Western Pacific, and Administrator of British New Guinea, 1888; Lieutenant-Governor, New Guinea, 1895; Governor, Lagos, 1899; Governor, Newfoundland, 1904; Governor, Queensland, 1909–14; knighted, 1889.

Mercer, William (1855–1932). Entered Colonial Office, 1879; called to Bar, Inner Temple, 1886; Senior Clerk, 1896; Principal Clerk, 1898; Crown Agent, 1900–20; Senior Crown Agent, 1920–1; knighted, 1914.

Moor, Ralph (1860–1909). Royal Irish Constabulary, 1882–91; Commandant of Constabulary, Oil Rivers Protectorate, 1891; Vice-Consul, 1892–6; Commissioner and Consul-General, Niger Coast Protectorate, 1896–1900; High Commissioner, Southern Nigeria, 1900–3; retired from colonial service and worked for Sir Alfred Jones, 1903–9; knighted, 1898.

Olivier, Sydney (1859–1943). Entered Colonial Office, 1882; General Secretary, Fabian Society, 1886–90; Acting Colonial Secretary, British Honduras, 1890–1; Auditor General, Leeward Islands, 1895–6; Senior Clerk, Colonial Office, 1897; Principal Clerk, 1904; Governor, Jamaica, 1907; Permanent Secretary, Board of Agriculture and Fisheries, 1913; Assistant Comptroller and Auditor of the Exchequer, 1917–20; Secretary of State for India, 1924; knighted, 1907; created first Baron Olivier, 1924.

Ommanney, Montagu (1842–1925). Trained as engineer, Royal Military Academy, Woolwich; employed by War Office and Admiralty, 1864–7; employed by Royal Military Academy, 1867–74; Private Secretary to Secretary of State for the Colonies Lord Carnarvon, 1874–7; Crown Agent for the Colonies, 1877–1900; Permanent Under Secretary, Colonial Office, 1900–7; knighted, 1890.

Selbourne, second Earl of (1859–1942). William Palmer; Private Secretary, at various times, to the Lord Chancellor, Secretary of State for War, and the Chancellor of the Exchequer; Parliamentary Under Secretary, Colonial Office, 1895; First Lord of the Admiralty,

1900; High Commissioner, South Africa, 1905–10; President, Board of Agriculture and Fisheries, 1915–16.

Strachey, Charles (1862–1942). Entered Foreign Office, 1885; transferred to Colonial Office as Senior Clerk, 1898; Principal Clerk, 1907; Assistant Under Secretary, 1924–7; knighted, 1926.

Wingfield, Edward (1834–1910).Called to Bar, Lincoln's Inn, 1859; entered Colonial Office as Legal Assistant Under Secretary, 1878; Permanent Under Secretary, 1897–1900; knighted, 1899.

Introduction

By the late 1890s diplomatic manoeuvring in Europe and military posturing in Africa had resulted in a British Empire in tropical Africa of which the British Government and people were largely ignorant. What was to be done with these new possessions? *The Colonial Office and Nigeria, 1898–1914* describes what was done with one important group of British tropical possessions – the Crown Colonies of Lagos, Southern Nigeria, and Northern Nigeria.* The Colonial Office tended to think of these territories as a unity, because they were physically contiguous, and called them Nigeria. (Before 1914 'Nigeria' was purely a geographical expression. However, it will be used here as a term to refer to the whole area, except when one of the three colonies is being specifically discussed.) In 1906 Lagos and Southern Nigeria joined to form the Colony of Southern Nigeria, and then in 1914 that combination and Northern Nigeria were amalgamated to form the Colony of Nigeria. The Colonial Office policies established before 1914 led to the creation of the political, administrative, economic, and financial infrastructure that was to carry Nigeria through the colonial period and into the post-independence era. Because Nigeria was the flagship of Britain's tropical empire these policies were often followed in other parts of British tropical Africa. Therefore an analysis of how this came about is important. The British–Nigerian story, and the Colonial Office's role in it, though specialised, is one that speaks for a number of problems which plague the Third World today.

Crown Colony Government in Nigeria and elsewhere in the British Empire was autocratic government. Officials at the Colonial Office and colonial governors in the field never pretended otherwise. In fact, autocratic, bureaucratic rule was the true legacy of British

* Technically speaking, Northern Nigeria and Southern Nigeria were Protectorates, not possessions, of the British Crown. This was, however, a difference without a distinction. By 1900 the Colonial Office treated Protectorates in almost every way the same as it did Crown Colonies. They were both non-self-governing dependencies. Therefore, for the sake of convenience, the two Nigerias will be called Crown Colonies throughout this book.

1

colonial government in Africa. In this book we shall examine the role of the Colonial Office in establishing and maintaining that legacy. However, it should be emphasised that Crown Colony Government in the British Empire of the late nineteenth and early twentieth centuries was an end in itself; no one imagined that it was the first step toward colonial political development. It should also be kept in mind that the Colonial Office did not administer, it supervised administration. Thus a good deal of the Colonial Office's work concerned not only the formation of policy but also the supervision of its implementation.

This study inquires into the formation and implementation of British policy for Nigeria after the partition and during the administrative occupation of Africa by the European Powers. It is done with special reference to the work of permanent officials at the Colonial Office (see Table I.1). The most important conclusion to emerge from this work is that the Colonial Office, before 1914, was in charge of the Colonial Empire. The Colonial Office fended off challenges from other Whitehall departments and from colonial governors who attempted to impose their own imprint on colonial policy. This accomplishment was the result of the attitude of the Colonial Office staff towards the Colonial Empire and their work as overseers of that Empire.

THE HISTORICAL CONTEXT

The context of this inquiry is British-occupied Nigeria from the Anglo-French Convention of 1898 to the 1914 Nigerian amalgamation. These years form a natural period in British–Nigerian history. The Anglo-French Convention settled the last major disputed area in West Africa – the boundaries of Northern Nigeria – and symbolised the end of the partition of West Africa. As one Colonial Office official said, 1898 marked 'the end of one period and the beginning of a new one in West African history'.[1] Until that time Britain's main interest had been partition and its diplomatic context: little consideration had been given to Nigeria's future. The tiny Colony of Lagos had been supervised by the Colonial Office since 1861, while the Niger Coast Protectorate – until 1894 the Oil Rivers Protectorate – and the territory of the Royal Niger Company came under the Foreign Office. These latter two territories later became, with some important border adjustments, respectively Southern and Northern Nigeria.

TABLE I.1   *Offices and office holders related to Nigerian business at the Colonial Office, 1898–1914*

Secretaries of State

Joseph Chamberlain	1895–1903
Alfred Lyttelton	1903–1905
Earl of Elgin	1905–1908
Earl of Crewe	1908–1910
Lewis Harcourt	1910–1915

Permanent Under Secretaries

Sir E. Wingfield	1897–1900
*Sir R. Herbert	Oct. 1899–March 1900
Sir M. Ommanney	1900–1907
Sir F. Hopwood	1907–1910
Sir J. Anderson	1910–1915

Parliamentary Under Secretaries

Earl of Selborne	1895–1900
Earl of Onslow	1900–1903
Duke of Marlborough	1903–1905
W. S. Churchill	1905–1908
J. E. B. Seely	1908–1911
Lord Lucas	March–Oct. 1911
Lord Emmot	1911–1914

Assistant Under Secretaries

H. B. Cox	1897–1898
R. L. Antrobus	1898–1909
G. V. Fiddes	1909–1915

Department Heads

R. L. Antrobus	1896–1898
W. H. Mercer	1898–1900
W. B. Hamilton	1900–1906
S. Olivier	1906–1907
C. Strachey	1907–1924

Senior Clerks

F. G. A. Butler
C. Davis
A. J. Harding
D. Malcolm
W. H. Mercer
C. Strachey

Junior Clerks

J. Anderson	G. Grindle
D. Baynes	R. Geikie
F. G. A. Butler	A. B. Keith
E. R. Darnley	E. Machtig
P. H. Ezechiel	J. Robinson
A. Gray	

* Herbert was Permanent Under Secretary from 1871–92 and was brought out of retirement after Wingfield suffered his stroke and before Ommanney took office.

In 1898 the Colonial Office was about to take over these two territories, and finally did at the beginning of 1900. To insure the smoothest takeover possible the Foreign Office proposed that an interdepartmental committee be set up to 'discuss the arrangements for . . . future administration'.[2] Joseph Chamberlain, Secretary of

State for the Colonies, took control of the committee and appointed his Parliamentary Under Secretary, the Earl of Selborne, to chair it. Chamberlain then set the terms of reference for the committee. It was to make recommendations on the following:

1. viz., the future administration of the 3 territories, Lagos, Niger Protectorate, and Niger Company's territory including Sokoto, etc. Is it to be united under one head?
If not, under how many administrations and with what limits?
What are to be the seats of government?
What arrangements for military forces?
What customs duties? There must be a customs union.
What other – if any – taxation?
What estimate of cost – and how provided?
2. What is to be our future policy for Sokoto, etc?
As to a Resident, As to Railways, As to Bornu, As to Rabeh.*
I do not suppose that we can make a definite settlement but a discussion will be of great value in opening up the questions to be decided.[3]

Henceforth, British Nigerian policy would centre, not on diplomatic negotiations but on the administrative occupation of Nigeria. The committee's report symbolised it; it was also in some respects a blueprint for this process.

The administrative occupation was completed, symbolically and actually, with the amalgamation of Southern Nigeria and Northern Nigeria on 1 January 1914, when Nigeria ceased being simply a geographical expression and became also a constitutional unit and an administrative unity. Regarding the amalgamation, it has been claimed variously that it was a sign of British confidence; that it was not meant to create a new nation; that it sowed the seeds of civil war; and even that it never really took place.[4] However, the point is that it

* Sokoto, in the northwest of present-day Nigeria, was in 1898 the political centre of the powerful Fulani Empire. Bornu was an ancient West African state which ran from the eastern border of the Fulani Empire to Lake Chad. When Chamberlain wrote his minute neither deemed itself subject to British control, even though the British held a paper sovereignty, recognised by the states of Europe, over the area occupied by each state. Rabeh, an adventurer from the eastern Sudan, had been a close associate of the Mahdi (who had had General Gordon killed at Khartoum). Rabeh had, in the middle 1890s, conquered Bornu. Both Bornu and Sokoto represented serious threats to the British position. What happened in Sokoto is discussed in Chapter 2, while the French fortuitously killed Rabeh and defeated his troops in a fierce battle in 1900.

represented the end of an era. In these sixteen years, from 1898 to
1914, the Colonial Office faced all the problems – administrative,
economic, and financial – attendant upon the establishment of new
colonies. For this reason, the period is especially suitable for a study
of the role of permanent officials at the Colonial Office as overseers
of Nigerian development.

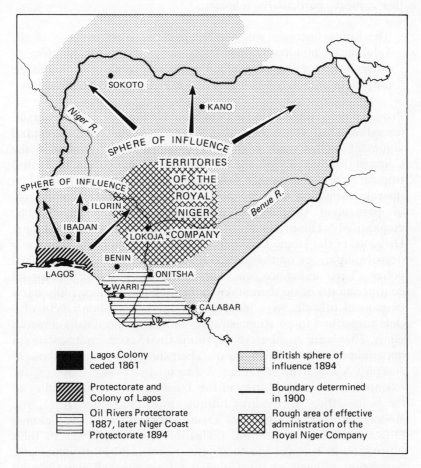

MAP 1 *The growth of British influence in Nigeria – to 1900*

SOURCE: Michael Crowder, *The Story of Nigeria* (revised and expanded edition,
London, 1966) p. 189.

THE ARGUMENT: SOURCES, REASONS, AND REASONING

This study is based primarily on Colonial Office and, to a lesser extent, Treasury records at the Public Record Office in London. Of particular value were the minutes attached to official and semi-official correspondence and other Colonial Office and Treasury documents. What A. Taylor Milne said about the minutes of permanent officials and political masters at the Colonial Office is, in this context, particularly relevant:

> The future historian will need to make a selective study of the voluminous minutes written upon almost every file in order to determine the influence wielded by the respective officials and the amount of authority which they . . . exercised upon their masters.[5]

Private papers of the Secretaries of State for the Colonies during this period were also consulted. Using Nigeria as a case study, the central argument of this work is that the Colonial Office controlled the Colonial Empire during the administrative occupation of British tropical Africa. Since other Colonial Office studies have focused on the role of the Secretary of State, it is fitting that analysis of the role of permanent officials concerned with Nigerian business be emphasised.[6] These officials, members of the First Class, or Upper Division, of the Home Civil Service, had a considerable, frequently decisive, influence on the formation and implementation of colonial policy. Their influence was not based on imperial ideological considerations, or on their stake in the Colonial Empire (only a few permanent officials were ideological imperialists). Permanent officials subscribed to an administrative and not a specifically imperial ethos. They were members of the Home Civil Service, not acolytes to imperial prophets and high priests. Their standards were not those of Joseph Chamberlain or Frederick Lugard but rather those of, for example, Sir George Murray of the Treasury, Sir Arthur Godley of the India Office, Sir Godfrey Lushington of the Home Office, and Robert Giffen of the Board of Trade. As members of the Colonial Office staff, officials' central obligation and loyalty was to their office, and its survival was their primary concern. More important, permanent officials at the Colonial Office believed the Colonial Empire to be their special preserve, their own special territory. In consequence, these officials resisted challenges to their Office's domination of the Colonial Empire, and did so successfully, out of a sense of Robert Ardey's 'territorial imperative'.[7] The affairs of the Colonial Empire were the affairs of the Colonial Office and officials there would brook no interference.

This being the case they worked to enhance the supremacy of their office over the Colonial Empire and over questions relating to it. The Colonial Office might engage in negotiations with the Treasury over financing a colonial railway or balancing a colonial budget, or struggle with a colonial governor over the use of the colony's income for economic development. The point to make, and one which will be argued throughout, is that the Colonial Office usually prevailed. Officials and political masters acted vigorously to assert and defend Colonial Office prerogatives. Even so, co-operation and not confrontation was, when possible, the Office's preferred stance.

An important sub-theme in this book concerns relations between the Colonial Office and Treasury *vis-à-vis* colonial public finance and development. In the past the Treasury has been presented as having an undue influence on colonial policy or, alternatively – and less frequently – very little influence. Research in the records of the Colonial Office and Treasury suggests that what frequently was obtained was a spirit of co-operation. What is perhaps controversial is the conclusion that when co-operation did not prevail, the Colonial Office did. Based on this study there seemed to be two poles to the Colonial Office–Treasury relationship: at one end there was co-operation, and at the other there was an independent Colonial Office. For the most part, however, the relationship was a constructive one characterised by a general desire to get the job done.

Indeed, on most matters Colonial Office staff was essentially flexible and pragmatic rather than ideological. This flies in the face of conventional wisdom which asserts that these men were members of a conservative upper middle class and therefore conservatives themselves whose impact could only be conservative. This was not the case, and their actions cannot in fact be assessed in these terms. To do so would be to mistake being cautious – which they were to an extreme – with being conservative. On one occasion they might act in a liberal or progressive way; on another their action would seem patently retrograde. For example, Colonial Office officials allowed the Southern Nigerian Government to lend £25,000 to a private company engaged in a search for petroleum in Southern Nigeria. At the time this was rather progressive, not to say ingenious. This is also true of officials' work on developing railways in Nigeria. On the other hand, their response to Governor Sir Walter Egerton's developmentally oriented budgets was decidedly conservative and fiscally orthodox. And their reaction to Sir Frederick Lugard's system of indirect rule was to strip it of any progressive merit and establish it as an exceedingly conservative precedent that would influence British tropical African government for decades. Superficially, inconsistency and contradiction seem the most obvious characteristics of officials' work – but only if one wishes to judge them in terms of conventional political philosophy. One can perhaps get closer to the heart of the matter by examining permanent officials' actions and reactions in a situation involving pure administration rather than substantive colonial issues. Such a situation occurred when Lugard proposed that he should remain in charge of Nigeria even when on leave. Officials engaged Lugard in a long and acrimonious dispute over this scheme of continuous administration. Permanent officials feared that if Lugard's proposal was accepted they might be eliminated from much of the decision-making process. They were not willing to allow this. One can see clearly that their intention was to dominate their area of concern – the Colonial Empire in its metropolitan and peripheral spheres.

THE PLAN OF THE BOOK AND SOME FINAL POINTS

This book is in the mainstream of recent work on the Colonial Office. It is also, one hopes, a positive contribution to British–Nigerian and to British administrative history. It is divided into three parts: (i) a description of how the Colonial Office operated and profiles of those who operated it (Chapter 1); (ii) case studies involving the Colonial Office and the formation and implementation of administrative, economic, and financial policies for Nigeria (Chapters 2 to 7); and (iii) a summary analysis which explains the actions of the Colonial Office staff and the impact such actions had on British colonial policies in Nigeria before 1914.

Three more points should be made. At times, Nigerians are referred to as 'natives'. This is not meant pejoratively and should not be taken as such. This usage, when it occurs, is a function of the historical context of this work. Second, because of the nature of this work – a series of topical case studies about various facets of the same subject – there is occasional unavoidable repetition. Third, although only one chapter actually begins with the year 1898 and only two end in 1914, it should be evident that the 1898–1914 dates are absolutely accurate in a general and symbolic sense.

1 The Colonial Office and Nigeria, 1898–1914

To fully explain what the Colonial Office did for Nigeria it is necessary to know both the workers and the context of their work. Therefore this chapter describes and explains the Colonial Office – its organisation, its purpose, and its procedures – and its personnel. This chapter also points out the similarity of the Colonial Office to other Whitehall departments, and emphasises the fact that the Upper Division clerks at the Colonial Office who handled Nigerian business were typical of Upper Division clerks throughout the Civil Service.[1] Once this is made clear, it is equally clear that Colonial Office officials operated essentially according to an administrative ethos, though their work was on imperial affairs.

OFFICE ORGANISATION AND WORK PROCEDURES AT THE COLONIAL OFFICE

The work of the Colonial Office was based on the written word – correspondence to and from colonial governors, other government offices, non-governmental organisations, and individuals. Thus the bulk of the work came from 'a despatch, a petition, a complaint, a request for instructions, or a communication'.[2] In as much as the Colonial Office's clerks, i.e. permanent officials, had any contact with the public, it was with those belonging to their natural constituencies – financial, commercial, scientific, and humanitarian organisations that had a specific interest in some part of the Empire. Members of these groups formed deputations that frequently met with the Secretary of State to make representations on some aspect of colonial policy. On a more informal basis, representatives of these groups might regularly visit and confer with permanent officials or the responsible Assistant Under Secretary. But outside of these occasions the permanent officials saw more paper in the Colonial Office than people.

The basic administrative unit in the Colonial Office was the Department, composed of four Upper Division clerks: the Head of the Department, a Senior and two Junior Clerks. The Department head was always a Principal Clerk. Senior and Junior Clerks were also known as, respectively, First Class and Second Class Clerks. With the exception of a General Department, the departments were organised geographically. Thus the business of the colonies and protectorates of Lagos, Southern Nigeria, and Northern Nigeria was handled by the Nigeria Department.* It was set up in 1898 in anticipation of the Colonial Office taking over from the Foreign Office the Niger Coast Protectorate and the Royal Niger Company's territory. These territories would become Southern Nigeria and Northern Nigeria in 1900. (Lagos had been under the Colonial Office since 1861.) The Colonial Office Permanent Under Secretary and the Assistant Under Secretary in charge of West African business supervised the Nigeria Department. These officials, as a group, were charged with the 'consultative and deliberative' (i.e. the policy-advising and intellectual) work of the Office.[3] Above them was the political head of the Colonial Office, the Secretary of State for the Colonies, and his Parliamentary Under Secretary of State (who existed outside the functional administrative chain). The mechanical work of the Office – filing, registering, copying, and typing – were done by Lower, or Second, Division clerks who were separated from the first division by an 'impassable gulf'.[4]

What was expected of the members of a Department? Junior Clerks were required to ensure that all relevant papers were attached to a file under consideration.[5] They were also permitted – and this was the intellectual attraction of the job – to read, research, and minute despatches and letters, and to draft replies. However, this aspect of the system did not meet with universal approbation. In 1888 Sir Robert Herbert, Permanent Under Secretary at the Colonial Office, suggested that Junior Clerks had abused this privilege by minuting 'too much'. He reluctantly admitted, however, that they did good work even though it was 'excessively laboured, as in India'.[6] In 1912 a member of the Royal Commission on the Civil Service asked Sir John Anderson, then Permanent Under Secretary at the Colonial Office: 'Is a young man of 23 who comes fresh from the university,

* For the sake of convenience, the term 'Nigeria Department' will be used throughout this book, although it was not in use at the Colonial Office until 1918. One may construct the complete story of the Nigeria Department's organisational development by consulting the *Colonial Office List*, an annual publication, for the years 1898 to 1918.

who has never had any work to do, and no business experience whatever, competent at once to advise the secretary of state on matters of policy?' Anderson: 'He is allowed to try.' The questioner followed this up by asking, 'That may account then for some of the official answers which we get in the House of Commons sometimes?' Anderson: 'Possibly.'[7] In fact, Junior Clerks substantively minuted only two sorts of files: those which could be disposed of departmentally and those which were in their area of expertise.[8]

All work done by Junior Clerks was seen by the Senior or Principal Clerk. The Senior Clerk in a Department was more experienced, but his routine duties might differ little from those of the Junior Clerks he supervised.[9] He could, however, dispose of certain matters without reference to the Principal Clerk, in whose absence he acted as Head of Department. The Principal Clerk, as Head of the Department, had absolute discretion.[10] It was of course understood that he would send on to his superiors files that involved important questions of principle or policy, as well as any files he thought the Assistant Under Secretary ought to see.[11]

The Assistant Under Secretary and Permanent Under Secretary, both appointed by the Secretary of State, were officials who, in the Treasury's words:

> must always be present as responsible advisers and executive officers of the parliamentary chiefs, and . . . become more and more necessary as the growth of the country and the increasing demands of legislation add to the duties of the Ministers.[12]

In 1898 there were four Assistant Under Secretaries – after 1911, two.[13] Individual Assistant Under Secretaries minuted files concerning matters beyond the official competence of Department Heads, and were responsible for securing 'uniformity of policy and continuity of procedure'.[14] Their experience enabled them to form 'an intimate knowledge of the secretary of state's policy' and to 'anticipate' his decisions.[15] They were crucial to the decision-making process, in part because they were the highest administrative officials who still had intimate knowledge of a specific geographical area.

The Permanent Under Secretary was the highest non-political official at the Colonial Office. His special function, said Lord Crewe, was to 'advise and inform' the Secretary of State on matters of policy.[16] As administrative head of the Office he was also responsible for the smooth running of the Colonial Office. Personal conferences were important adjuncts to his work. For example, in 1906 Lord Elgin noted that Permanent Under Secretary Sir Montagu Ommanney could come freely and frequently into his office; Elgin was convinced that this helped the work get done.[17] Although personalities, outside events, and other factors influenced the Secretary of State in his decision-making, the Permanent Under Secretary's institutional position dictated that the Secretary of State turn to him for advice on colonial policy. The Permanent Under Secretary was also expected to negotiate for his department in government circles, and, within the Colonial Office, to 'compose matters of difference which naturally arise between co-equal heads of departments'[18] as well as between the Secretary of State and his Assistant Under Secretaries.[19]

A typical work-day at the Colonial Office in the late nineteenth century would start at 11 a.m. At that time at least one Upper Division Junior Clerk was expected to be in attendance in each department. He usually had nothing to do in the morning, but business picked up later in the day and generally he stayed to 7 or 7.30 p.m.[20] In the years immediately preceding the First World War the routine had not changed greatly; however, Junior Clerks were expected to come in before 11 a.m. and they *did* have work to do.[21]

All communications received at the Colonial Office were registered and sent to the appropriate department. In most cases the method used to handle the problem posed was to allow clerks at each level to minute the file – that is, to develop a précis and analysis of the problem and a prescription for its resolution. The file would be examined and taken care of – depending on the matter's complexity and importance – by a Junior, Senior, or Principal Clerk, Assistant Under Secretary, the Permanent Under Secretary, or the Secretary of State. In theory, no matter would rise higher than its own importance. Thus relatively unimportant matters could be disposed of by a Junior Clerk, while very important matters were decided by the Secretary of State. Matters that fell between these extremes would be handled by Senior Clerks and their superiors who, it should be emphasised, had substantial latitude in deciding matters on their own.

In 1905 Sir Augustus Hemming wrote to the *Spectator* decrying the system of administration in British Government which gave a Junior Clerk authority to substantively minute documents. He asked, 'what can be the value . . . of the views of a clerk of perhaps six months' standing on matters of, it may be, high imperial policy?' and signed himself 'Ex-CO'.[22] In 1912 the same Royal Commission that had doubted the ability of young clerks to 'advise the secretary of state' also had doubts about the Colonial Office's decision-making process. For example, the Bishop of Southwark, a member of the Commission, complained that 'a document had to go through a very large number of different hands' before a decision was made on it. He asked if this was essential and wondered if there was 'any waste of time or energy or material in that process?'. Sir John Anderson assured the Bishop that a matter of importance received all the Office expertise necessary to solve the problem.[23] Nevertheless, R. B. Pugh, a modern critic, has suggested that as the Colonial Office's business and responsibility grew, this process did impede the efficient dispatch of business.[24] But it did have the advantage of ensuring that all Colonial Office expertise was utilised on a given piece of business. Despite the occasional criticism, officials at the Colonial Office, and their masters, thought it a good system that functioned well.

POLITICAL MASTERS: THE SECRETARIES OF STATE, 1898–1914

Joseph Chamberlain was the dramatic exception in social, religious, and educational background, as well as political achievement, to the other four men who were Secretary of State for the Colonies during the period. Chamberlain's family had been in business since the early eighteenth century. His formal education ended when he left the University College School at Birmingham at the age of 14. After amassing a fortune in his uncle's firm, he retired from business at 38 to devote his time to politics. After three terms as Mayor of Birmingham he was elected to Parliament in 1876. From that point, he began to move from the position of an ambitous domestic radical to that of an ambitious imperialist radical. The transformation was completed when in 1895 he became Secretary of State for the Colonies.

Chamberlain's background, experience, and business acumen were as unique at the Colonial Office as his evangelical rhetoric. Treasury Permanent Secretary Sir Edward Hamilton thought that Chamberlain was 'not born, bred or educated in the way which alone secures the necessary tact and behaviour of a real gentleman'.[25] Attitudes like this may have made many of Chamberlain's goals difficult to achieve. He felt that British possessions in West Africa were undeveloped estates valuable for Britain's future as well as for the indigenous inhabitants. This assessment dictated the necessity for development. Believing that substantial responsibility for such development belonged with the state,[26] Chamberlain focused Colonial Office attention on West African affairs and 'inspired the beginnings of . . . modern administration and development' there.[27] Those who worked under Chamberlain noted two qualities that raised him well above the average head of office: the ability to seize the essentials of a complicated subject and the ability to delegate authority with confidence. He wrote 'concise' minutes and 'commonly accepted the advice of his under secretaries'. When he did not follow staff recommendations he felt it important to explain personally why he had 'upset their conclusions'.[28] Chamberlain's description of the Anglo-Saxon race – 'proud, persistent, self-asserting, and resolute' – was no mean description of himself.[29] He left the Colonial Office in 1903 to pursue his Tariff Reform campaign, and the Colonial Office would never see the likes of him again. His successors over the period of this study were neither exceptional men nor exceptional in their interest in the Empire.

The social background of the four Secretaries of State who followed Chamberlain was aristocratic and upper class. Three went to Eton (Alfred Lyttelton, the Earl of Elgin, and Lewis Harcourt) and one to Harrow (the Earl of Crewe). Lyttelton and Crewe went on to Cambridge, while Harcourt was prevented from going there on account of illness. Elgin went to Balliol College, Oxford. Of the four, only one, Crewe, was a politician of the first rank, but none was of Chamberlain's calibre. Alfred Lyttelton, appointed Secretary of State in 1903, was a successful lawyer, the son of Lord Lyttelton, and a nephew of Gladstone. He was said to possess a 'personal charm which all sorts of men found irresistible'.[30] Lyttelton was elected to Parliament in 1885. His appointment as Secretary of State may have been inspired by his personal friendship with Balfour, as well as his political innocuousness. However, Balfour's first choice, Lord Milner, had also recommended Lyttelton for the post.[31] Judging from his private papers and biography, Lyttelton was not particularly interested in West Africa or Nigeria.[32] However, he accepted the initiatives set in train by Chamberlain, endeavouring to work in partnership with his staff and allowing them considerable latitude. But he could be firm and even independent, as when he accepted Sir Frederick Lugard's scheme of continuous administration in the face of almost unanimous disapproval from his staff.

In December 1905, when the Liberals took over, the Earl of Elgin became Colonial Secretary. He had been, like his father, Viceroy of India. Imperial service was a family tradition; his maternal grandfather had written the Durham Report; and his father had also been Governor of Jamaica and Governor-General of Canada. Lord Elgin's imperial service was taken up more from duty than ambition, and Nigeria did not particularly interest him. He thought the Colonial Office staff first-rate.[33] His contemporaries did not hold him in high regard. Chamberlain said, 'I do not know him personally, but he appears to be weak and he had that character in India.'[34] In spite of such remarks, Ronald Hyam, in a revisionist examination of Elgin at the Colonial Office, has concluded that Elgin had 'wide experience, unwavering administrative courage, unimpeachable honourableness. . . . Sometimes he was pedestrian, sometimes unduly cautious, sometimes unimaginative, but he was never weak, never lethargic and never slavishly dependent on his officials.'[35]

When Asquith became Prime Minister, Elgin was rather unceremoniously dumped from the Liberal Government. He was succeeded by the Earl of Crewe. Crewe's maternal grandfather was Lord Crewe, and his father the first Lord Houghton. Crewe counted for more in his party than did any of the others – with the exception of Chamberlain. He excelled in the art of muting political differences while enlarging areas of agreement. In doing this he combined 'calm judgment with strong conviction and . . . discouraged extreme views . . . and exercised a healing influence among his colleagues.'[36] Nicholas Mansergh suggests Crewe had no particular interest in imperial affairs. Although he remained incurious about the Office machinery as long as it operated efficiently,[37] he was a stickler for conventions regulating the relationship between political masters and civil servants.[38] His Private Secretary called him 'a capable and charming chief'.[39]

The last Secretary of State in this period was Lewis Harcourt. His grandfather-twice-removed had been the first Lord Vernon; his great-grandfather was the Archbishop of York; and his father, Sir William Harcourt, was the famous Liberal politician and statesman. Harcourt acted as his father's Private Secretary, served as trustee on the board of several organisations involved with aesthetic and scientific matters, and entered Parliament in 1904. He was the first Secretary of State since Chamberlain to have a special interest in tropical Africa.[40] Judging from correspondence between Harcourt and his staff, their relationship was friendlier and more informal than was usually the case. One of them, Frederick Butler, told him on the occasion of Harcourt's leaving the Colonial Office: 'I can never forget the great kindness which you always shew me, and always have shewn me, and not least in what you say to me and to others about my work.'[41] Ralph Furse, who did personnel work at the Colonial Office from 1910 to 1948, remembered Harcourt as 'subtle, apt for intrigue, rather malicious, but a good master and a kind friend. He looked like an elegant dilettante; actually he was a hard and thorough worker.'[42]

PARLIAMENTARY UNDER SECRETARIES

While the Secretary of State represented the Colonial Office in one House of Parliament, the Parliamentary Under Secretary represented the Colonial Office in the other. Beyond this he had but a limited function – he might chair special committees of inquiry, or attend ceremonial functions to relieve the Secretary of State of tiresome duties. Although the later careers of four of the seven Parliamentary Under Secretaries from 1898 to 1914 cannot be termed enduring ministerial successes, two, the Earl of Selborne and J. E. B. Seely, did achieve higher office and some success. Selborne became First Lord of the Admiralty, and British High Commissioner in South Africa. Seely in 1912 was appointed Secretary of State for War but became a liability to the Government for his handling of the Curragh Incident and resigned in 1914. The seventh, Winston Churchill, did of course achieve fame and power. Being an ambitious young man, Churchill kept up a constant stream of memoranda, suggestions, and proposals which, combined with his behaviour, drove Lord Elgin to say that Churchill possessed 'a distinct desire to set me aside'.[43] That Churchill could not accomplish this was due as much to the authority inherent in the position of Secretary of State as to Elgin's own strenuous assertions of self.[44] The position of Parliamentary Under Secretary, though often interesting, was seldom influential in policy deliberations.

PERMANENT UNDER SECRETARIES

The Permanent Under Secretary was appointed by the Secretary of State. In selecting this official the Secretary of State could go outside of the Office or promote from within. Four men served as Permanent Under Secretary for the Colonies between 1898 and 1914. Their backgrounds were all professional and upper middle class. Only one was a career Colonial Office official. The first was Sir Edward Wingfield, a barrister.[45] A product of Winchester, Oxford, and Lincoln's Inn, he was called to the Bar in 1859 and practised until 1878. Then, at the age of 44, he was appointed Legal Assistant Under Secretary at the Colonial Office. Nineteen years later, in 1897, he became Permanent Under Secretary. Wingfield had not been Chamberlain's first choice for the position. None the less he did a creditable job. Indeed in 1899 Chamberlain asked the Treasury to permit Wingfield to stay on past retirement age because of his 'extensive and general grasp of the work . . . the value of which it is impossible to overrate'.[46] In point of fact the Colonial Office had recently lost several of its most experienced officials, and because of the increased workload due in great measure to the South African War, had made frequent changes in organisation and personnel. It could ill afford to have to break in a new man. Ironically, six months later Wingfield suffered a stroke which partially paralysed him and forced his retirement.

His successor, Sir Montagu F. Ommanney, was the son of a banker and naval agent. Like Wingfield, Ommanney did not begin his professional life as a civil servant. Educated at Cheltenham College and the Royal Military Academy, Woolwich, he was commissioned in the Royal Engineers in 1864. Ten years later he became Lord Carnarvon's Private Secretary, and in late 1876, Carnarvon appointed him Crown Agent for the Colonies because, Ommanney later said, 'it was thought that my qualifications as an officer of the Royal Engineers might be useful in a department which has to deal largely with contract business and with questions of the supply of material.'[47] As Crown Agent for twenty-three years, Ommanney gained considerable knowledge and experience of railway financing and construction. He was respected as a diplomat and negotiator in Whitehall,[48] and was also successful within the Colonial Office as a co-ordinator and office administrator. He was not a stern head of office, but one who always displayed 'an even temper and great kindliness of heart'. His known strengths were in business, finance, and engineering, and as Permanent Under Secretary under Lyttelton and Elgin, he furthered public works projects, especially railway and port construction in the Crown Colonies.[49] Ommanney has been generally underrated, but he was an important civil servant. This study will offer a chance to examine in some detail his work and its impact on colonial development.

Sir Francis Hopwood, the next Permanent Under Secretary, took office in early 1907, left in 1910, and returned in 1911 for the Imperial Conference. His father was a barrister, and Hopwood himself, educated at King Edward School, Louth, trained as a solicitor. When he was 25 years old (1885) he entered the Board of Trade as Assistant Law Clerk. In 1901 he had risen to Permanent Secretary. Hopwood was interested in the position of Permanent Under Secretary at the Colonial Office as early as December 1905,[50] and was Elgin's first choice for the position. He had general 'bureaucratic expertise', wide contacts and experience throughout the civil service, personal acquaintance with most leading politicians and even personal friendship with the King.[51]

The years 1907–10 were crucial to the Liberal Government's policy toward the defeated Boer republics. It was the Government's hope to reweave the constitutional fabric of Southern Africa in such a way as to satisfy both imperial and local needs. Resolving the problems involved meant dealing with South African whites who controlled, or would soon control, responsible governments there. It was important to have a diplomatic, tactful, and flexible Permanent Under Secretary such as Hopwood, addressing himself to these delicate problems.

However, in a letter to Campbell-Bannerman on 11 December 1906, Elgin seemed to have second thoughts about Hopwood, suggesting that Sir John Anderson be chosen. He feared that Hopwood was unfamiliar with the Office, and that it would be 'a long time before he can have the knowledge to enable him to become the most useful of secretaries'. Elgin wavered because Anderson had served on permanent staff 'with distinction' since 1879, and had been a colonial governor.[52] But after discussing it with the Prime Minister,[53] he offered the job to Hopwood, saying, 'I am not offering a bed of roses. It means . . . an amount of responsibility more varied than I think any other Department can show.'[54]

Hopwood's appointment met with some disapproval. G. E. Buckle, editor of The Times, noted that the Office had acquired a gifted public servant, but, in a congratulatory note to Hopwood, sympathised 'with the feeling that prevails widely in the Colonial Service, that the permanent head of that office should have been associated with the service throughout the principal part of his career'.[55] However, when Elgin left office, he admitted to Crewe that he could not have had a better Permanent Under Secretary; that Hopwood 'never spares himself – he never quarrels – his judgement is correct and quick – and he lays himself out to help his chief in every possible way'.[56] Unlike his two predecessors who, on leaving the Office, left public life, Hopwood still had a considerable career ahead of him as Additional Civil Lord at the Admiralty (1912–14), as member of several committees and boards during the First World War, and as member of royal commissions and boards of directors after the war. He became Lord Southborough in 1917.

Hopwood was succeeded by Sir John Anderson, who was the first Permanent Under Secretary at the Colonial Office to be produced by the civil service open competition.[57] He entered the Colonial Office in 1879, and had become a Principal Clerk before being appointed Governor of the Straits Settlements and High Commissioner for the Federated Malay States. He returned to the Colonial Office in 1911 as Permanent Under Secretary. Anderson's experience as a permanent official, as Secretary to the Colonial Conference in 1897 and 1902, and as Governor of a Crown Colony, was of direct relevance to the job of Permanent Under Secretary. His reputation as a 'quick worker – willing and able to make up his mind and express it – a most essential quality for the post' was an added attraction.[58]

The fact that Anderson succeeded Hopwood reflects Elgin's and Harcourt's different levels of imperial and political experience. Elgin, a former Viceroy of India, had already been Colonial Secretary for a year when he appointed Hopwood. In contrast, Harcourt's first ministerial post was insignificant, and the colonial secretaryship was only his second post. Thus, Elgin, an experienced imperial public servant, would be complemented by a 'meticulous bureaucrat',[59] whereas Harcourt, with no imperial experience, might best be served by a seasoned member of the Colonial Office staff.

PERMANENT OFFICIALS CONCERNED WITH NIGERIA, 1898–1914: A STATISTICAL PROFILE

Who a man is, almost invariably goes a long distance in explaining what he does (not all the way of course – we must know the context in which he worked). A group profile of the permanent officials concerned with Nigeria, from the Assistant Under Secretary to the Junior Clerks, will help lay the groundwork for appraising and evaluating their work. In this group were twenty-one men: their names have come from the *Colonial Office List* (an annual publication) for the years 1898–1914. They tended to be upper middle

TABLE 1.1 *Basic information on permanent officials concerned with Nigerian business, 1898–1914*

Name	Father's occupation/ social status	Pre-university education	University education and degree earned	Class and date of degree	Subject(s) studied	College attended	Professional training	When and how recruited to civil service	Dept first recruited to if other than Colonial Office	Date entered and left Colonial Office	Highest rank at Colonial Office	Highest or last rank in public service or related Colonial service
John Anderson, first Viscount Waverley, 1882–1958	fancy stationer	George Watson's College, Edinburgh	1. Edinburgh (a) B.Sc. (b) M.A. 2. Leipzig*	1. (a) With great distinction, 1903 1. (b) First Class, 1905	1. (a) mathematics, natural philosophy and chemistry 1. (b) mathematics and natural philosophy	Not applicable	None	1905: open competition	not applicable	1905–1912	Junior Clerk	Permanent Under Secretary, Home Office (1922–32); Governor of Bengal (1932–38); Chancellor of the Exchequer (1943–45)
R. L. Antrobus, later Sir Reginald, 1853–1942	clergyman	Winchester	Oxford. B.A.	Second Class, 1876	classics	New College	None	1877: open competition	not applicable	1877–1909	Assistant Under Secretary	Crown Agent for the Colonies, (1909–18)
Denman L. H. Baynes, 1885–1918	admiral	Clifton College	Cambridge, B.A.	First Class, 1908	natural science	Clare College	None	1908: open competition	not applicable	1908–1915	Junior Clerk	
F. G. A. Butler, later Sir Frederick, 1873–1961	clergyman	Bradford Grammar School	Oxford. B.A.	First Class, 1896	classics	Trinity College	None	1896: open competition	Admiralty, 1896–1897	1897–1917	Senior Clerk	Deputy Under Secretary, Foreign Office (1932–38)
Hugh Bertram Cox, 1861–1930	clergyman	Westminster	Oxford (a) B.A. (b) B.C.L.	(a) First Class, 1883 (b) Third Class, 1884	(a) classics (b) civil law	Christ Church	barrister	1886: special assistant to Attorney General	Attorney General's Office, 1886–1897	1897–1911	Legal Assistant Under Secretary	Official at Board of Inland Revenue
E. R. Darnley, 1875–?	barrister	Dulwich	1. Cambridge, B.A. 2. London, B.Sc.	1. First Class, 1897 2. Second Class, 1898	1. mathematics 2. science	1. Trinity College 2. not applicable	None	1898: open competition	not applicable	1898–1933	Assistant Secretary	
C. T. Davis, later Sir Charles, 1873–1938	engineer	Christ's College, Brecon	Oxford. B.A.	First Class, 1896	classics	Balliol College	None	1896: open competition	Admiralty, 1896–1897; Board of Inland Revenue, 1897	1897–1925	Assistant Under Secretary	Permanent Under Secretary, Dominions Office (1925–30)
P. H. Ezechiel, later Sir Percy, 1875–1950	army officer		1. Bombay, unknown 2. London unknown 3. Cambridge, B.A.	1. unknown 2. unknown 3. First Class, 1897	1. unknown 2. unknown 3. mathematics	1. not applicable 2. not applicable 3. Trinity College	barrister	1898: open competition	not applicable	1898–1905	Junior Clerk	Secretary, Crown Agents Office (1905–20), Crown Agent for the Colonies (1920–37)
G. V. Fiddes, later Sir George, 1858–1936	gentleman	Dulwich College	Oxford**	not applicable	classics	Brasenose College	None	1881: open competition	not applicable	1881–1921	Permanent Secretary	

Name, dates	Father's occupation	School	University, degree	Class, year	Subject	College	Barrister	Entry	Early post	Later post	Final post / notes
Roderick Geikie, 1874–1910	geologist	Harrow	Cambridge, B.A.	First Class, 1896	history	King's College	None	1896: open competition	Local Government Board, 1897–1899	1899–1910 Senior Clerk	Official, National Insurance Commission (1912–19) and Insurance Department, Ministry of Health (1919–21)
A. Gray, later Sir Alexander, 1882–1968	unknown	Dundee High School	1. Edinburgh (a) B.A. (b) B.A. 2. Göttingen* 3. Paris*	1. (a) First Class, 1902 1. (b) First Class, 1905	1. (a) mathematics 1. (b) political economy	not applicable	None	1905: open competition	Local Government Board, 1905–1909	1909–1912 Junior Clerk	
G. E. A. Grindle, later Sir Gilbert, 1869–1934	gentleman	Kensington School	Oxford, B.A.	First Class, 1891	classics	Corpus Christi College	barrister	1893: open competition	Local Government Board, 1893–1896	1896–1931 Deputy Permanent Under Secretary	
W. A. B. Hamilton, later Sir William, 1844–1920	admiral	Harrow	None	not applicable	not applicable	not applicable	barrister	1864: limited competition	not applicable	1864–1909 Chief Clerk	
A. J. Harding, later Sir Alfred, 1878–1953	lodging house keeper	Christ's College, Brecon	Cambridge, B.A.	First Class, 1900	natural science	St John's College	None	1901: open competition	not applicable	1901–1928 Assistant Secretary	Director of Colonial Audit, (1928–1941)
A. B. Keith, 1879–1944	advertising agent	Royal High School, Edinburgh	1. Edinburgh B.A. 2. Oxford (a) B.A. (b) B.A.	1. First Class, 1897 2. (a) First Class 1900 2. (b) First Class, 1901	1. classics 2. (a) classics 2. (b) oriental languages	1. not applicable 2. (a) Balliol College 2. (b) Balliol College	barrister	1901: open competition	not applicable	1901–1914 Junior Clerk	
E. G. S. Machtig, later Sir Eric, 1889–1973	unknown	St Paul's	Cambridge, B.A.	First Class, 1911	classics	Trinity College	None	1912: open competition	not applicable	1912–1930 Assistant Secretary	Permanent Under Secretary, Dominions Office and Commonwealth Relations Office (1940–1949)
D. O. Malcolm, later Sir Dougal, 1877–1955	banker	Eton	Oxford, B.A.	First Class, 1897	classics	New College	None	1900: open competition	not applicable	1900–1912 Senior Clerk	
W. H. Mercer, later Sir William, 1855–1932	designer and gentleman	unknown	Oxford, B.A.	Second Class, 1878	classics	Wadham College	barrister	1879: open competition	not applicable	1879–1900 Principal Clerk	Crown Agent for the Colonies, 1900–1920. Senior Crown Agent, 1920–1921
Sydney Olivier, later Lord Olivier, 1859–1943	clergyman	Tonbridge	Oxford, B.A.	Second Class, 1881	classics	Corpus Christi College	None	1882: open competition	not applicable	1882–1907 Principal Clerk	Governor of Jamaica (1907–12); Secretary of State for India (1924)
J. R. W. Robinson, 1880–1919	cotton broker	Marlborough	Oxford, B.A.	Third Class, 1903	classics	New College	None	1904: open competition	Chief Secretary's Office, Dublin, 1904–1905	1905–? Junior Clerk	
C. Strachey, later Sir Charles, 1862–1942	Indian civil servant	unknown	Cambridge**	not applicable	unknown	King's College	None	1885: Foreign Office Competition	Foreign Office, 1885–1898	1898–1927 Assistant Under Secretary	

* not in a degree course
** no degree earned

class, public-school trained, and university-educated at Oxford and, to a lesser extent, at Cambridge. As might be expected, with the exception of a small number who qualified as barristers, few had any postgraduate education. Overwhelmingly they were recruited through the Civil Service Commission's open competition system, initiated in 1870 and gradually adopted by most departments of state shortly thereafter. The basic data from which these general statements come can be seen in Table 1.1. (This table is also the source for Tables 1.2 to 1.5.)[60]

Broken down, this information illustrates and properly highlights each point made in the general comments above. Regarding the official's class background, the designations 'upper middle class' and 'lower middle class' are those used by Kitson Clark in *The Making of Victorian England* – the middle class was everyone in-between the nobility or landed gentry and the manual labourers.[61] Those in the lower middle class were primarily retail shopkeepers and wage-earning clerks in government, law, and commerce. Those in the upper middle class were in higher-income groups or in important professional, commercial, or industrial positions.[62]

These definitions place Colonial Office permanent officials primarily in the upper middle class. This can be seen by looking at Table 1.2. Three of these men – William Baillie Hamilton, Dougal Malcolm, and Charles Strachey – also had connections with the nobility and landed gentry.[63] Nine had fathers in prestigious occupations – the Church, the Bar, and the highest ranks of the Civil Service and the armed forces;[64] and the remaining five had fathers in the important professional, commercial, or industrial positions. I have simply assumed that George Fiddes's and Gilbert Grindle's fathers were upper middle class because they are mentioned as being gentlemen in the alumni lists of Oxford University.[65] Of the three who fit into the lower-middle-class category, all are from the north of Great Britain – two from Scotland and one from Yorkshire.

When we turn to the pre-university, secondary-level education, we see that they were overwhelmingly public-school boys. Table 1.3 vividly illustrates this. Of the three about whom no information could be found, Charles Strachey, given his family background, probably did attend some sort of public school. Regarding Mercer, no good guess can be made. P. H. Ezechiel hardly had time to attend secondary school – he received the first of his three BA degrees at the age of 14.

British public schools in the Victorian and Edwardian eras were

TABLE 1.2 *Fathers' occupations*

Upper middle class		Lower middle class	
Clergyman	– Antrobus Butler Cox Olivier	Advertising Agent	– Keith
		Fancy Stationer	– Anderson
		Lodging House Keeper	– Harding
Gentlemen	– Fiddes Grindle		
Naval Officer	– Baynes Hamilton	Unknown	– Gray Machtig
Army Officer	– Ezechiel		
Banker	– Malcolm		
Barrister	– Darnley		
Cotton Broker	– Robinson		
Designer, university educated	– Mercer		
Engineer	– Davis		
Indian Civil Service	– Strachey		
Scientist	– Geikie		

finishing institutions for a social, political, and administrative elite.[66] It was the intensity of experience in the public schools which accounted for their influence on students. For the most part a public school was what sociologists call a total institution:

a place of residence and work where a large number of like-situated individuals cut off from the wider society for an appreciable period of time, together lead an enclosed, formally administered life.[67]

The public schools, as institutions, varied in reputation, but all produced 'public school gentlemen'.[68] In any period it has been

TABLE 1.3 *Public schools attended*

Bradford Grammar School (a)	Butler
Christ's College, Brecon (b)	Davis
	Harding
Clifton College (c)	Baynes
Dulwich College (c)	Darnley
	Fiddes
Dundee High School (d)	Gray
Eton (e)	Malcolm
George Watson's College (f)	Anderson
Harrow (e)	Geikie
	Hamilton
Marlborough (c)	Robinson
Royal High School, Edinburgh (g)	Keith
St Paul's (e)	Machtig
Tonbridge (c)	Olivier
Westminster (e)	Cox
Winchester (e)	Antrobus

Notes: Of the remaining four officials, Grindle went to Kensington School, a non-public secondary school, and the other three (Ezechiel, Mercer, and Strachey), if they did attend secondary school, seemed to have left no record of it.

This table indicates which secondary schools were attended by the permanent officials concerned with Nigerian affairs at the Colonial Office, and indicates which of the schools were public. I have attempted to determine if, in each case, each school was recognised in the mid- and late nineteenth century as a public school.

(a) *Whitaker's Almanack*, 1892, 271.

(b) Brian Gardner, *The Public Schools: An Historical Survey* (London: Hamish Hamilton, 1973) p. 66.

(c) Listed in the *Public Schools Yearbook*, 1889.

(d) J. C. Stocks, 'Education in Dundee', in *Dundee and District* (Dundee: Local Executive Committee of the British Association for the Advancement of Science, 1968) p. 364.

(e) One of the nine leading public schools investigated by a Royal Commission from 1861 to 1864. 'Report of H.M. Commission appointed to inquire into the Revenues and Management of certain Colleges and Schools and the Studies pursued and Instruction given Therein', *Parl. Papers*, 1864, XX (Vol. I).

(f) Gardner, *The Public Schools*, pp. 139–40.

(g) Ibid, pp. 54–7.

difficult to recognise what is meant by the term 'gentlemen'. In 1929 Sir Charles Strachey, then a retired Colonial Office clerk, wrote to his cousin Lytton that 'Thanks to Anita Loos, it is now much easier to identify a gentleman.'[69] This is of course a reference to Anita Loos's *Gentlemen Prefer Blondes*. However, a more serious meaning of the

term revolved around educational and social attributes.[70] Public
schools created a milieu in which the sons of the upper and upper
middle classes became acceptable to, by becoming indistinguishable
from, one another in education, attitudes, and accent.[71] The elite
produced by these schools felt that the world was its oyster. A critic
of this education, however, wrote in 1913 that public-school boys left
school 'saturated with class prejudice . . . it is the one thing they are
really successfully taught'.[72] Be that as it may, the non-academic
functions which public schools served were most appreciated. The
Clarendon Commission in 1864 spoke for the ruling establishment
when it said:

> These schools have been the chief nurseries of our statesmen; in
> them . . . men . . . have been brought up on a footing of social
> equality, and have contracted the most enduring friendships, and
> some of the ruling habits of their lives; and they have had perhaps
> the largest share in moulding the character of an English
> gentleman.[73]

The Colonial Office Upper Division clerks, English gentlemen to a
man, looked out at the world primarily through the prism of class, not
race. A small incident illustrates this. Throughout 1901 the Colonial
Office received complaints about living-conditions on the steam-ships
carrying colonial civil servants out to Nigeria. Many of the complaints
dealt with the question of who should travel by what class. The
Assistant Under Secretary's analysis not only dealt with the problem
posed but clearly showed his view of what the onboard class structure
should be:

> The difficulty seems to arise from the fact that there are at least 3
> classes of European passengers – to say nothing of the natives, and
> only 2 classes of passages. The question whether we should send
> foremen of works and others 1st class is not so much one of
> expense as one of discipline and dealing fairly with the higher
> officials. It is bad for discipline that the higher and lower officials
> should travel in the same class; and it is never allowed in the army;
> and it is unfair to the higher officials to inflict upon them the
> inconvenience and discomfort of being berthed and having to be at
> table with persons whose habits and manners are different from
> theirs. This runs all through. The gentlemen do not like being
> thrown into such close contact with the artisans, and the

respectable artisans object to being compelled to associate with the foul-mouthed and drunken ones; and all three classes objected to being associated with negroes of various degrees.[74]

It was not good for morale, P. H. Ezechiel, Junior Clerk, argued, to allow anyone who had the money to go first-class. If this were done, a foreman in the public works department of a colony, who received better pay than a secretariat clerk, would probably go first-class. This would no doubt have bothered the secretariat clerks who were usually gentlemen. Ezechiel's solution to this problem was to devise a list indicating which positions were in which social class and then rigidly adhere to it. The basis of any such classification had to be social status and not salary.[75]

With one exception – Hamilton – all these officials went to university. Out of this group of twenty, eighteen attended either Oxford or Cambridge (see Table 1.4). Several (Gray, Anderson, Keith, Ezechiel, and Darnley) attended more than one university, but only two of the group – Anderson and Gray, who studied in Scotland and on the continent – missed the Oxford/Cambridge experience. All but one of the twenty, Strachey, were in honours-degree programmes. All but two, Strachey and Fiddes, actually completed their degrees. (Had Fiddes taken his degree examination he quite likely would have done well. After all, he placed first in the Civil Service competition in 1881.) The eighteen who did finish earned a total of twenty-three bachelor degrees: eleven from Oxford, six from Cambridge, three from Edinburgh, two from London, and one from Bombay. In this group there were fifteen first-class, three second-class, and two

TABLE 1.4 *Universities attended*

Oxford (11)	Antrobus, Butler, Cox, Davis, Fiddes, Grindle, Keith, Malcolm, Mercer, Olivier, Robinson
Cambridge (7)	Baynes, Darnley, Ezechiel, Geikie, Harding, Machtig, Strachey
Other Universities* (9)	Anderson (Edinburgh and Leipzig) Darnley (London) Ezechiel (Bombay and London) Gray (Edinburgh, Göttingen, and Paris) Keith (Edinburgh)

* It should be noted that Ezechiel and Darnley also attended Cambridge, and that Keith attended Oxford.

third-class degrees (the class is unknown for the other three degrees). That so many in the Nigeria Department received a first-class degree represented a significant and substantial achievement. Clearly the clerks of the Colonial Office were second to none in intellectual ability. The assumption was that this intellectual capacity could be translated into administrative accomplishment. It is the burden of this book to show that this happened.

There was, however, no obvious connection between what these men studied and their work at the Colonial Office. One exception was H. B. Cox, the Legal Assistant Under Secretary, who studied law as well as classics at Oxford. Thirteen studied classics, and of that number eleven were at Oxford (see Table 1.5). Indeed Oxford classicists formed the largest element in the Nigeria Department. As Shaw's Lady Britomart said, 'Nobody can say a word against Greek; it stamps a man at once as an educated gentleman.'[76] Five studied mathematics. Kitson Clark has noted that 'intensive drill in the old-fashioned type of mathematics' as taught at Cambridge was an important support to a proper classical education,[77] and was considered especially helpful in developing logical thought.[78]

Clearly these men were, in terms of their academic subjects, a close-knit traditionally educated group, not at all in the vanguard of academic or practical study.[79] No specialists were produced who were specifically trained for overseeing the undeveloped estates. Rather, they were generalists who, in the British view, were ideally suited to supervise the work of administrative specialists. Just as public-school education had been a socialising experience – producing gentlemen, with not only an education, but a caste identity and an ideological base – so university education continued the process on a more sophisticated level. Upper-middle-class young men who had been taught the importance of such things as discipline, leadership, authority, manners, and accent, were now given a broader sense of their own identity.

Only six of the twenty-one could claim any professional training, all as barristers; one, H. B. Cox, studied and practised law directly after university. The other five qualified for the Bar after some time in the Civil Service. They were P. H. Ezechiel, G. A. Grindle, W. B. Hamilton, A. B. Keith, and W. H. Mercer.

All but two (Cox and Hamilton) of the permanent officials concerned with Nigeria were chosen through open competition. The foundations for this system of recruitment were being laid in the 1850s and were put into effect in 1870. The first officials in the

TABLE 1.5 *Subjects studied by universities attended*

Subject	University			
	Oxford	Cambridge	Other	Total
Classics	Antrobus Butler Cox Davis Fiddes Grindle Keith Malcolm Mercer Olivier Robinson	Machtig	Keith (Edin.)	13
Mathematics		Baynes Darnley Ezechiel	Anderson (Edin.) Gray (Edin.)	5
Science		Baynes Harding	Anderson (Edin. and Leipzig) Darnley (London)	4
Economics			Gray (Edin.)	1
History		Geikie		1
Civil Law	Cox			1
Oriental languages and Literature	Keith			1
Unknown Subjects		Strachey	Ezechiel (Bombay and London) Gray (Göttingen and Paris)	3
Total	13	8	8	29

Colonial Office generated by this new system were brought in in 1877. Open competition recruitment was based on written examinations administered by the Civil Service Commission up until the First World War, after which, part of the examination consisted of an oral interview in which a certain number of points could be earned.[80] Originally, anyone aged 18 to 24 could sit for the examinations, but in 1895 the minimum age was raised to 22. The Civil Service Commissioners wanted men with a 'thorough education, keen intelligence and capacity for development' and therefore set examinations which tested the candidates' general ability. With examinations as the sole means of entry there was concern that large numbers of 'quick-witted youths without breeding' might thus enter the Upper Division of the Civil Service.[81] But the examination itself prevented this from happening: it was based on the degree examinations given at Oxford in classics, and at Cambridge in mathematics and science. Obviously, candidates from Oxford and Cambridge who were familiar with the nature of the examinations had an enormous advantage. Therefore it was not surprising that men whose family traditions included, and whose finances allowed, study at these universities, were more likely to do well than any other group. At almost any time in the period 1870–1914 graduates from Oxford and Cambridge would make up at least 75 per cent, and usually more, of the annual entrants to the Upper Division of the Civil Service.[82]

To demonstrate graphically the advantage that, for example, a classicist had in the examination process, here are the subjects one could be examined on, and the maximum points allowed for each, in the 1881 competition:

English	1,500	(history – 500, literature – 500, composition and précis – 500)
Greek	750	
Latin	750	
French	375	
German	375	
Italian	375	
Mathematics	1,250	
Natural Sciences (5)	1,000	
Moral Sciences	500	
Jurisprudence	375	
Political Economy	375	
	7,625	

George Fiddes scored first in this year with 1,810 points. Approximately 1,400 of his points came from the English, Greek, and Latin examinations.[83] Two other Oxford men in the Nigeria Department placed first in the civil service examination: Olivier in 1882 and Keith in 1901. Another, Antrobus, placed second in the 1877 competition.

John Anderson, of the University of Edinburgh, was the only other clerk in this group to place first (in 1905).[84] He is also the exception who proves the rule – he was the only one who did not study classics as his university subject.

The sort of official who would emerge from this background and this recruitment system was not immediately apparent in the mid nineteenth century. There was some criticism of the new system. Sir James Stephen, who as Permanent Under Secretary at the Colonial Office from 1836 to 1847 had done more than any person to create the method by which business was transacted there, harshly criticised the idea of recruitment by open competition. He feared that a system based on the degree examinations at Oxford and Cambridge would produce large numbers of over-qualified over-achievers. He feared that the Upper Division of the Civil Service would become the equivalent of an army composed entirely of generals. Far from insuring the efficient dispatch of government business it 'would insure bitter jealousies and enduring quarrels, and would render impossible all cordial cooperation among them [the officials] in the discharge of their common duties'.[85] The very same intelligence and talent which would insure a high score on a competitive examination might disqualify a candidate from becoming a permanent official. Talents which were 'excellent gifts for a combatant in the open fields of professional competition', might be 'ill-suited, and even inconvenient, to one who is to be entombed for life as a clerk in a Public Office in Downing Street'. In short, the public service did not need 'statesmen in disguise'. Stephen believed that what was needed were 'intelligent, steady, methodical men of business'.[86] He didn't believe such men could be found through the proposed examination system. In fact, this system annually brought into the civil service the cream of the crop of British university graduates, mostly from Oxford and Cambridge. Their talents for analysis and clear expression, coupled with their native ability and intelligence, created a civil service '*corps d'élite*'. If it included few statesmen, it did include, in the Colonial Office as well as in other departments of state, many able and sound 'men of business'.

PERMANENT OFFICIALS CONCERNED WITH NIGERIA: A LOOK AT SOME INDIVIDUALS

As instructive as it is to know statistical information, it is also worthwhile to flesh out these facts. Something must be said about the men as individuals – at and away from their work. The highest rank held in this group was Assistant Under Secretary of State in charge of West African (and thus Nigerian) business. H. B. Cox held this post during 1897–8, Reginald Antrobus until 1909, and George Fiddes to 1916. Cox came to the Colonial Office after practising law for many years; he was appointed as (Legal) Assistant Under Secretary with responsibility for general legal advice and the business of certain colonies. Cox greatly enjoyed the latter work and was disgruntled when it was taken away in the reorganisation of 1907. Elgin suggested to his successor that Cox's unhappiness would lessen considerably if Lord Crewe could 'grease the wheels a little' by conferring with Cox, and showing an interest in his work.[87] This must have been done, for Cox remained another three years. His accomplishments were varied and went beyond mere legal skills. His *Times* obituary noted his ability not only to play the organ but to take it apart and reassemble it.[88]

Antrobus, son of a clergyman and married to a clergyman's daughter, was one of the first clerks brought into the Colonial Office by open competition.[89] Chamberlain said Antrobus worked 'like a horse' during the Niger crisis and negotiations of the late 1890s. Lord Elgin was impressed by Antrobus's knowledge of the colonies. He considered his work 'very thorough' and thought it an asset that Antrobus wrote shorter minutes than many of his colleagues.[90] But Antrobus was considered a slow worker compared with his successor, George Fiddes. Fiddes was quick to get to the heart of a question, 'and could not appear but intolerant of anything like slowness or slackness in others'.[91] He was one of the few imperialists who worked on West African business; he was not universally admired for this – his colleague Sydney Olivier called him a 'rabid, narrow-minded jingo'.[92] Ralph Furse, who entered the Colonial Office in 1910, stated that most people in the Colonial Office 'feared him; many disliked him'. He also recalled that Fiddes had 'cold blue eyes, a clear logical brain and a sharp . . . viperish tongue'.[93]

Five men served as Head of Nigeria Department in the sixteen years covered by this study: Antrobus, William Mercer, Sir William Baillie Hamilton, Sydney Olivier, and Charles Strachey. Hamilton, as mentioned earlier, entered the Office under the limited competition system. He was an older man, with aristocratic and upper-class connections that most of the clerks did not have (his father was an Admiral, and his mother the sister of the first Duke of Abercorn). He had 'an antiquated prejudice' against the open competition system, not because it had failed to produce men of ability, but because he felt these men were not as 'suited for command' as non-competition officials had been and were.[94] Hamilton's official minutes sometimes rather colourfully reflected his interests in riding, hunting, and the army: in 1901, when minuting a file on French incursions into Nigeria while in hot pursuit of their African enemies, he wrote:

> As regards . . . the endemic violations of our territory, I suppose we ought to remonstrate with them, but I am afraid it will be difficult to bring anything home to them. There is an old-established maxim in foxhunting to the effect that you may follow your fox into another man's country, and kill him in any way you can . . . and I am afraid the French would argue on analogous lines.[95]

Hamilton is probably the only clerk in this group who was sent on a secret mission for the Colonial Office, and the only one to write a novel.[96] In his novel, a simple romance with a happy ending, the main character is an official who describes his career as 'an attendance [at work] of a few hours a day, with unlimited leave and ample opportunity for playing cricket'.[97]

Of the other three heads of the Nigeria Department, Mercer and Olivier entered the Colonial Office through open competition, whereas Strachey went first to the Foreign Office, which still refused to recruit by open competition, and then transferred to the Colonial Office. Mercer, was 'gnomelike' in appearance, with a 'small body topped with a large head'.[98] He was in charge of the Nigeria Department when much of the planning for Nigeria's future took place, and held decided views. He argued against Lugard's desire to keep the West African Frontier Force at or near full strength, for fear that 'it would encourage him to contemplate military operations which from our point of view it is most important to avoid, but which have a fascination for every officer in the force'.[99] In the Colonial Office, Mercer's reputation was one of 'great efficiency, a dogged tenacity, and an imperturbability in which no emergency could cause a tremor'. He was also the author of the theory that the best way to keep up with the work was to divide the number of files into the number of minutes in the working-day and spend the resulting quotient on each file.[100]

Olivier was of French Huguenot descent. Of a dramatic turn, he habitually wore a velvet cape that was considered 'in defiance of usage'.[101] (Perhaps theatricality ran in the family; he was uncle to Sir Laurence Olivier.) His friend and fellow Fabian, Bernard Shaw, described him as a 'Spanish grandee'.[102] His intellectual arrogance and impatience with those less gifted made him unpopular at the Office, and he further alienated his colleagues with advanced views on socialism, race, and a host of other issues. After eight years at the Colonial Office he lost interest in the work there, and took a temporary position in the West Indies. He then went back and forth between work at the Colonial Office and in the colonial service. He was involved with Nigerian affairs from 1904 to 1907, and during the period published, among other things, a short story called 'The Empire Builder' which Henry James admired.[103] He also wrote several books of non-fiction on conditions in British tropical Africa and the British West Indies. Olivier was respected, if not liked. A colleague of his wrote that his work was good and able 'in spite of his tone, which no one personally objects to more strongly than I do'.[104]

Charles Strachey was described by a colleague as 'acute and whimsical'.[105] These characteristics are perhaps illustrated by Strachey's great interest in gypsies which occasionally prompted him to go and live with them.[106] The Strachey family was distinguished by its imperial, administrative, and literary qualities. An earlier ancestor, William Strachey, had combined both qualities as secretary to, and then historian of, the Virginia colony.[107] The administrative inheritance, however, mostly manifested itself in service to Britain's Indian Empire: Sir Henry Strachey served as Clive's secretary; three of his sons and four of his grandsons served the East India Company. Two of the grandsons, Richard and John, were influential civil servants in India in the 1860s and 1870s, particularly in the fields of financial and administrative reform.[108] Two of Sir John's sons had careers in the Indian Civil Service. The third son, Charles Strachey, went into the Foreign Office, where he interested himself in the affairs of African Protectorates and served as secretary to the Uganda Railway Committee. This experience was important to his work on railway policy when he was transferred to the Colonial Office in 1898.[109]

The remainder of this group served as senior and junior clerks in the Nigerian Department. John Anderson, for example, a Scot, was at the Colonial Office for seven years before going to the National Insurance Commission. He went on to make a great mark on public administration in Great Britain. Lord Salter, himself a distinguished public servant, once called him 'the greatest administrator of his time'.[110] He served in later years as Permanent Under Secretary at the Home Office and Lieutenant-Governor of Bengal. Then he went into politics just before the outbreak of the Second World War. During the war he became Chancellor of the Exchequer, and afterwards was rewarded for his service to the state with a peerage. He is not to be confused with the Sir John Anderson who was Permanent Under Secretary at the Colonial Office from 1911 to 1916. Gilbert Grindle exemplifies the official who once having chosen a career in the Colonial Office remained there to make his way up the ladder of promotion. In 1892, while still at Oxford, he won the Chancellor's English Essay Award for his paper, 'The Destruction of Paganism in the Roman Empire'. Entering the Home Civil Service in 1893 through open competition, he worked at the Local Government Board for three years before transferring to the Colonial Office. Four years later he was promoted to Senior Clerk, and in 1909 to Principal Clerk. In 1916 he became Assistant Under Secretary, and in 1925 Deputy Permanent Under Secretary. His obituary in *The Times* described him as 'one of the "quiet" men of the Colonial Office, little seen or heard, but getting through great quantities of business in the background'.[111]

Another senior official in the Nigerian Department was Alfred John Harding. 'A ponderous Yorkshireman', he was a Cambridge mathematician and a 'meticulous bureaucrat', a formidable combination.[112] A born schoolmaster, he never overlooked a slip. He was actively involved in planning and implementing the amalgamation of Northern and Southern Nigeria.[113] After twenty-seven years in the Colonial Office he left to become Director of Colonial Audit. Additionally there was Frederick Butler, who after twenty years in the Colonial Office, left it for the Foreign Office. From 1897 to 1907 he was closely associated with Nigerian business. One of his colleagues remembered him as one who insisted that all minutes should end with a recommendation – even if the recommendation suggested doing nothing.[114]

These men and others like them set the tone of the Colonial Office in the late nineteenth and early twentieth centuries. Anyone who did not conform to this 'tone' or found themselves at odds with it was eventually eased out of the Office's mainstream, or eased themselves out. An example of the former would be Sydney Olivier's Colonial Office career, and of the latter Sidney Webb's.[115] H. E. Dale – himself a permanent official who had served in the Colonial Office and in the Agriculture and Fisheries Department – said that these clerks created a civil service 'composed mainly of men who entered the service by the same road after the same kind of education, belong[ed] to the same social class, and . . . [led] personal lives of a very similar nature'.[116] Distinct individuals all; yet there were limitations on that individuality – limitations established, as should be clear, by their background, education, and method of recruitment.

NIGERIAN GOVERNORS

The power of a Governor in a Crown Colony was substantial. Chosen by the Secretary of State, the Governor was a colony's chief administrator, and, on occasion, executive head of specific departments. He could appoint an Executive or Legislative Council, and sometimes was empowered to pass legislation himself. He was in charge of the colony's legal administration in the early stages, when the colony was first being established. Later, when a separate judicial system was set up, he retained the Crown's power of clemency. A Governor could issue orders as to a military expedition's objectives within his colony, but could not actually command the expedition. To these very specific powers, one must add the reserve power, which authorised the Governor, should an emergency arise, to take whatever steps were necessary for the safety of the colony. As A. H. M. Kirk-Greene has noted, 'all power and responsibility [in a colony] were centered on the governor and he personally dominated the whole administration'.[117] There were limitations of course. The Governor was controlled by the Colonial Office, which could veto his recommendations and legislation, dislocate his budget, and criticise his clemency. In the final analysis a Governor of a particular colony was the conduit of the Secretary of State's will.[118]

Regarding governors, permanent officials seemed to hope for the best and expect the worst. William Baillie Hamilton, after thirty-four years at the Colonial Office, did not expect governors to be 'exceptionally brilliant in any one particular respect', but thought that if men could be found who combined 'fair administrative ability with some common sense, tact, decision, knowledge of the world and "of men and things", and above all, with the power of exercising personal influence', all would be well.[119] All too frequently, however, or so permanent officials sometimes seemed to think, colonial governors were mediocre, inferior types, financially extravagant, and 'prone to disregard instructions . . . and to public indiscretions'.[120] With few exceptions, they were considered second-rate.

Between 1898 and 1914, seven men served as Governor in Nigeria (see Table 1.6). All seven were knighted for their service to the Empire, and one – Sir Frederick Lugard – became a peer. These men were different from the permanent officials in the Nigeria Department. They were separated to some extent by birth, but mainly by education, professional training and experience. Whereas the overwhelming majority of permanent officials were English, born in England, less than half the governors could make this claim: Lugard, though English, was born in India; McCallum and Mac-Gregor were Scots. Bell, a native of the British West Indies, was of French extraction, and Girouard was French Canadian.[121]

Where their fathers' occupations were an indicator, they were not that different from the permanent officials. Girouard's father was a Judge of the Supreme Court of Canada; Lugard's a missionary in India; McCallum's a Major in the Royal Marines Light Infantry; and Moor's a surgeon; all upper–middle-class occupations. Although I could discover nothing about the occupations of Bell's and Egerton's fathers, given the sort of education they were able to give their children, they were also probably upper middle class. Separated from the rest was MacGregor, whose father was a crofter, periodically on poor relief, at that.[122]

The difference between Nigerian governors and permanent officials in the Nigeria department becomes marked when the governors' secondary and post-secondary education is examined. With two exceptions, each governor's secondary education was private, and non-public school. Girouard, McCallum, and Moor were taught privately, Bell at Brussels and Paris. Only Egerton and Lugard attended public schools (Tonbridge and Rossall respectively). Mac-Gregor spent only two terms in secondary school – the Aberdeen Grammar School. Since he did not begin until he was 19, one assumes his character was fully formed by the time he entered Aberdeen University. None of the governors had the classical education of the permanent officials. Three – Bell, Egerton and Moor – had no higher education at all. MacGregor spent a year at King's College, Aberdeen, and did poorly.[123]

The educational background of the remaining three illustrates the fact that military men were a substantial part of the pool from which colonial governors were drawn. Girouard studied at the Royal Military College, Kingston, Canada; Lugard attend the Royal Military College, Sandhurst, in 1878, but only for two months (he would have stayed the normal length of time had not all members of

TABLE 1.6 *Nigerian Governors and High Commissioners, 1898–1914*

Lagos: Governors	*Northern Nigeria:*
Henry McCallum (1897–1899)	*High Commissioners*
William MacGregor (1899–1904)	Frederick Lugard** (1900–1906)
Walter Egerton (1904–1906)	Percy Girouard (1907–1908)
Southern Nigeria:	*Northern Nigeria: Governors*
High Commissioners	Percy Girouard (1908–1909)
Ralph Moor* (1900–1903)	Hesketh Bell (1910–1912)
Walter Egerton (1904–1906)	Frederick Lugard (1912–1913)
(Amalgamated) Southern Nigeria:	*(Amalgamated) Nigeria:*
Governors	*Governor-General*
Walter Egerton (1906–1912)	Frederick Lugard (1914–1919)
Frederick Lugard (1912–1913)	

* Moor, from 1896 to 1900 was Commissioner and Consul-General for the Niger Coast Protectorate (which was incorporated into Southern Nigeria when the Colonial Office took over the territory in 1900).
** Lugard was, from 1897 to 1900, Her Majesty's Commissioner for, and Commander-in-Chief over, British Imperial troops in the Nigerian Hinterland.

his class been called to active duty when war with Russia was feared); and McCallum studied engineering at the Royal Military Academy, Woolwich. In the case of Lugard and McCallum, family connections further emphasise the military element. Three of Lugard's uncles were army officers, the most prominent being General Sir Edward Lugard, who made a name for himself in the Sikh Wars and in the Indian Mutiny, and later became Permanent Under Secretary at the War Office. Even Lugard's father, a chaplain on the Madras establishment, held the rank of Lieutenant Colonel.[124] McCallum's father and grandfather were Majors in the Royal Marines Light Infantry, and he himself retired a full Colonel in the Royal Engineers. Lugard and Girouard both received the Distinguished Service Order – Girouard for his work in the Sudan on the Dongola Expeditionary Force, and Lugard for his work as transport officer in the Third Burmese War.[125]

In professional training and experience the governors also differed markedly from permanent officials. They were not, with the exception of Bell and Egerton, career civil servants. Bell started out as a clerk in the Barbados government at the age of 18; Egerton as a Cadet in the Straits Settlements at the age of 22. Bell served in Grenada, the Gold Coast, Seychelles, St Kitts and Dominica, and held governorships in Uganda, Northern Nigeria, the Leeward

Islands, and Mauritius before he retired. Egerton at first worked strictly in Britain's eastern Empire, moving steadily up the promotion ladder from Cadet to Resident. He was then asked to head the administration of Lagos and Southern Nigeria. When the two amalgamated, he continued as Governor until 1912 when he was appointed Governor of British Guiana. He remained in that position until he retired from colonial service in 1919.

It was Girouard's, Lugard's, and McCallum's military skills that brought them to service in the Empire. Girouard's first position was a a Canadian Pacific Railway engineer. He left Canada when he received a commission in the Royal Engineers, and subsequently held several important positions in railway administration and construction in the Empire.[126] It was due to this experience that he was appointed High Commissioner in Northern Nigeria.[127] Lugard, after almost ten years' active service, mostly in India, went on the inactive list, after which he became an imperial soldier of fortune. Employed first by the African Lakes Company, and then by the Imperial East Africa Company, he explored, fought Arab slavers, and played a central role in bringing Uganda into the Empire. In 1895 Chamberlain asked him to raise a force in West Africa to show to the French Britain's intention to protect and assert its rights there. As a result of this work, Lugard was appointed first Northern Nigerian High Commissioner. In 1907 he became Governor of Hong Kong, but returned to Nigeria in 1912 for the remainder of his colonial service career.

McCallum combined his engineering and military training with colonial administration almost from the beginning. Four years out of Woolwich, he became Private Secretary to the Governor of the Straits Settlements. Over the next twenty years he served in the East – Hong Kong, Singapore, and Penang – as engineer, army officer, and colonial administrator. With his appointment as Governor of Lagos, he became solely a colonial civil servant, and was successively Governor of Newfoundland, Natal, and Ceylon before retiring.

MacGregor started his colonial service as a doctor in the Seychelles government. There, and then in Fiji, he gradually became more an administrator than doctor, finally being made Administrator of New Guinea. After that, he was Governor in Lagos, Newfoundland, and Queensland before retiring. Moor came to the colonial service circuitously. He entered the Royal Irish Constabulary, rising to the rank of District Inspector before resigning to become Commandant of Constabulary in the Oil Rivers Protectorate. Over a four-year period he changed from police specialist to general administrator. When the Protectorate was transformed into the Niger Coast Protectorate, he was appointed Commissioner and Consul-General (in effect, governor), and when the Foreign Office handed over the territory to the Colonial Office, Moor stayed on as first High Commissioner of Southern Nigeria until he retired in 1903.[128]

A certain amount of built-in friction existed in the relationship between colonial governors and permanent officials. The Governor – the man on the spot – saw his own colony's needs and demands as primary, whereas Colonial Office officials had their eyes on the demands and needs of the Empire as a whole. These different angles of vision – though focused on the same subject – produced a fairly predictable pattern in a Governor's correspondence with the Colonial Office. Initially officials would be impressed with the ability, intelligence, and devotion to duty shown by the new man. Eventually, mutual criticism and dissatisfaction set in.

Some minutes on Sir Ralph Moor's correspondence provide an example of this process. When Moor first became High Commissioner the permanent officials could not have been happier. But two years later, Butler told Antrobus, 'I have heard from officers who have lately returned from Southern Nigeria that the effects of the climate on Sir R. Moor are becoming very noticeable.'[129] And the next year it was worse:

> The tone . . . is characteristic of Sir R. Moor's most recent communications. He has lately been very quick to imagine that the wishes and convenience of the local authorities have been deliberately ignored by the Colonial Office.[130]

The way in which governors approached their work, as much as what they actually did, often diminished officials' respect for them. In 1910, Sir Walter Egerton wrote to the Colonial Office stating that the salary offered one of his subordinates was 'niggardly',[131] and should be revised. It was one thing for Egerton to suggest that someone have his salary increased; it was quite another to call the salary level 'niggardly'. Assistant Under Secretary Fiddes was incensed:

> the Governor should be called to order. He has an unfortunate tendency to let his pen run away with him, and to lecture the secretary of state in a way which is not quite seemly.[132]

Harcourt agreed, and suggested Egerton's 'epistolary style should be remembered if there is in future any question of his promotion'.[133] Egerton's next and last governorship was a definite step down from Southern Nigeria. When Sir Hesketh Bell became embroiled in a controversy and stated his own opinions publicly before checking with the Secretary of State, Fiddes told him that he had 'treated the secretary of state very badly'. Bell protested, saying he had been misunderstood. Fiddes did not want to argue but wished to bring home to Bell that 'the question at issue was . . . his method of handling the matter'. Bell believed that this attitude of the permanent officials was an influential factor in bringing about, in Bell's own words, his 'reduction, before expiration of the usual term of a governor's appointment, from a second to a third class administration [the Leeward Islands] and the diminution of emoluments by nearly £1,500 a year'.[134]

Most governors were willing to be convinced that permanent officials were not 'abnormally obstructive' to their work.[135] One of them, however, after only a brief experience of the Colonial Office and its methods, seemed not only to expect obstruction, but to enjoy it. Sir Frederick Lugard seemed to relish doing the very thing that would most irritate the permanent officials, apparently in a spirit of tit-for-tat. To his brother he wrote that:

> the incompetence and the indifference of the Colonial Office have thrown very great obstacles in my way, and have trebled the difficulties. They angered me . . . and I have written two letters which will I expect anger *them*. I am curious to see the results.[136]

Lugard thought conflict with permanent officials a zestful addition to his work. 'I really do believe,' he told his wife,

> I should like my work less if I had not this Colonial Office obstruction to contend against! – It is essentially a part of the difficulty to be overcome, and anything that lessened the difficulty, would lessen the interest in the work.[137]

Lugard's untidy administrative habits annoyed and exasperated permanent officials. He drove Butler, a Junior Clerk in the Department and therefore the first to read and minute Lugard's despatches, to distraction. Butler referred to one of Lugard's despatches as 'unsatisfactory and inconclusive', and found it 'impossible to see what General Lugard wishes to be done on it'.[138] On another he wrote, 'This is a hopeless despatch. I can't make out at all what Sir F. Lugard is driving at.'[139] Butler was not alone in these sentiments. P. H. Ezechiel complained that 'General Lugard's vicious habit of mixing up several subjects in one letter or despatch has brought the correspondence into a state which cannot be described as anything but chaotic.'[140] But these traits, no matter how frustrating, did not, except in extreme cases, count as matters of substance. When Lugard stepped too far out of line, he was firmly shown his place and put in it. His biographer, Margery Perham, tells what happened when Lugard, while a serving Governor, publicly supported the Ulster protestants in their anti-Home-Rule struggle. He was officially reprimanded and the Secretary of State's confidence in him was severely undermined.[141] On another occasion, when Oliver Howard was appointed Senior Resident in Bornu, Northern Nigeria, Lugard 'deprecated' the appointment in an official despatch because of his youth and lack of experience. This angered Hamilton:

In thus criticising an appointment made deliberately by the Secretary of State, Sir F. Lugard has overstepped the brink of his function as High Commissioner; and if it had been anyone else, one would have been inclined to suggest that he should be politely told to mind his own business. But Sir F. Lugard is such a very peculiar person, and we have got so into the way of putting up with his peculiarities, that I suppose that the usual allowance must be made for him on this occasion.

While writing his minute, Hamilton must have decided that Lugard perhaps should not have the 'usual allowance' made, He went on:

Sir F. Lugard's criticism amounts to an implication that the secretary of state is not sufficiently conversant with the conditions of Northern Nigeria to make appointments without first consulting him, and this, to put it mildly, is not quite the attitude to be assumed by the Administrator of a Protectorate toward the secretary of state.[142]

A calming influence generally, Antrobus suggested that he should have a quiet talk with Lugard when he arrived home on leave. Chamberlain asked him to tell Lugard, 'I regret that he should have written such a letter.' After the interview, Lugard became quite apologetic about his action and 'much distressed to think that he had written something of which Mr. Chamberlain disapproved'. The Nigeria Department officials were no doubt pleased by this.[143]

Governors distrusted permanent staff, and the staff had little respect for the governors. The permanent officials believed that the 'best and brightest' of the civil service recruits either entered the Home Civil Service as they had done, or the Indian Civil Service. Their different backgrounds, and the different contexts in which they worked, guaranteed that they would frequently rub one another the wrong way. Governors tended to think that all Secretaries of State were under the thumb of their permanent officials. In 1910 Sir Charles Bruce, who had served as colonial governor in Mauritius, maintained that:

> Every secretary of state, however well-intentioned, energetic, and capable he may be, is likely sooner or later, to become the medium, conscious or unconscious, through which the permanent heads of the office will carry out their policy.[144]

The actual relationship between the Secretary of State and his officials, as we shall see in the case studies in the next section of the book, was much more complex than Bruce's simplistic rendering might lead one to believe. None the less it indicates and emphasises the governors' perception of that relationship and consequent suspicion and unease when making proposals to the Colonial Office. The governors knew everything was filtered through permanent officials who were the official eyes and ears of the Secretary of State.

Lugard's angry comment that 'one never knows where one is with this more than damned Colonial Office'[145] fairly represents the governors' feelings toward permanent staff. And Frederick Butler's sarcastic comment about how to read Lugard's despatches – first one had to try 'to ascertain . . . what, if anything, Sir F. Lugard means by what he actually says'[146] – fairly represents the staff attitude towards most governors. For the most part, however, they all realised they were part of the same system, and had to do the best they could, with what they had, to make it work.[147]

CONCLUSION: THE COLONIAL OFFICE AND WHITEHALL

This chapter contains the foundations for the next six chapters – case studies of the Colonial Office's work on the formation and implementation of administrative, financial, and economic policies in Nigeria from the late 1890s to 1914. The underlying assumption of these pages is that the context of action, and the background of the actors, is a crucial key to correctly understanding action itself. It should be noted that two other departments – the Treasury and the Crown Agents for the Colonies – were involved so frequently in Nigerian affairs that they became, practically speaking, part of the Colonial Office context itself. These departments will be discussed when and as they relate to particular topics.

A last point to make, and one important to the thesis of this book, refers to the Colonial Office as a part of Whitehall. There should be no doubt that the Colonial Office and its permanent officials were typical of a great department of state at the turn of the century. It, and they, did not exist in an isolated enclave for governing the Colonial Empire; the Colonial Office and its staff were part of the British administrative mainstream. In demonstrating this, four aspects of a Whitehall department should be examined: its organisation; its decision-making and work procedures; the function of its Upper Division clerks; and the background of those clerks.

First, regarding organisation, A. Lawrence Lowell, author of *The Government of England*, wrote in 1908 that:

> Although in origin and legal organization the departments of state are very unlike, yet the growth of custom, and the exigencies of parliamentary life, have, for practical purposes, forced almost all of them into something very near one common type. Whatever the legal form of the authority at their head, the actual control is now in nearly every case in the hands of a single responsible minister, usually assisted by one or more parliamentary subordinates, and supported by a corps of permanent non-political officials, who carry on the work of the office.[148]

This was true whether one was talking about the Treasury, the Board of Trade, the Colonial Office, or any other department of state. Second, with few exceptions, the decision-making and general work procedures described earlier in this chapter were the same for other departments.[149] Lowell again bears witness to this, noting, after describing the system, that:

> Each permanent official thus performs a double service for his

immediate superior. He collects all the material that bears upon a question, presenting it in such a form that a decision can be readily and quickly made; and he acts to a certain extent as a reader, examining a mass of papers that the superior would be quite unable to go through, and making up his own mind how far they contain anything that requires his chief's attention. This system runs throughout the department, from the junior first-class clerks to the parliamentary head, each official deciding what he will submit to his superior; in the same way the minister himself determines when he will settle on his own authority, and what he had better lay before the cabinet.[150]

This procedure was true no matter what department one was discussing.

Third, across the Civil Service Upper Division, clerks performed similar functions and carried out similar tasks. A few late nineteenth-century examples from testimony of senior officials in three departments, including the Colonial Office, demonstrate this. Sir Reginald Welby, Treasury Permanent Secretary, explained that Upper Division clerks were:

charged with the *deliberative* and *executive* [his emphasis] work of the Treasury, i.e., they consider the merits of proposals submitted to the Department, and compose letters sanctioning, criticising, or refusing them, as the case may be.[151]

H. Calcraft described the clerks of the Board of Trade as undertaking:

the more important general work of the [Board of Trade] departments to which they were attached, such as the preparation of memoranda and precis, drafting letters, etc.[152]

Richard Ebden of the Colonial Office said that Upper Division clerks there dealt with:

the political, financial, administrative, and other business arising in the four geographical divisions of the office . . . They are authorised to dispose at once of minor business . . . As regards remaining business their duties are to submit for consideration, as far as they are able to do, the course to be taken on the various questions arising, or to present the subject matter in a shape to facilitate the forming of a decision, to draft letters and despatches, carrying out the decisions arrived at, and to prepare precis and memoranda on important questions.[153]

Clearly, although the language differed, the work described was very similar.

Fourth, regarding background, the available evidence generally reinforces what has already been said. Upper (or First) Division clerks were university men. This can be seen by looking at Table 1.7.[154]

TABLE 1.7 *Universities attended by open competition recruits to the upper division of the civil service in 1877, 1895, and 1910*

Year	Oxford	Cambridge	Others	Privately educated	Total
1877	6	2	1	1	10
1895	10	1	0	0	11
1910	13	8	8	0	29*
Totals	29	11	9	1	50

* There were only twenty-eight upper division recruits in 1910: one attended two universities.

The total of First Division open competition clerks, taken into the Civil Service in the years 1877, 1895, and 1910 respectively, was forty-nine. Out of this group only one did not go to a university – he was privately educated. This puts the Colonial Office's Nigeria Department on a par with the rest of the Civil Service: twenty out of the twenty-one permanent officials who served in that Department between 1898 and 1914 went to university. When we look at the sample years of 1877, 1895, and 1910 we see that these men overwhelmingly attended Oxford or Cambridge, mostly the former. Toward the end of this period this tends to lessen a bit, but the number and percentage is still sufficiently high so that the basic contention is not undermined. By comparison, at the Colonial Office, eighteen of twenty who attended university attended Oxford or Cambridge, again mainly the former. In terms of the subjects studied, the Upper Division recruit in general resembled to a high degree his Colonial Office counterpart, especially in the most numerically significant category – classic graduates. This is especially so for Oxford men: if we combine the figures for 1895 and 1910 we see that twenty-two out of twenty-three Oxford recruits to the Upper Division of the Civil Service studied classics. In the Nigeria Department the number was eleven out of eleven. The social background of the First Division recruit was generally about the same as that of the Colonial Office clerk: they all come from the upper-middle reaches of society. As A. Lawrence Lowell pointed out in 1908, a listing of the occupations of the fathers of the successful candidates contained no peers and only a few tradesmen.[155]

The conclusion to be drawn is obvious: the Colonial Office, organisationally and administratively, and in its decision-making process, was hardly different from other departments of state. Additionally, Upper Division clerks in the Colonial Office in no important way differed from their colleagues across the Civil Service. There was no reason to expect that Colonial Office staff would develop an imperialist ethos. And they did not. What did develop in the Colonial Office (and the rest of the Civil Service) was an administrative ethos in which permanent officials had a high degree of loyalty to the state, to the government of the day, and to their own department. However, this loyalty never interfered with a civil servant's ability to approach critically all proposals put before him. They were required to master the details of administration and policy implementation. This was an important ingredient of permanent officials' influence, for as Sir Henry Taylor wrote, 'details make the substance of public affairs'.[156] Permanent officials were wedded to their routine and painstakingly cautious in their methodology. By any standard they were efficient and competent. However, they were different from their counterparts in the private sector. Why was this? As one permanent official said in 1908, the Civil Service, as opposed to the man of business in the private sector, was

> invariably subject to fixed limitations – the rules of the service, estimates and status; the business is not his private business, and he must deal with it under direction.

This did not mean that civil servants were unimaginative or lacking in energy and initiative. 'Government business,' the writer continued, rather loftily,

> is conducted on honest, and usually sound, lines, and, if it does not propagate the type of worker who flourishes by crushing his rivals, it encourages steady application and disinterested character.[157]

It also inculcated a cautious approach to the business of their Office. One should not read 'conservative' for 'cautious', even though 'cautious' was a byword among officials. To do so would give permanent officials in the Upper Division a reputation not necessarily deserved. A person could be cautious in his approach to work and yet the results of that work might be, in ideological terms, liberal *or* conservative, progressive *or* reactionary. In the final analysis, permanent officials were all, or tended to be, cautious administrative pragmatists. This was true whether a clerk worked in the Treasury, the War Office, the Board of Trade, the Colonial Office, or any other office of state.

2 Crown Colony Government in Nigeria, 1897–1914

In 1910, Sir Charles Bruce, author and colonial administrator, characterised Crown Colonies as:

> Colonies not possessing responsible government, in which the administration is carried on by public officers under the control of the Secretary of State for the Colonies.[1]

These 'public officers' were almost always white. This was not so on narrowly racist grounds but from larger considerations of policy. Rulers of empires – ancient, medieval, or modern – have always assumed that beyond a certain level colonial administrators had to be from the imperial metropolis. This notion effectively excludes the imperialised, no matter what their qualifications or racial origins. This age-old imperial view was also found in the British Colonial Office. In 1910, Charles Strachey, Principal Clerk in the Nigeria Department, commented on a complaint by Henry Carr, a black West African who was also Senior Inspector of schools in Lagos Colony. Carr had expressed dissatisfaction because:

> in practice, the coloured man in West African found it impossible to rise so high or so rapidly as the white man, even though his qualifications were as good or better.

Strachey's response was:

> On the general question of blacks it is necessary to recognise that the administration of the West African Colonies is British and that as long as this is the case no native African can expect to be appointed to any but subordinate posts.

48

Strachey then continued his argument, and in doing so took it beyond classic administrative common sense and into racial realms:

> Apart from this general fact [as given above] it is also the case (1) That the native African is rarely if ever so well 'qualified' – using the word in a wide sense, and not merely as meaning academic qualifications – as an Englishman to fill a post involving the exercise of authority.
>
> (2) That Englishmen object to work under Africans. This applies to all classes of Englishmen, but it may be said in particular that the number of men of the artisan class . . . willing to serve in West African – already embarrassingly small – would be reduced to *nil* if they were informed that they would have to take their orders from Africans.
>
> (3) That the natives generally are accustomed to see authority in the hands of Europeans, and regard it as a matter of course. If a white man were subordinated to a black, he would no doubt lose the respect of the natives.[2]

Clearly, race was an element in this policy, but it was not the only element or even the controlling element.

Within Bruce's definition of a Crown Colony there were several distinctive groups.[3] The least-advanced Crown Colonies were those in which the Governor, or High Commissioner, ruled as a despot, with no legal need to consult his subordinates or those over whom he ruled. The expectation was that the despot would be enlightened. If he were not, the Colonial Office would show him the error of his ways. In the period 1898–1914 both Northern and Southern Nigeria were in just such a situation. Lagos Colony was somewhat more developed – it had a Legislative Council with native and European (mercantile) representation on it. However, colonial government officials appointed to it by the Governor remained a majority. The most advanced type of Crown Colony might have a partly elected legislature, but the Governor was in no way responsible to it. In short, although the Governor ruled his colony, we should emphasise that the policy on which he based his rule was something hammered out between himself and the Colonial Office.

The significance of Crown Colony Government was that it provided a secure framework within which to develop and administer a territory such as Lagos or Northern or Southern Nigeria. With this in mind, we can turn to a discussion of the Nigerian Crown Colonies and the early development planning for what was called in the 1890s the Niger Territories. Several administrative problems that presented themselves to the Colonial Office in its Nigerian work, and which had important consequences for both Nigerian and African history during and after the colonial period, will then be discussed. They deal with the military dimension of Crown Colony Government; the origin, development, and consequences of indirect rule in Northern Nigeria; the 1906 and 1914 amalgamations in Nigeria; and finally Lugard's scheme of continuous administration.

EARLY PLANNING FOR NIGERIA

One of the first Colonial Office efforts, in May 1897, was permanent official Herbert J. Read's 'Memorandum on British Possessions in West Africa'.[4] Discursive in nature, it assessed the situation in British West Africa and proposed for Nigeria a wide range of policy goals. There were three administrations there – Lagos Colony, the Niger Coast Protectorate, and the Royal Niger Company – working within 'inconvenient and unscientific boundaries'. Read suggested that all three areas should be placed under Colonial Office administration and eventually amalgamated into one large colony.[5] He also suggested a variety of projects for the region – for example, the development of a quasi-military police force similar to the Royal Irish Constabulary, the creation of a small army of four or five thousand natives to be led by British officers, construction of a railway from the coast to Kano, and the establishment of a coin-based currency to replace cowries and slaves. Additionally Read thought that the development of natural resources in Nigeria should be encouraged.[6] There is no indication that this long memorandum (forty-eight pages) influenced British policy. Nevertheless, its very existence proves that in the 1890s the Colonial Office was aware that West Africa posed problems for the British Empire and felt impelled to do something constructive about these problems. Read's memorandum is an early indication of the Colonial Office's desire to develop the 'undeveloped estates'.

In the summer of 1898 the Niger Committee, whose origins and purpose have been discussed in the Introduction, met and issued its report. The report was one of the most important documents to issue from the Colonial Office on the future of Nigeria. G. N. Uzoigwe has rightly characterised it as 'an essential document to the understanding

of the post-1898 political and economic developments in Nigeria'.[7]
The report differed from Read's memorandum in that its purpose was
to provide the Colonial Office with guidelines for the development of
Nigeria.[8] It addressed itself, at Chamberlain's request, to the
question of the future administration of the three Niger Territories –
should they be amalgamated, and, if so, when and by what
process – as well as a host of other questions concerning the
administrative, military, economic, and financial development of the
territories. On the key question of amalgamation the Committee
recommended eventual amalgamation under a Governor-General,
but only under certain conditions.[9] Until these conditions were met
there must be at least two, and possibly three, separate colonies; that
is, in addition to Lagos Colony, there should be a Maritime Province
and a Soudan Province.[10] The latter two eventually became Southern
and Northern Nigeria respectively. The Committee's policy goal,
total amalgamation, was not immediately possible. The report also
proposed that each colony be divided into conventional divisions and
districts and administered by British colonial servants. One member
of the Committee, Sir Henry McCallum, Governor of Lagos,
recommended that native chiefs be organised in village and district
councils as a part of each colony's administrative structure. Indirect
rule was an obvious and natural solution to the imperial problem of
how to govern huge territories with severely limited resources. This
method of ruling through native authorities was already a familiar
and acceptable one to the Committee,[11] despite the fact that in later
years the concept of indirect rule was attributed to Sir Frederick
Lugard. The Niger Committee's report was a blueprint for the future,
and much of British Nigerian policy over the next several decades was
an outgrowth of, and an elaboration on, the Committee's recommendations.

The Colonial Office sent a draft of the report to McCallum and
Moor (administrative head of the Niger Coast Protectorate and
Committee member) for their comments before it was formally
accepted. While the Committee had been deliberating McCallum had
supported the view that only two colonies – a northern and southern
one – should be formed from the Niger Territories. On reflection,
however, he decided that because of the poor communication and
transportation system between Lagos and the rest of Nigeria, there
should be two southern colonies and a third in the north. Although
McCallum insisted that his main concern was the most efficient
administration of the colonies it is equally possible that he was

attempting to protect his position. He may have feared that Lagos would be absorbed by a southern Nigerian colony and his job would be jeopardised. Moor, on the other hand, argued that the southern territories could and should be governed by one man. All it required was the 'formation of a competent staff, and the proper splitting of the territories into divisions'. However, he reminded the Committee that 'The European element of the colonial administration is too small and individually changing to really govern the natives', and emphasised the need for indirect rule.[12]

Sir Frederick Lugard, the first High Commissioner of Northern Nigeria, while not a member of the Committee, also had plans for northern Nigeria. In early 1899, Reginald Antrobus, Assistant Under Secretary, conferred with Lugard and found his outlook on Nigeria 'too vague and expansive'. Antrobus suggested to the Permanent Under Secretary that Lugard be advised to lower his expectations and work within available funds. Lugard was asked to submit a statement to Secretary of State Chamberlain concerning his policy goals for northern Nigeria.[13] This statement dealt with a number of topics, but was particularly concerned with the immediate requirements of the situation rather than such long-term eventualities as amalgamation. For example, he wanted to occupy the country at once, to develop a transportation system which would make resource exploitation possible, to encourage agricultural and mineral development, and to prevent – by force if necessary – slave-raiding and slave-dealing. Regarding the last, permanent officials did not object to the suggestion of the use of force, but Mercer and Antrobus felt that for Lugard to use troops 'as he found prudent and necessary' would not be wise. Chamberlain agreed, saying that, 'Col. Lugard must always remember that we know general situations . . . and a just war may be most impolitic if commenced at the wrong time.'[14] Over the years the Colonial Office was to become very familiar with Lugard's tendency to attempt too much too soon. For the moment, however, the Office was reassured because, as Antrobus noted, 'This seems to be on the right lines. Col. Lugard does not now dwell, as he used to do, on the needs of an establishment comparable to those of the Gold Coast or Lagos.'[15]

Antrobus himself should be heard from. From 1898 to 1909, as Assistant Under Secretary in charge of Nigerian business, he was the senior permanent official most closely associated with Nigerian policy. Although he had been a member of the Niger Committee, the Committee's report did not indicate his views. However, a month before the Niger Committee met, Antrobus had outlined the probable results of its deliberations. In his view it was quite enough to expect the Colonial Office to arrange the administrative takeover of the Royal Niger Company. Therefore, Lagos and the Niger Coast Protectorate (soon to be Southern Nigeria) must continue for some time to be administered under the existing arrangements,[16] and not expect to be united. Amalgamation would come – but later rather than sooner. Antrobus clearly expected the new colonies to have minimal administrations, i.e. they should make extensive use of the native authorities, and maintain only a small European staff. The two main goals of the colonial governments should be improved means of communications – especially by railway – and the protection of traders.[17] Finally, the area that would soon be Northern Nigeria was not ready for a full-fledged colonial establishment, no matter what Lugard seemed to want. On this point Antrobus wrote that, 'the more money we spend on salaries of officials the less chance we shall have getting funds eventually . . . which will be required for the development of the country'.[18] The Colonial Office, Antrobus believed, had to be on guard against the immodest visions to which most governors seemed prone. Neither the Colonial Office, nor the colonial governments, had access to unlimited funds. In general, Antrobus felt that those interested in colonial development should not attempt to accomplish more than could reasonably be expected.[19]

All of this early planning – by the Niger Committee, by Nigerian governors, and by permanent officials concerned with Nigeria – helped shape the context within which decisions regarding Nigeria were made over the years. Concurrent with this planning for the future was the actual establishment of the Crown Colony governments of Southern and Northern Nigeria. (Lagos Colony had been established in 1861, and in the 1890s had steadily expanded its authority to the north and to the east.) In 1898 and 1899 names were discussed for the two new colonies. Sir George Goldie, head of the Royal Niger Company, suggested 'Niger Soudan' and 'Niger Coast' respectively. Antrobus thought that, strictly speaking, the base names for both should be 'Negrita', but since 'Nigeria' had by then become a familiar term they should stick with it. He favoured 'Southern Nigeria' and 'Northern Nigeria' or 'Lower Nigeria' and 'Upper Nigeria'. Chamberlain favoured the former two titles, and Southern Nigeria and Northern Nigeria were the names agreed on.[20] The Colonial Office decided, because of certain legal aspects of the situation, to call the governors of the new colonies 'high commissioners'. However, functionally speaking, it made little difference. They were the administrative and executive head of a colony's government. Ralph Moor, who had been head of the Niger Coast Protectorate, became High Commissioner when Southern Nigeria came into being. By mid-1898 it was clear that Lugard was the choice for High Commissioner in Northern Nigeria.[21] The Royal Niger Company's administration over that territory had been at best minimal and at worst non-existent. Consequently Lugard was very busy throughout late 1898 and all 1899 arranging for staff and supplies to be sent out to Northern Nigeria, but at last the work was done. On 1 January 1900 the Colonial Office took over the Niger Company's and the Niger Coast Protectorate's territory. All three Nigerian colonies were now in place.

THE MILITARY DIMENSION OF CROWN COLONY GOVERNMENT

During the administrative occupation of a British African Crown Colony the military could have at least three functions: internal security; pacification; and defence against external aggression. In a generally peaceful colony such as Lagos there was little need, by 1900, for an active military establishment. This was not the case in Southern and Northern Nigeria. For several years at the turn of the century the main function of the military was to subdue, i.e. pacify, the tribes and peoples that had not yet submitted to British overrule. Only when this had been done could traditional Crown Colony administration begin. Clearly the military had an important role. It established by a show of, or use of, force the precondition (submission to British rule) necessary to setting up Crown Colony Government.

Obviously the Colonial Office had no active role in the military campaigns; it was instead responsible for advising on the wisdom and timing of involvement in a colonial war. It functioned as the political co-ordinator of certain aspects of a colonial military campaign. To carry out this function it was vital that the Colonial Office be fully informed as to the purpose, planning, and progress of any expeditionary force. What follows are discussions of the work the Colonial Office did regarding military affairs of Southern and Northern Nigeria. These discussions are not, and are not meant to be, narrative histories of military campaigns in colonial Nigeria. They are selections from the military history of Nigeria to illustrate certain points.[22] In Southern Nigeria, Sir Ralph Moor and Sir Walter Egerton co-ordinated all important phases of their campaigns with the Colonial Office. In Northern Nigeria, Lugard did not. As always he operated differently. He tended to keep his military plans to himself, thus causing problems and anxiety for the Colonial Office.

Moor's expedition against the Aros was the only major campaign in the South after 1898 and the Colonial Office considered it the very model of a major military campaign. Moor may have been less enthusiastic – he had to request permission three times and it took two and a half years for his request to be approved and the expedition carried out. Moor first sought approval of the military expedition into Iboland (eastern Nigeria) in September 1899, a few months before the Colonial Office formally took over Southern Nigeria. Moor wished to destroy the political and commercial stranglehold of the Aros, and to abolish slavery in the area.[23] Although Moor convinced the Colonial Office that this must be done, he did not convince officials there that it had to be done immediately. Strachey's reaction was typical. He was willing to admit that an expedition was necessary but, given that Southern Nigerian troops were not at full strength, he felt it made no sense to embark on the expedition. His immediate superior, William Mercer, agreed that no critical situation existed. Perhaps the Aros were not as hostile as had been thought. Anyone, Mercer noted, could come up with a reason to justify an expedition, 'but the kind of ingenuity that is wanted is that which discovers means of avoiding expensive expeditions and of promoting commercial intercourse by other methods'. Antrobus, however, was not sanguine about the chances of a peaceful resolution of the situation. Moor's view, that it would be better to go to the heart of the situation at once and break the power of the Aros, had great force. What militated against it was the current situation: the Foreign Office was about to relinquish responsibility for the area, the Southern Nigerian military was being reorganised, and further afield the South African War had just broken out. Since the Aro problem was not an actual emergency, the Colonial Office felt they should not permit Moor to launch an expedition. Secretary of State Chamberlain found this analysis persuasive, saying 'the people on the spot ought to know best – but they are sometimes too much in a hurry'. He also hoped that the Aros could be brought gradually under control without war. However, before he definitely turned down Moor's request, Chamberlain wanted to have the opinion of two Nigerian experts – Sir George Goldie and Lugard.[24] Goldie came down firmly on Moor's side: 'I do not believe that anything but force can effectively destroy or even weaken the influence of the Long Juju [the phrase he used to describe the Aro leadership and power generally] over its present large sphere of influence.'[25] Lugard agreed but thought the moment inopportune. He was taking over a new colonial government and did not wish to be forced to lend his soldiers to Southern Nigeria when he might need them. This clinched the case; Moor's request was turned down, but with the understanding that when the time was right the Colonial Office would not object.[26]

In the spring of 1900, Moor again proposed the expedition, this time for the following December, and was given provisional authority to proceed. The expedition could only go forward if the British position in the South African War and, now, the Ashanti War greatly improved.[27] At the Colonial Office's request Moor submitted a military plan and cost-estimate in June. Mercer chose this opportunity to use his earlier argument that the expense of military expeditions might on occasion make them unnecessary if there was another way out. The proposed expedition should be judged on commercial facts – i.e. 'How far would the trade and revenue of Southern Nigeria benefit from a successful expedition, taking into account the permanent expenditure which new territory is likely to bring?' Over time, trade and revenue from the area would grow whether or not an expedition took place. Therefore, Moor's campaign should not be allowed. The Aros were great traders, and their hostility arose not surprisingly from a fear that they would lose their trade if the area was opened up and taken over by the British. If his analysis was correct, continued Mercer, then 'it may be possible that with judicious handling this may be kept fairly quiet and reasonable until the time arrives for effective administration'.[28] Mercer emerged from this analysis as one strongly committed to the idea of peaceful penetration. His colleagues, however, were very pessimistic. Antrobus argued that 'unless the expedition is carried out trade will suffer and the [Southern Nigerian] revenue will fall off'; in which case the Secretary of State seemed to feel that the expedition should go sooner rather than later. The only question then was whether the men and the money would be available in December.[29]

In July and August it began to be clear that the Ashanti War, at least, was being won, but slowly. The result was, as Baillie Hamilton put it, that:

we have come absolutely to the bottom of our resources as regards officers, even if we were to succeed in scraping together a few Canadians or other militia officers (half of whom would probably be unfit for the work) they would be without men to command.

He was unhappy with this conclusion. 'It would be a great pity to give it up', he said, 'but what are we to do?'[30] What they did was to withdraw the provisional permission to go ahead. Antrobus explained the situation to Moor personally and Moor accepted this, but warned that the Aros, by their own action, might force his hand.[31]

In June 1901, Moor sent in a third proposal for the expedition. By this time the Ashanti campaign was over and so more troops were available, but there were raised eyebrows at the Colonial Office over Moor's estimates. He had estimated that in his first two proposals the expedition would require 900 to 1,200 men and would cost £5,000 to £6,000. Now Moor wanted 1,550 native soldiers, 75 British officers and non-commissioned officers, 7 medical officers, 5 political officers, and 2,100 carriers. Estimated cost was £35,000. However, Southern Nigeria was very healthy economically and in consequence had large surplus reserves. Baillie Hamilton observed that the 'details appear well and carefully thought out' and said they should approve the expedition – particularly as it would probably be the last large military campaign that Southern Nigeria would undertake. Antrobus concurred, saying:

> The main reason for taking action now is that, if we do not undertake the operations at the time which suits us best, the Aros may force our hands and compel us to engage in a punitive expedition at some most inconvenient time.

Chamberlain was also convinced that the time had come to settle the Aro question:

> Otherwise we shall be allowing the worst kind of slave raiding in our Protectorate and shall run the risk of a great stoppage of trade.[32]

And so, flying the flags of civilisation and commerce, the Colonial Office finally authorised the expedition to begin in December 1901. Over the summer the Aros conveniently made some slave raids on neighbouring tribes, providing the Colonial Office and the Southern

Nigerian Government with, as Nigeria Department member Butler termed it, 'the technical justification for the expedition' which, as he further noted, had 'already been decided to be necessary on more general grounds'.[33] The expedition began and ended right on schedule. It was very successful. In fact, the military power of the Aros turned out to be a myth, and their power was sufficiently broken to allow the effective administrative occupation of south-eastern Southern Nigeria to take place.

The Colonial Office could not have been happier with Moor. Butler thought it 'a great thing in an unknown West African territory to have brought elaborate military operations to a successful conclusion within a few days of the time predicted'. Chamberlain too was pleased; the expedition had gone like clockwork and had caused no political problems in London. The 'Long Juju', which Chamberlain had characterised as 'an extraordinary combination of superstition and arbitrary government', was no more.[34] In the two-and-a-half years that elapsed between the planning and the execution of the expedition, the Colonial Office and Moor had worked together well as a team. The Colonial Office wanted assurance that the expedition was justified – or at least could be justified, that Southern Nigeria could pay for it, and that Moor would keep them informed at all stages of planning and action. This last point was seen as especially important should questions be raised in the House of Commons about pacification policy. Moor fulfilled the permanent officials' hopes and at the same time got what he wanted. Indeed his approach to military action was greatly appreciated at the Colonial Office.

As Baillie Hamilton had predicted, the Aro expedition was the last major expedition in Southern Nigeria. However, when Moor resigned in 1903 a substantial portion of the northeastern section of Southern Nigeria still remained outside British administration. Moor's successor, Sir Walter Egerton, quickly embarked on, with the blessings of the Colonial Office, a policy of sending out pacification patrols annually. For the most part the patrols did not involve the use of force so much as they did the threat of force if submission was not made. At the beginning of each dry season the Southern Nigerian troops would establish a central base on the edge of the area they were to take over. Then small columns of soldiers would be sent out to different parts of the unoccupied country. Usually this show of force was enough, and the area would soon be open for the introduction of district administration and commercial development. Egerton claimed that by this method 'within a year of the occupation of a district the political officer in charge is generally able to travel in any direction without a military escort'.[35]

The Conservative Government, in power from 1895 to 1905, had accepted this policy without question. When the new Liberal Government came in, the Parliamentary Under Secretary, Winston Churchill, questioned the policy. In an early example of Churchillian prose, he said:

> These warlike operations are so much accepted as a matter of course in the dry season, that one would imagine only ordinary autumn manoeuvres were in question. It is clear that the scope and character of British activities in Nigeria require to be more definitely confined and the whole question and policy to be brought under review.

The 'serious, indefinite and ever-expanding' responsibilities might soon mean that they were gravely overcommitted in Nigeria.[36] Secretary of State Lord Elgin ignored Churchill, thus graphically illustrating the relative impotence of the Parliamentary Under Secretary no matter how capable the individual holding that post might be. Indeed the annual patrols, once started, seemed to have a life and a momentum all their own.[37] What Elgin and the Colonial Office wanted most was to be consulted before the patrols started, and to have a chance to approve, modify, or reject the governor's proposals. Egerton had, as had Moor before him, co-operated fully in this. Egerton's annual patrols continued until all Southern Nigeria was under civil administration.

Northern Nigeria, however, was a different story. The conquest of the country was carried out while Sir Frederick Lugard was High Commissioner (1900–6). Lugard was a secretive person who had an almost obsessive need to be in control of a situation. He was most reluctant to allow the Colonial Office to supervise his work, especially in military affairs. John Flint has called him, correctly, an 'autocrat'.[38] Although only 10 per cent of Northern Nigeria was in British hands in 1900, the Colonial Office was not interested in rapid occupation. Most of Northern Nigeria was part of the Fulani Empire, with its religious and political capital at Sokoto, and its commercial centre at Kano. Both the political head and permanent officials at the Colonial Office realised the need to eventually occupy the north; but they were also aware of the obstacles – financial as well as military and political.[39] They also realised that, as Antrobus warned, 'The nation doesn't like a policy which involves us in little wars.'[40]

When Lugard was first appointed, permanent officials feared that he might be influenced by the strong military element in Northern Nigeria.[41] Butler described the sentiments of this group as being:

> that the native should do as he is told or be 'smashed', coupled with a lurking desire that he will choose to be 'smashed' and so afford an opportunity for the display of the qualities in which the military man excels.[42]

Too late the officials discovered that, in fact, Lugard was this military element's leading spirit, and was himself convinced that the best basis for British rule in Nigeria was conquest. Before Lugard went out to Nigeria, Antrobus did his best in private conversation to impress upon him that he had to go slowly because the Colonial Office did not have access to unlimited funds. None the less, Antrobus felt that Lugard 'still wants to begin on a larger scale than seems to me either practical or desirable'.[43] The home government would not favour a too-precipitous conquest of the northern territory because it could not immediately finance and staff an occupying administration. Lugard was told not to start military operations without first receiving approval from the Secretary of State.[44] This was British policy in Northern Nigeria.

However, Lugard, unlike Moor and Egerton, was uninterested in observing proper procedure or in soothing official fears. He wanted to conquer the peoples and rulers of Northern Nigeria and he was sure that the Colonial Office staff did not have the same wisdom as he did. Consequently, he deliberately refrained from informing the Office of his military plans until they were complete or impossible to halt. Butler described early military operations of Lugard's in Northern Nigeria as follows:

> In the case of Bida and Kontagora, we had news of the aggressive action on the part of the two Emirs; then came a lull in our information; and next we had a telegram saying that they had been defeated and expelled. There was not a word in advance about the military preparations and the intentions to attack at the particular time.[45]

Of course, when his expeditions were successful, the Colonial Office staff did not complain that he had kept them uninformed. However much Lugard favoured this 'policy of silence' it made the Colonial Office very unhappy.[46]

Kano and Sokoto were the most significant targets in Northern

Nigeria. Consequently Lugard's decision to embark on an expedition against them represented a major step for the future of British rule in Northern Nigeria, but the Colonial Office only learned of his plans accidentally. In February 1902, Antrobus assured his colleagues that it was 'no part' of Lugard's policy to 'upset the existing situation in the North'.[47] Six months later, however, an expedition was being planned, and one of Lugard's staff members, Reginald Popham-Lobb, wrote to his mother that 'we are going to smash Kano after the rains in December . . . It will be the last big expedition in the Protectorate, I expect, and I am in hopes of going up with it.'[48] At that point, Mrs Popham-Lobb knew more than the permanent officials at the Colonial Office.

Lugard clearly intended to leave the Colonial Office in ignorance until the campaign was over, or at least well under way. However, a news story in *The Times* on 5 December 1902, and a second one carried by the Reuters News Agency a few days later, announced preparations for the imminent campaign against Kano.[49] As the news spread in England, questions were raised in the House of Commons, and a leading merchant, J. A. Hutton, protested Lugard's policy as unnecessary and bad for West African trade. The Colonial Office was anxious to reassure West African merchants that Northern Nigeria was *not* engaged in an unnecessary little war; but first they had to discover what Northern Nigeria was engaged in.[50] The Colonial Office, totally in the dark, despatched a telegram immediately. Until Lugard replied, complained Ommanney, 'we are open to the charge of having been less well informed on this important subject than the outside public'.[51] The Colonial Office was reluctant to admit ignorance because:

It may be of importance hereafter to be able to show that we acted with full knowledge and not merely on what could be implied from the very general statements contained in [Lugard's] . . . despatches.[52]

Aside from their reluctance to lose face and their natural concern about military activity in Northern Nigeria, Colonial Office staff found themselves in a situation in which they could not carry out their function of co-ordination, supervision and policy-advising, because they were not fully informed.

On 23 December, Lugard replied to the Colonial Office telegram: he referred the Colonial Office to several vague references made in earlier despatches and letters which he suggested should have told the reader his plans. Butler and everyone else in the Office felt this was 'rather unfair' of Lugard. They could hardly have gathered from incidental and scattered allusions in previous correspondence 'the full extent and importance of his plans with regard to the great Hausa States of the North'. Butler began to have a strong sense of *déjà vu*: 'Sir Frederick Lugard,' he said, 'has tried to follow his favourite policy of keeping silence until the coup has been made.'[53] Lugard argued convincingly that he was well equipped with troops and supplies. Ommanney grumbled that 'If the information furnished by this telegram had been given earlier, our public position would have been stronger than it is.'[54] Partly reassured by Lugard's telegram, the Colonial Office decided not to interfere. Permanent officials felt that they had no choice except to approve Lugard's expedition and justify it if it was attacked.[55] If it were to fail they would of course disown him. The Colonial Office did call up other West African troops but Lugard decided to do without their assistance and ordered the expedition to move on without them.[56] This was exactly in character. Hoping to cover themselves at Lugard's expense the permanent officials sent Lugard another telegram stating that:

> even though approving generally of the policy pursued in Northern Nigeria . . . military operations should be avoided, if possible. The information in possession of His Majesty's Government is not so complete as they could have wished.[57]

Lugard however, an old hand at this game, responded by innocently asking if he should recall the expedition, knowing full well that the advance publicity had made this impossible. Lugard had forced the Office's hand. Two days after the campaign had actually begun, on 19 January 1903, the Colonial Office formally approved the expedition. That same day a regular despatch arrived from Lugard, dated 12 December, informing the Colonial Office of his intended expedition. When it had been sent, Lugard knew that it would not reach London for four or five weeks after the expedition had started.[58]

In any case, opposition from Kano and Sokoto was almost non-existent, and the reserves from outside proved unnecessary. The success of the Kano-Sokoto campaign broke the back of any large-scale opposition to the imposition of British rule in Northern Nigeria. Lugard implied that the Colonial Office had over-reacted and made a mountain out of a molehill. Ommanney vigorously disagreed:

Sir F. Lugard does not seem to realise that it was precisely his failure to supply the Secretary of State with information which gave rise to the exaggerated impression of great danger to British rule in Northern Nigeria and . . . at the same time prevented us from correcting that impression.[59]

Clearly, Lugard's main aim was to conquer the Hausa states. However, Lugard eventually produced an acceptable justification for the campaign: the murder of one Captain Moloney by an official of the emirate of Keffi. The official had fled to Kano and the ruler there would not return him to the British. Lugard's annual report would later say that:

If the life of a European can be taken with impunity the prestige of the Government would be gone, and prestige is another word for self-preservation in a country where millions are ruled by a few score.[60]

Chamberlain ended all Colonial Office debate on the subject by saying that he had spoken to Lugard and there was no need to take further action.[61]

Three years later, it became obvious that either Chamberlain had not spoken forcefully enough or Lugard had not been listening. In early 1906, Lugard telegraphed that he had sent a punitive expedition into Munshi, or Tiv, country, one of the few remaining areas in Northern Nigeria that had not fully accepted British rule, and that a despatch was on its way explaining the whole situation. Permanent officials, having been through all this before, thought it well to wait until the despatch arrived. However, the Secretary of State, Lord Elgin, and his Parliamentary Under Secretary, Winston Churchill, were not willing to wait. Churchill asked why Lugard could not confine himself to defensive operations while the Colonial Office considered the situation in light of all the information he could supply. Elgin added that when he had been Viceroy in India it had been customary to obtain government sanction for all military expeditions. Lugard was told that approval was denied until the Office received more information.[62] He promptly telegraphed back asking if he should recall the expedition. At the same time he wrote in injured tones to his wife:

With great difficulty I have got together a thoroughly efficient force. It is already practically on the spot and capable of dealing with the whole Munshi tribe. Not a word from the CO all this time. Now, when all the expense of transport has been incurred and men have worked day and night to do it, they wire they do not approve, and pending full information the expedition is to do nothing.[63]

Of course there had been 'not a word' from the Colonial Office because officials there had no idea he was getting together 'a thoroughly efficient force'. The Head of the Nigeria Department, Olivier, was resigned and matter-of-fact in his advice to Elgin:

I gather from this telegram that the expedition is already well on its way. We can either leave this unanswered until the mail brings Sir F. Lugard's despatch, or telegraph again to suspend operations now under way until the despatch has been received and considered.
I think we should let things take their course.

He also pointed out, as Lugard had, that:

If the millions of people [in Nigeria] who do not want us there once get the notion that our people can be killed with impunity they will not be slow to attempt it. They have no conscience nor compunction in this matter.
If we don't want to have to shed blood we should not be there.

It is interesting to note that Olivier, a Fabian socialist, used the word 'impunity' in the same imperialist way Lugard had used it to justify the Kano–Sokoto expedition. At a certain basic level, it would seem, all members of the British establishment supported the continuance of Empire. At any rate Olivier convinced Elgin; the expedition was allowed to continue and to do its job.[64]

Lugard saw himself as a martyr in all this manoeuvring. He thought he had been let down; this was not empire-building but bureaucratic nit-picking. On the other hand Colonial Office officials thought that Lugard had been secretive and had once again blackmailed them into supporting his judgement without sufficient independent data. Lugard was simply unwilling to operate according to procedures. After this incident, and over the next few years, the policy in Northern Nigeria followed that of Sir Walter Egerton's in Southern Nigeria – annual pacification patrols that opened up the area to British trade and administration.[65]

The Colonial Governor's military decisions played a crucial role in the administrative occupation of British tropical Africa. What happened in Nigeria happened, with variations, in British Crown Colonies in Africa and elsewhere. In some cases large forces were required; in others the threat of force was enough. The result was the submission of the African natives to Britain's sovereignty and the imposition of British rule. No matter what words and phrases were used to explain and justify the process by which Britain created an empire in Africa, it was a power struggle. The imperial administrative occupation of a territory was not an automatic process. In the Nigeria Department Frederick Butler realised this. Commenting on Lugard's military policy, he wrote in 1902 that conflict was

the natural and almost inevitable outcome of contact between British officers exercising a real power in the country and native states which have been long accustomed to undisputed sway.[66]

In carrying out military action the colonial Governor and his units had, so to speak, only a ground-level view. The Colonial Office alone could see the larger picture. Empire-wide considerations – military, economic, political, and strategic – inevitably coloured the situation in a given colony. A Governor might wish to authorise a military operation that, on its own merits, made sense. Certainly Moor saw his proposed expedition against the Aros in 1899 and 1900 in these terms. However, the Colonial Office considered such requests in terms of larger imperial needs. They knew that compared with the Ashanti War and the South African War the Aro expedition was not so urgent as Moor thought. In military matters the Colonial Office–Southern Nigeria relationship was a model of how a thing should be done. The Colonial Office–Northern Nigeria relationship was a model of how a thing should *not* be done. Lugard had purposely kept information from the Colonial Office. He had no intention of allowing global concerns to interfere with his plans in Northern Nigeria. Lugard himself was very lucky. All his campaigns – against Bida, Kontagora, Yola, Kano, Sokoto, etc. – were successes. As long as this was so, the Colonial Office had no real criticism to make that would effectively restrain him. Even Ommanney admitted that Lugard's policy seemed to have been justified by its success.[67] Along these lines the Assistant Under Secretary, George Fiddes, in 1911, commented on the actions of a Northern Nigerian officer in charge of an unsanctioned pacification patrol. In words applicable to Lugard and his expeditions, Fiddes noted that since the patrol had not run into any trouble it could not handle they would do nothing (except perhaps congratulate the officer in charge), but if the officer had been killed or wounded 'we should have said "what inexcusable rashness" '.[68]

Nothing succeeds like success. However, Lugard's behaviour inevitably stamped him as being uncooperative and potentially unreliable. This could not help but affect the way the Colonial Office viewed his proposals and requests in other areas. Fortunately, however, for the Colonial Office, there were more Moors and Egertons than there were Lugards.

INDIRECT RULE IN NORTHERN NIGERIA, 1900–1914

In British colonial administrative history the importance of indirect rule – in theory and in practice – should not be underestimated. Indirect rule, as it developed in Northern Nigeria before 1914, became the most influential model for local government in other British Crown Colonies. By the 1930s practically all of British tropical Africa, outside of the urban areas, had accepted indirect rule as the basic mode of local government. Traditionally Sir Frederick Lugard has been credited for this achievement. However, Mary Bull's important 1963 article, 'Indirect Rule in Northern Nigeria, 1906–1911', began to change this.[69] Bull argued convincingly that while Lugard was out of Nigeria between 1906 and 1912 senior officials in Northern Nigeria – called Residents – channelled the evolution of indirect rule into very conservative lines. Despite strenuous efforts upon his return in 1912, Lugard was unable to regain control of the development of indirect rule. Thus it was the Resident's model of indirect rule that was adopted throughout British tropical Africa. At its heart was the Native Treasury system, an administrative innovation of the Northern Nigerian Residents, which gave the local Native Administration, and therefore the Resident, institutional protection against and quasi-independence from the colony's central government.

One hitherto unexamined reason for the acceptance of this more conservative version of indirect rule is that Colonial Office staff adopted the more conservative interpretation as their own, and therefore were willing to defend what had become the status quo and to defend it successfully against Lugard's attacks. It is this crucial aspect of the story of indirect rule that has not been told. Its telling here will clearly highlight the very important role the Colonial Office played in the development of indirect rule.

The basic idea behind indirect rule was exceedingly simple. The imperial power should rule its possessions through indigenous leaders, governing through, as much as possible, indigenous authority structures. As simple as this was, there was more than one way to implement indirect rule. Here we will examine two: Lugard's way, and that of the Northern Nigerian Residents. Michael Crowder has very properly called the two methods, respectively, interventionist and non-interventionist approaches to indirect rule. In defining the two terms Crowder has written that:

> Indirect rule as conceived by Lord Lugard was to be a dynamic system of local government. The indigenous political institutions, under the guidance of the resident European political officer, would be continually developing into more efficient units of administration, responding to and adapting themselves to the new situations created by colonial rule. However, many of Lugard's successors followed a policy of minimal interference in the process of local government, preferring to let the traditional political institutions develop along their own lines rather than along lines laid down or suggested by the European administrator.[70]

Lugard came out to rule Northern Nigeria with firm and fixed ideas on how the job should be done. They had been formed by his experience in Uganda in the early 1890s.[71] A clear expression of these ideas by Lugard himself can be found in a memorandum he wrote in the late 1890s. 'In the early stages of British rule,' he noted,

> it is desirable to retain the native authority and to work through and by the native emirs. At the same time it is feasible by degrees to bring them gradually into approximation with our ideas of justice and humanity. . . . In pursuance of the above general principles the chief civil officers of the provinces are to be called Residents which implies one who carries on diplomatic relations rather than Commissioners or Administrators.[72]

Lugard saw indirect rule as a means to an end. (It is interesting to note that the Colonial Office initially feared that Lugard might destroy the influence of the native rulers and govern the country by white officials.)[73] It took Lugard three years of military campaigning before he could devote himself to developing and implementing his notions of indirect rule. In a speech to the elders of Sokoto after the conquest, he described his concept of indirect rule:

> The Fulani in old times . . . conquered this country. They took the right to rule over it, to levy taxes, to depose kings and to create kings. They in turn have by defeat lost their rule which has come into the hands of the British. All these things which I have said the Fulani by conquest took the right to do now pass to the British. Every Sultan and Emir and the principal officers of state will be appointed by the High Commissioner throughout all this country. The High Commissioner will be guided by the usual laws of succession and the wishes of the people and chief, but will set them aside if he desires for good cause to do so. The Emirs and chiefs who are appointed will rule over the people as of old time and take such taxes as are approved by the High Commissioner, but they will obey the laws of the Governor and will act in accordance with the advice of the Resident.[74]

In his system there would not be:

> two sets of rulers – British and Native – working either separately or in cooperation, but a single government in which the Native Chiefs have well defined duties and an acknowledged status equally with the British officials.[75]

> [The goal to achieve through indirect rule was] to regenerate this capable race of Fulanis and mould them to ideas of justice and mercy so that in a future generation, if not in this, they may become worthy instruments of rule.[76]

Lugard saw indirect rule as a tool for progress in an uncivilised land. He realised that the key people in carrying out this policy were his own British Residents stationed in the emirates and districts of Northern Nigeria. They had to be men of strong principles and of devotion to British rule. They had to be empathetic with native ideas, customs, and prejudices, yet they should not let their empathy turn into identification. Residents had to be loyal conduits of the High Commissioner's policy, yet never be seen to impose policy. In short, the Resident had to preserve the prestige of the Emir while ensuring that he ruled in accordance with the High Commissioner's policy. During his years as High Commissioner in Northern Nigeria Lugard did a great deal to convert his theory into administrative fact. On the basis of these efforts he made an early reputation as an able and innovative administrator. Colonial Office staff contributed little to Lugard's development of indirect rule beyond encouraging it as the most practical approach. The Colonial Office wanted colonial administrators to govern 'through native rulers, making them comply with our wishes, if necessary by force'.[77] The Colonial Office favoured indirect rule but was not at the time committed to any particular form.

The change in the Colonial Office's viewpoint was due to the creation of the Native Treasury system. Although the Native Treasury system was conceived and developed by Northern Nigerian Residents, it was anticipated in late 1905 by Sydney Olivier, a senior official in the Nigerian Department in London. Lugard suggested reimposing the old tax system (from the pre-British days) on the now-conquered province of Northern Nigeria, and then turning over the proceeds, or a substantial portion, to the local native ruler. Olivier opposed the idea. The Northern Nigerian taxation system was already oppressive; there was no need to give the Emir both the money and a free hand in spending it. Instead, the colonial government should control the spending:

If . . . it is necessary that we should provide the present rulers an income, I would limit it once and for all by a maximum, and make it a civil list with a definite understanding as to whom it was to be paid to, and on account of what public functions. That civil list will in course of time no doubt come up to be reconsidered; if their work is neglected or diminished, their annuities may to that extent be made terminable.[78]

Although Olivier did not contemplate the role colonial administrators might play, what he discussed later became the Native Treasuries.

After Lugard left Northern Nigeria in 1906 indirect rule was remoulded and redirected. Lugard's successors, Sir Percy Girouard and Sir Hesketh Bell, in the matter of indirect rule were content to be guided by the men Lugard had appointed as Residents in the chief Northern Nigeria emirates and districts. The ones most important to this process were John Burdon (1866–1937), Charles Temple (1871–1929), Charles Orr (1870–1945), Richmond Palmer (1877–

1958), and Hanns Vischer (1876–1945). The work of Temple and Palmer were especially important and should be examined here.

'Above all,' wrote Marjory Perham, 'there was Temple who had been Girouard's friend and chief of staff and had been given a very free hand with the northern administration as Bell's deputy governor.'[79] He was responsible for convincing Girouard and Bell that the Resident was the key to any proper system of indirect rule. He argued that the role of the Resident was to protect the natives of Northern Nigeria from outside influences while they developed in their own way at their own pace. The British were not in Northern Nigeria to westernise the African. Temple was considered something of a fanatic on his interpretation of indirect rule.[80] A. H. M. Kirk-Greene has characterised him as leading the 'rigid school' of 'ultra-conservative' indirect rulers, and thus being responsible for its fossilisation.[81]

Temple's views are best found in his book, based on his experiences in Northern Nigeria, called *Native Races and Their Rulers*. It has, since its publication, become a classic expression of the conservative, non-interventionist, school of indirect rule. On the Resident's work with an emir he wrote that:

[The Resident's] main object, one which he must ever bear in mind, is to create a situation resembling as far as possible that which existed, or might be imagined to have existed, were a thoroughly able, well-meaning, liberal-minded Emir ruling over a unit untouched by foreign influence. He must as far as possible keep his authority in the background and concealed, if not from the emir and his immediate entourage, at all events from the people generally. At the same time he must be on the alert to stamp out and if possible forestall the growth of the thousand and one measures by which oppression and malpractices can be exercised.[82]

Temple felt that the less the governor and the Colonial Office interfered, the better. He warned that the Resident's

work may be rendered abortive, either by a wrong orientation of the general policy laid down by the [Colonial] Government or by over centralization, that is to say, the curtailment of the executive power of the Residents, rendering necessary a reference of too many questions to Headquarters. Such references operate adversely in two ways, first they entail great delays in the execution of orders, secondly, they lower that moral prestige of the Resident among the natives on which he must chiefly depend as his main asset to enable him to carry out his duties successfully.

Finally he wrote that:

> Given a fairly free hand however, and a rightly decided main policy, a Resident can properly be held responsible for practically all administrative matters within the areas under his jurisdiction. Moreover, beyond affording him the help that a free hand and a sound policy gives, Headquarters can do little to assist him, though much may be done to thwart him.[83]

Thus the role of the Governor was to loyally support the Resident in whatever he did! This sort of argument, powerfully persuasive to his fellow Residents in Northern Nigeria, was equally so to officials at the Colonial Office. Temple's notion of indirect rule and the role of the Resident became accepted as the ideal to be achieved. For obvious reasons, it is this approach that Michael Crowder described as non-interventionist.

The single institutional development that allowed the emergence of the Resident as the most powerful official on the local and regional scene in colonial Northern Nigeria was the Native Treasury, also called the Beit-el-Mal. We have already seen how Olivier at the Colonial Office partially anticipated this development. It was also implicit in Lugard's early work. He established Native Administrations as the chief ruling institutions in each emirate and district. They were run and staffed by the traditional rulers who in turn were advised by a Resident. To operate effectively there had to be some way to account for revenue and expenditure. Lugard appreciated the problem but realised that the more formalised the local financial arrangements were the less control his central government would have over the native administrations and their advisers (the Residents). Consequently, he never did much with the idea.

When Lugard resigned in 1906, Richmond Palmer, the junior Resident in Katsina District, began to experiment with indirect rule, and his efforts earn him a place in its history. Palmer persuaded the Emir to accept the idea of western-style accounting and establishment of a special native finance office to keep track of the revenue and expenditure of the native administration and plan its budget. He thus created the first Native Treasury.[84] The system worked as follows. Revenue was paid by the taxpayers of the district or emirate to the Native Administration which kept its share – at first 50 per cent, except for Sokoto which kept 75 per cent and the pagan districts which kept only 25 per cent, and passed the rest on to the colonial government. Expenditure was divided into three categories: a fixed amount for the Emir; a second fixed amount to cover the salaries of various officials in the Emir's government; and finally the remainder, if there was one (and increasingly there was), to be used for special purposes, usually public works. Not all the funds in this last category were to be spent. Some part was saved, and consequently, in most Native Treasuries a surplus, or a contingency fund, began to develop. The establishment of a Native Treasury imposed a higher level of financial and bureaucratic efficiency on the Native Administration than had been the case. Furthermore, it modified and eventually ended the Emir's heretofore almost absolute control over native revenue.[85] This was revolutionary. It should be emphasised that Palmer did not – nor did any of his fellow Residents – see the Native Treasury as a means to westernise the native ruling class. Quite the contrary: they saw it as a device by which they could protect the native from westernising influence that might come from above, i.e. from the colonial central government. Functional control over the Emir's funds shifted to the Resident. This made sense because the Resident in each district was responsible for assessing the taxable value of the land and for seeing that the tax was collected. Therefore it seemed logical that he take responsibility for supervising expenditure. Implicit in the Resident's power to supervise expenditure was his right to veto, a right that made the Resident the most important and powerful official in the structure of indirect rule.

Palmer's achievement was quickly copied by his fellow Residents across the colony when they saw how powerful a tool the Native Treasury was in establishing and maintaining their position.[86] Palmer, Temple, and the other Residents, in doing this, accomplished two very important things: (i) they secured a qualified independence from the central colonial government for themselves and for the Native Administrations; and (ii) they institutionalised the dependence of the Emirs and chiefs upon themselves. The ideological purpose of the Residents' action, in as much as there was one, was to secure for the indigenous inhabitants the right to preserve their own non-western way of life and to develop in their own way at their own pace. This may sound paternalistic and patronising in the late twentieth century, but it should not be seen as hypocritical. The

Residents were wholly sincere in their belief in the non-interventionist approach to indirect rule.

As the Native Treasury system developed, the Colonial Office became converted to the non-interventionist approach to indirect rule it underpinned. For example, A. J. Harding, Senior Clerk in the Nigeria Department, endorsed Temple's belief when he wrote:

> we are in N. Nigeria – certainly in the Mohammedan States of the North – to supervise the administration of the country on native lines – not to try to turn it into an English country.[87]

It is also no coincidence that this conversion occurred when Charles Strachey was Senior and then Principal Clerk in the Nigeria Department. Strachey and Temple were close friends with similar views on the implementation of indirect rule. Strachey, like other clerks in the Department, realised that the Native Treasury system was crucial to the conservative approach. In early 1913 he wrote, 'I am convinced of the importance of keeping up the system of the Beit-el-Mal . . . as an integral part of the method of indirect rule.'[88] Indeed, the Native Treasury was considered the heart of the system. Consequently the Colonial Office clerks were prepared to support and, if necessary, defend it vigorously.

When Lugard returned to Nigeria in 1912 to amalgamate Northern and Southern Nigeria into one colony, he found he did not care for the Native Treasury system and the new approach to indirect rule it gave support to. The new approach, or at least new to him, represented a degree of decentralisation in relation to himself as Governor that he was not prepared to accept. By emphasising the authority of the Resident and the Native Administration he worked with, it greatly cut into Lugard's own power as Governor. Lugard began his attack on the Native Treasury system when he presented the 1913 Northern Nigeria estimates to the Colonial Office. Clearly he intended to resume control of indirect rule. To this end he introduced three measures: (i) he required that the Native Administrations' expenditure (up to this time only listed as a lump sum) be itemised; (ii) he absorbed the Native Administrations' current annual surplus, nearly £54,000, into the central administration's revenue estimates; and (iii) he merged the Native Administrations' reserves into the general reserves of the colony. The effect of his proposals was to assert his right to control the Native Treasuries and Administrations and to actually assume that control. Harding, one of the extreme proponents of non-interventionist indirect rule, pointed out that itemising expenditures might open a Pandora's box:

> trifles for Mohammedan feasts, upkeep of mosques, etc., though fit and proper expenditure for a Mohammedan Emir . . . might lead to missionary and other protests if they were paid out of money which was even in appearance part of the Protectorate funds.[89]

It should not be done.

He went on to insist, regarding the second point, that the Native Administration's revenue did not belong to the colonial government and it would be a 'breach of faith' to treat it as such. He elaborated on this by vigorously asserting that:

> Neither the Secretary of State nor the Governor has any legal or moral right to decide how the Emir of Kano or Sokoto spends his revenue. The resident and the Governor may advise him how to do it and help him not to waste it – but it is the expenditure of his Government, not of theirs.
>
> If the Emir were to persist in extravagance and improper expenditure (judged from a central African Emir's standard) it would be for the Governor with the sanction of the Secretary of State to depose him in favour of a better ruler. But while he is ruler, he should be treated as a ruler and not a petty native official. The Court and people of a Mohammedan state cannot be expected to understand English methods of financial control of government expenditure or to respect a native ruler who cannot spend – or even waste to a reasonable extent – money without the prior sanction of an outside European authority.[90]

Harding's insistence that the Emir be seen as a native ruler and not as a petty official violated Lugard's notion, mentioned earlier, that there should not be two sets of rulers – one British, the other Nigerian – in his system of indirect rule. None the less it seemed crucial to the non-interventionist approach. Strachey, however, pointed out that although the Native Treasury system worked well and was essential to indirect rule, the Native Treasuries themselves were not as free from controls as Harding implied. He stopped short of recognising the Native Administrations as independent states. To him they could properly be characterised as 'something like

municipalities over whose finances a certain but not a detailed control
is exercised'. It had been understood when the system was adopted
that the Emirs would receive large sums, and that since they no
longer had to spend large amounts on armies, something would have
to be done to prevent them from squandering their shares. The
Native Treasury took care of this; a fixed amount went to the salaries
of the Emir and his civil servants, while the remainder was spent,
under advice from the Resident, on various public works projects.
Anything left over became part of the individual Native Treasury's
surplus reserve.[91]

Regarding these reserves, Lugard argued that the original purpose
of such funds was to have money in the emirate or district
immediately available in case of emergency. Now, however:

> There is no longer any necessity for the Native Administrations to
> effect an insurance of their own. They have entered into the
> heritage of Nigeria as a whole. If their surplus balances are
> absorbed into the common fund for the development of the
> country, they are assured that the common surplus will be freely
> expended in case of their need.

To this Strachey simply responded 'It is their money.'[92] Fiddes
thought Lugard's proposal was such a breach of faith with the
Northern Nigerian chiefs and Emirs that he must have done it under
some misapprehension. He suggested that action be deferred until
Lugard came home, and Lugard was so informed in February 1913.[93]

In Northern Nigeria Lugard accepted an invitation to discuss the
question of the surplus reserves as well as the other proposals, in June
when he returned to England. His basic position, as stated in his reply
to the invitation, was that:

> The ideal at which I would aim *in the present state of development*
> [Lugard's emphasis] is the maximum of European control consis-
> tent with the fostering of a keen interest in their own financial
> affairs by the Native Administrations. Whether in the future we
> shall be able to advance a step beyond this, and enable them to
> 'build up for themselves an efficient system of account and audit',
> remains to be seen. . . . In my judgment it would be a . . . grave
> mistake to allow the Native Administrations to strike off on a line
> of independence, as separate entities separate from the central
> British administration.[94]

Meanwhile, Colonial Office officials further discussed how best to approach Lugard's proposals. Harding elaborated on a point Strachey had made previously:

> In Northern Nigeria the Protectorate Government has full power, legislative and executive, in the last resort, but just as His Majesty's Government doesn't interfere in every detail with County Council and Municipal expenditure or include such expenditure in the Civil Service Estimates, though the revenues of these local governing bodies are raised by virtue of Acts passed by Parliament, so the Protectorate Government should as far as possible let the native Governments run along under the guidance of the Residents and only interfere when really necessary.[95]

Strachey himself was especially concerned with the way Lugard was attempting to manipulate the reserve funds. If the funds were growing too large the situation could be corrected by allocating more to the central government and less to the native administrations. However, it would be treachery to go back on their word and seize control of the reserve funds without due process. 'I believe,' he said, 'that this question is of the utmost importance to the preservation of the principle of indirect rule which has worked so admirably up to the present.' Strachey noted that the policy of ruling through Native Administrations had been 'Statesmanlike' when Lugard had inaugurated it a decade and more ago, and it still was. Lugard had 'very properly' received a great deal of credit for this and, as Strachey cleverly put it, 'we really cannot allow him to tamper with his own reputation in this way'. Only Sir John Anderson, the Permanent Under Secretary, who had himself been a colonial governor from 1904 to 1911, seemed sympathetic. Like Fiddes, he was sure it was all simply a misunderstanding which the June conference would clear up.[96]

The conference was held at the Colonial Office on 19 June 1913. The conclusions reached represented a signal victory for the permanent officials in their campaign to preserve the Native Administrations and Native Treasuries. In attendance were Strachey, Fiddes, Anderson, and Lugard. At the meeting Anderson and Fiddes found that they had not misunderstood Lugard; he really wished to curtail the autonomy of the Native Administrations and Treasuries. Consequently he was told that he must cease and desist, and to make certain that there could be no misunderstanding on Lugard's side, the conclusions of the meeting were put in writing. These notes, drafted by Harding and sent to Lugard in early July, clearly stated that the revenue and expenditure of the Native Treasuries should not appear on the general estimates submitted to London but should – after being prepared by the Emirs and their staff under the supervision of Residents, and approved by the Governor – be sent separately to the Colonial Office for informational purposes only. Additionally, the Native Treasuries' accumulated surplus reserves could not be considered part of the general surplus reserves of the colony, but had to be treated as a trust. The revenues which came from this trust would be credited to the Native Treasuries. However, if necessary, the Governor had the authority to change the proportion of the gross revenue kept by a Native Treasury. He was also to leave the Native Treasuries' current surplus alone. Lugard had been told in no uncertain terms that he could not interfere with the Native Administrations, and especially not with the financial heart of the Native Administration, the Native Treasuries. In short, he could not interfere with the system of indirect rule as it was then evolving. Knowing Lugard, no one in the Colonial Office felt confident that he had taken the message to heart. Sir John Anderson said, after the conference of 19 June:

> I don't know whether we have convinced him. He looks at the question as if he were to be perpetual Governor of Nigeria and from the standpoint of one in whom the natives have implicit confidence not only as regards his zeal for their welfare but as regards his wisdom in providing for it.
>
> We must look at it from a more general point of view.[97]

The Colonial Office and the Northern Nigerian Residents – Temple and Palmer – had, according to Lugard's biographer, out-Lugarded Lugard 'with a vengeance'.[98]

How did Lugard react to this? Of course he was sure that what the Residents had done, and what the Colonial Office had defended, was a 'grave mistake' and as a result the provinces would become too independent of the central administration. Therefore he felt obligated to protect the Colonial Office and the Residents from themselves. The fact that he definitely refused to accept the Colonial Office's decision did not become evident until late 1913 when Strachey was touring Northern Nigeria. Strachey wrote privately to Harding in London:

I want to warn you to be particularly careful about scrutinising all Sir F. L.'s proposals about the Native monies. He has never spoken to me about it and indeed I have hardly had more than general talk at meals with him since I got to Lagos on December 29th. But I learn from Temple, Palmer and others that he wants or intends to spend some of this money on 'general services': i.e. the Bida or Kano Native funds may be used to pay for works or salaries not only outside their provinces but in (old) Southern Nigeria. . . . This I am sure is *wrong* [Strachey's emphasis] and contrary to the spirit at any rate of the arrangement come to when the Emir and others were put on salaries. The rest of the money (admitted to be theirs) was to be spent under supervision within the province.[99]

Thus alerted by Strachey's warning, permanent officials were able to catch Lugard only a few months later when he attempted to use £46,301 from the Native Treasuries as a grant-in-aid to the colonial government. While this was not a large amount, Lugard was trying to establish a precedent. Harding was amazed at Lugard's effort and called it 'dishonest'. It would make a mockery of the agreements concerning revenue-sharing which had characterised the relationship between the Native Treasury and central colonial government, and throw open 'the whole revenues of the Native Administrations . . . to the depredations of the Protectorate Government'. Fiddes called it 'an unpleasant business'; Anderson noted, 'this sort of thing savours too much of trickery'; and Harcourt agreed.[100] Lugard was not allowed to do this. The Colonial Office staff had worked as one in resisting him.

But Lugard did not give up, and until he left Nigeria he tried one way after another to obtain the revenues of the Native Treasuries and to curb the independence of the Native Administrations.[101] In all these efforts he failed. The Colonial Office was on guard and prepared for any attack Lugard might launch against the Native Treasury system. That system had become the new orthodoxy which would be protected until it flourished. Charles Strachey saw something of its future early in 1913 when he noted that 'the "Beit-el-Mal" system has many outside admirers'. It had been discussed favourably by members of the Northern Nigerian Lands Committee, and the West African Lands Committee (where it was suggested that the system be introduced into the other British West African colonies).[102]

By 1914 the permanent officials and their political masters were totally committed to non-interventionist indirect rule in both theory and practice. They believed that local administration in the colonies should be by Africans, along African lines, supervised by a British Resident. To permanent officials the essence of indirect rule was decentralisation, and the Native Treasuries symbolised that principle. Believing this they energetically resisted and successfully thwarted all of Lugard's attempts to redirect the evolution of indirect rule. The interventionist approach, which Lugard tended towards, would not survive.

Scholars have blamed Lugard for the consequences of indirect rule. For example, the distinguished imperial historian John Flint, in 1978, wrote that:

Through his [Lugard's] policies, and in his writings, he did more than any other individual to fix the concept of indirect rule firmly in British policy as a conservative philosophy, hostile to the ambitions of educated Africans and those influenced by Christian missionaries, to urban growth, to the spread of the money economy, and to the vision that new African nations were in the making.[103]

Few would disagree with Flint's list of consequences stemming from the 'conservative philosophy' of indirect rule. However, the evidence and argument developed in this section should clearly demonstrate that Lugard was not the responsible party – except in a minor sort of way. Therefore, when we talk about the origins of indirect rule in the British empire during the European occupation of Africa, when we talk about the consequences of this policy for British tropical Africa, and when we wish to apportion responsibility, we should hand out the larger shares to the Northern Nigerian Residents discussed above and to the Colonial Office. In this latter context we should name Harding, Strachey, Fiddes, Anderson and Harcourt. Only a much smaller share should go to Frederick Lugard. The record should now be clear on this.

THE AMALGAMATIONS OF 1906 AND 1914

The general arguments in favour of amalgamation were administrative, financial, and economic. Administratively, it made little sense to have three contiguous territories with three expensive administra

80

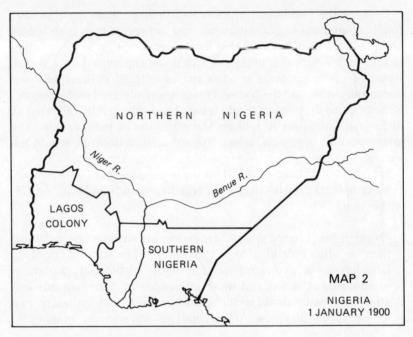

NORTHERN NIGERIA

Niger R.

Benue R.

LAGOS
COLONY

SOUTHERN
NIGERIA

MAP 2

NIGERIA
1 JANUARY 1900

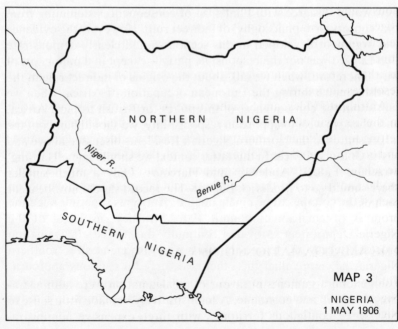

NORTHERN NIGERIA

Niger R.

Benue R.

SOUTHERN NIGERIA

MAP 3

NIGERIA
1 MAY 1906

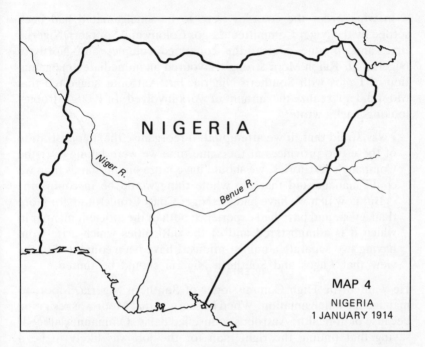

MAP 4

NIGERIA
1 JANUARY 1914

tions when one could do the work. Financially, in an amalgamated Nigeria, Southern Nigeria's economy would produce sufficient revenues to cover Northern Nigeria's deficit and free it from Treasury control. Economically, Nigeria's development was delayed because its three separate administrations made rational deployment of resources impossible.

Antrobus, Fiddes, and Strachey were the three officials most active in the amalgamation of Nigeria. Antrobus assisted Chamberlain in setting up the Niger Committee which recommended amalgamation, and he represented the Colonial Office on that Committee. In 1904–6 he adapted Egerton's amalgamation scheme to the Crown Colony model and suggested that a single person be appointed Governor in each of the colonies to be amalgamated. Antrobus superintended the progress of amalgamation until 1909. Strachey, as Head of the Nigeria Department, provided continuity during the amalgamation process. Because he feared the financial consequences for Southern Nigeria, he, more than the other two, urged a cautious approach. Fiddes's main contribution was to neutralise Treasury control over Nigeria while obtaining five years of imperial grants-in-aid for Nigeria.

In what order the colonies were to be amalgamated had been settled by the Niger Committee: Lagos Colony and Southern Nigeria, first; and, in due course, the combined colonies and Northern Nigeria. Sir Ralph Moor strongly favoured an immediate amalgamation of Lagos with Southern Nigeria, but Antrobus suggested that Moor did not realize the amount of work involved. In 1900 Antrobus, looking back, wrote:

> I was afraid that, if we attempted to reorganise the administration of these two provinces at the same time we were taking over the Company's territories, we should have more on our hands than we could manage and that the whole thing would be in confusion.
>
> But now that we have had the Niger Coast Protectorate for more than a year and have had experience both of the efficient manner in which it is administered and of the difficulties which arise from having two separate administrations, I have been converted to the view that Lagos and Southern Nigeria should be united.

He wanted the High Commissioner of Southern Nigeria, Moor, to manage the amalgamation. When he learned that Moor was resigning because of ill-health, Antrobus counselled delay. Ommanney agreed, saying that finding the right man for the job was likely to be a problem for some time. With amalgamation of the southern colonies put off, the Colonial Office thought 'it would be as well to make it a regular practice that each Governor or High Commissioner should consult or inform the others in all matters affecting common interests.'[104]

By mid-1904 the situation had changed, and Antrobus, who had wished to unite the two southern colonies as early as 1900, now felt optimistic enough to initiate Office proceedings on the project. He did so with a memorandum titled 'Amalgamation of Southern Nigeria and Lagos'. He did not think it would be wise to amalgamate the two just yet, but it would be equally unwise not to investigate the possibilities. The best way to do this was to appoint Sir Walter Egerton, Governor of Lagos, High Commissioner of Southern Nigeria. He would then be in a position to go impartially into the problems amalgamation might raise, especially regarding the fiscal union 'which is the principal object to be accomplished'. Egerton was competent and had not been so long in Nigeria 'as to be exposed to the suspicion of an inclination to favour S. Nigeria at the expense of Lagos'. The Permanent Under Secretary, Sir Montagu Ommanney, endorsed the idea; Egerton would:

thus be placed in a position which will enable him to study the whole question of the organisation required for the administration of the joint territory and in the course of a few months he should be able to furnish very useful advice on the subject.[105]

Antrobus seems to have showed some originality by suggesting that the same person become governor of both colonies. His solution may in retrospect have been obvious, but he was the only one to suggest it.

Egerton was chosen to replace Moor, who retired, and thus became chief executive of both Southern Nigeria and Lagos. Egerton submitted his amalgamation proposal in January 1905. His colonial administrative experience up to the time of his appointment as Governor of Lagos had been in the British Far East. His proposal is a good example of how ideas from one part of the Empire were transmitted to another:

> The scheme I now submit is not one of complete amalgamation but is desired to effect a rather more complete amalgamation than that which at present exists between the Colony of the Straits Settlements and the Federated States of the Malay Peninsula. If the future of the dual administration proves as successful as that of its Eastern counterpart my scheme will be fully justified.[106]

Egerton wanted the scheme approved immediately so that he could begin implementation before he came home on leave. However, the scheme's central elements were not acceptable to the Colonial Office. Those Colonial Office officials mainly concerned with Nigerian business saw serious flaws in the scheme and thought it best that Egerton come home to discuss the problems before amalgamation took place. Despite Antrobus's statement that the principal object was to establish fiscal union, Egerton wished to present separate estimates, i.e. separate budgets, for the two main divisions of the colony after amalgamation. He also expected the Lagos Legislative Council to continue as the legislative authority for Lagos Colony only, while he, as Governor, ruled Southern Nigeria without a legislative council. Understandably, the Colonial Office staff found a 'certain unreality' to his amalgamation scheme. Antrobus outlined the Colonial Office concerns as follows:

> The weak point of Mr. Egerton's scheme is his proposal that the revenues and the legislation of the two protectorates should

continue to be separate. If this were done, I do not see how any loan could be raised on the security of the combined revenues; for they would not be combined, and there is this further difficulty that a loan raised on the security of a protectorate will not be admitted by the Treasury as a trustee investment. Moreover, Mr. Egerton's point that the Lagos Council can hardly be given control over the revenues and legislation of S. Nigeria should, I think, be met by putting representatives of S. Nigeria on the Lagos Council. The present arrangement, under which S. and N. Nigeria are each placed under the control of an officer who is not bound to consult anyone, cannot continue indefinitely, and the merchants have more than once represented that there ought to be some sort of Council in Southern Nigeria. I would therefore have one legislature and one treasury.[107]

Although Ian Nicolson, in his administrative history of Nigeria, complains that 'there is little on record of the Colonial Office deliberations' regarding Egerton's amalgamation proposal and the subsequent decision taken, surely he is wrong.[108] Nicolson may not have seen Antrobus's memorandum on amalgamation or Ommanney's minute which recommended that Egerton should submit the proposal in the first instance. Nicolson does quote from a minute by Antrobus but gives the impression that the decision to unite the finances and legislatures of the two territories was the result of the conference between Egerton and the Colonial Office, rather than a suggestion by Antrobus. However, Antrobus made his suggestion in July, and it was endorsed by Ommanney at the same time, while the conference was not held until November when Egerton returned home and met with the permanent officials at the Colonial Office. At the conference, his Far Eastern experience was no match for Antrobus, Strachey, and Ezechiel, and he was persuaded to accept Antrobus's proposal regarding finance and legislatures.[109] Out of this meeting came a final amalgamation plan which Elgin approved. The scheme was put into effect on 1 May 1906. The result of the deliberation in the Colonial Office from June 1904 to May 1906 was a partial fulfilment of the Niger Committee's own amalgamation proposals. The initiative, as to timing and as to the actual shape of much of the plan's final form, came from the Colonial Office, mainly from Antrobus. This was good practice for the Colonial Office, for inevitably, in the not-too-distant future, the larger amalgamation of the new Southern Nigeria and Northern Nigeria loomed.

Sir Frederick Lugard played a major role in this second and more important amalgamation in Nigerian history.[110] As High Commissioner of Northern Nigeria he was interested in the idea of amalgamation with a richer colony. He himself, when Northern Nigerian High Commissioner, proposed amalgamation between Northern Nigeria and Lagos, and later between Northern and Southern Nigeria. Both proposals were turned down at the time because Lugard did not seem to appreciate that the revenue of a combined administration might not cover its expenditures.[111]

However, in 1905 he sent a greatly detailed, lengthy memorandum to the Colonial Office outlining a plan for the amalgamation of Lagos, Northern, and Southern Nigeria. He admitted that it would be irksome for all of Nigeria to be under Treasury control, but pointed out that the actual number of Nigerian colonies under Treasury control would not increase: there was one at the time – Northern Nigeria – and there would still be only one after amalgamation. From this point of view Treasury control could be taken in stride.[112] However, the Colonial Office saw Treasury control in a different light and was opposed to extending it to a larger area. Although Lugard's amalgamation proposals were rejected this time (they were hardly taken seriously), they were actually not that different from the 1913 scheme.

During the years that Lugard was out of Nigeria (1906–12) the Colonial Office held to its goal of an amalgamated Nigeria. As early as 1907 Girouard was warned that his term as High Commissioner in Northern Nigeria might be for sixteen to eighteen months only because the Colonial Office hoped to begin the amalgamation of Northern and Southern Nigeria at the end of the period.[113] And in 1909 a question on amalgamation was raised in the House of Commons. Fiddes recommended a non-committal answer, but noted that 'it seems to be a matter of common knowledge that such a proposal is in the air'.[114] After seeing the 1911/12 Northern Nigerian estimates – which required a £365,000* Treasury grant (the highest since 1904/5) – Fiddes realised the Treasury would soon want to discuss amalgamation. It would be, he felt, to the Colonial Office's advantage to seize the initiative in working out a deal whereby Treasury money, without Treasury control, would facilitate amalgamation.[115]

In response to Fiddes's comments Strachey calculated that the

* later reduced to £347,000.

annual deficit of an amalgamated colony, and thus the annual grant-in-aid, would be at least £250,000. If one assumed that the new Nigeria could afford to decrease this by £20,000 a year, then an amalgamated Nigeria would still be subject to twelve-and-a-half years of Treasury control before it could become self-supporting. Strachey's view was that it would hardly be worth joining the two if the new entity was in a chronic state of financial distress. His colleagues rejected this analysis as being unduly pessimistic. Fiddes preferred to ignore the obstacles and aim for the results. He reminded everyone that Treasury support was essential; therefore the crucial point was how they were to present amalgamation to the Treasury. His own view, one which was later adopted, was that the Treasury would be more willing to pay a fixed number of large annual grants than to continue the yearly grant indefinitely.[116]

Over the next several months Fiddes, Sir John Anderson, and Harcourt discussed the matter thoroughly. They decided finally that amalgamation should take place in the coming year and they should ask the Treasury to provide Northern Nigeria an annual grant-in-aid of £100,000 for the next five years, after which no further requests for assistance would be made. However, during those five years the Treasury would exercise no control over the expenditure of these grants.[117] The Treasury's initial response was favourable and after some hard negotiation agreement was reached.[118] It took effect with Northern Nigeria's 1913/14 fiscal year and continued through the first four years after amalgamation, ending in 1918. No doubt the Treasury and Colonial Office were pleased with the new arrangement. Treasury officials were rid of Northern Nigeria as a drain on imperial funds, and Colonial Office staff was pleased that a portion of the colony's revenue was fixed for the next five years. Additionally, the Colonial Office had eliminated any possible Treasury interference.

Besides the financial condition of Northern Nigeria, there were other obstacles to the final amalgamation which had to be surmounted. The unhealthy climate mentioned first in the Niger Committee Report was a serious problem, but by 1906 this was no longer a threat to Europeans.[119] Another problem, the lack of transportation and communication, was removed in 1911 when the railway to Kano was completed. A last obstacle to amalgamation was the appointment of a Governor capable of handling the combined administration. Unaware that what he was proposing was already being done, Strachey suggested that one person be appointed as

Governor of the two colonies to be joined and directed to devise a plan for amalgamation. This was the same procedure that had been used with the amalgamation of Southern Nigeria and Lagos and it was natural that it be used again.[120] Meanwhile, Harcourt and Anderson had already arrived at the same solution and had even chosen the Governor (Sir Frederick Lugard).

At the time there was still considerable interest, in Parliament and elsewhere, in the development and exploitation of the tropical empire. After amalgamation Nigeria would become one of Britain's largest and potentially wealthiest African colonies. The appointment of a Governor charged with the task of devising an amalgamation plan and carrying it out might well have political ramifications, and had to be done carefully. The person chosen had to be one in whom the Secretary of State had great confidence, someone he could support against criticism in and out of Parliament. The Secretary of State, Harcourt, in consultation with Sir John Anderson, chose Lugard. Although permanent officials liked some, though not all, of Lugard's ideas, they had built up a considerable antipathy toward Lugard during his tour of duty in Northern Nigeria (1900–6). His unorthodox and administratively untidy ways exasperated them. However, Harcourt and Anderson decided that they could not have Lugard's ideas without Lugard. In August 1911 Anderson told Lugard that they were anxious to amalgamate the Nigerian administrations; 'But our difficulty is to get the right man for the job. We are agreed that you are that man.'[121] Harcourt added his own brand of persuasion:

I know that your heart has always been in the work there in Nigeria and that I could not anywhere obtain so admirable an administrator for this great reorganisation – in fact, if I cannot secure your help, I think I shall let the project drop for the present, as its success must depend on the *quality of the man whom I could obtain to carry it out.*[122]

Lugard badly wanted the job, but initially held back both because he did not wish to be separated from his wife, whose poor health prevented her living in West Africa, and because he hoped to have his scheme for continuous administration accepted by the Colonial Office.[123] He finally accepted the position in December 1911. When announcing the appointment in Parliament, Harcourt said:

Though I have been convinced ever since I came to the Colonial Office that . . . amalgamation was desirable, I frankly admit that I should not have thought the moment opportune unless I had happened to know and been able to command the services of the one man marked out for this great work, Sir Frederick Lugard. I have been able . . . to induce him . . . to take up what will shortly become the Governorship of the combined Nigerias. . . . I am sending him, so far as I am concerned, with a free hand to examine the situation as to its developments since his last visit, to plan and to organise the amalgamation, to examine the administration, the financial, and the commercial possibilities, and then to return here and to discuss with me the probabilities of the future.[124]

Lugard was formally appointed governor of Northern and Southern Nigeria in May 1912. He left for Nigeria in September for a survey, returned to England in the spring, and presented his amalgamation plan to the Colonial Office on 9 May 1913. The essence of his plan was as follows:[125] Amalgamated Nigeria was to be divided into Northern and Southern provinces. The original colony of Lagos (a strip 110 miles long and from four to twenty miles wide) was to be detached from the Southern Province and separately administered, and the Southern Nigerian Legislative Council restricted to Lagos. The Governor-General* would legislate for the rest of Nigeria with the advice of an executive Council, composed of officials from his staff. There would be two Lieutenant-Governors, one for Northern and one for Southern Nigeria, and an Administrator for Lagos. Some departments would be fully amalgamated; others would be supervised by deputy heads with separate establishments in the North and South and come directly under the respective Lieutenant-Governors. The only significant unifying institution would be the Governor-General, who would be in a 'strongly authoritarian position', as all financial estimates would originate with him.[126] Provincial and district administration generally would remain the same with some important reorganisation being recommended for the South.

The Colonial Office assessed the scheme. Strachey, as Head of the Nigeria Department, spoke for all of his colleagues when he said 'Speaking generally, the scheme appears to be on sound lines, and although open to criticism in certain respects and requiring further

* Lugard insisted on being called Governor-General, and the title was approved on the understanding that it would be abolished when his term expired.

explanation in others, will, I believe, be found to work well'.[127] Lugard did ask for special authority to enact laws without submitting them to the Colonial Office. When this was not sanctioned, he blustered that he would assume Harcourt had lost confidence in him if the Colonial Office did not favourably reconsider this. This statement was typical of the game of bluff Lugard habitually played with the Colonial Office. Sir John Anderson, who had extensive experience with both the Colonial Office and colonial government, felt the matter concerned common sense, not confidence. He insisted on Colonial Office review of Crown Colony legislation, but at the same time was anxious to save Lugard from losing face:

> I do not think that one man however well and able should have the uncontrolled power of legislating for millions of people, and that is what Sir F. Lugard claims, as his Ex. CO. may consist of only two of his officials who are not likely to offer any very strenuous opposition to a masterful Governor like Sir F. Lugard. Reference to the Secretary of State coupled with the publications of the draft gives time for the public to object, and that is the main thing we want to secure.
>
> If it is the necessity for formally submitting the drafts that hurts Sir F. Lugard, I should be quite prepared to omit that provision provided that the period of publication of the draft prior to enactment is extended from one month to two. If an eye is kept on the Gazettes as they come in this will enable us to warn him of any objections we may entertain to legislative proposals, and also give Liverpool and Manchester an opportunity of voicing their objections.[128]

Anderson's common-sense solution reveals the Colonial Office's determination to control colonial policy. Harcourt approved; Lugard was satisfied; and permanent officials continued their supervision of Nigerian legislation.

Amalgamation of Southern and Northern Nigeria took place on 1 January 1914. Professor John Flint has criticised the Colonial Office for its role in amalgamation because:

> There was scarcely any discussion in London concerning the fundamental significance of amalgamation. Even in 1912 imaginative men might have seen the union of north and south as a great advance in Britain's Nigerian mission, as the first step towards a new nation.[129]

This is an easy criticism to make, but not very discerning. In fact it is ahistorical, forcing the Colonial Office of 1912–13 to act according to principles not yet adopted, to principles of a later age. To talk of 'Britain's Nigerian mission' is to miss the point of empire, and to establish, as it affected Nigeria, some sort of Whig interpretation of British imperial history. In as much as one can talk of the 'mission concept' in those days, one might have exhorted the Colonial Office to carry out Britain's 'imperial' mission: the Colonial Office did not have a 'Nigerian' mission. The role of the Colonial Office was to see that the Colonial Empire was ruled on sound lines and opened to commercial development and exploitation – not to found new nations. The Colonial Office supervised Crown Colony Governments that were autocracies, and officials in those Crown Colonies had no notion of being anything else but part of that autocracy.

One official, A. J. Harding, did try in a modestly philosophical way to put the scheme into an interpretative framework. However, Harding's comments, rather than being aimed toward any particular purpose, seemed to be speculative musings:

> Sir F. Lugard's proposal contemplates a state which it is impossible to classify. It is not a unitary state with local government areas but with one Central Executive and one Legislature. It is not a federal state with federal Executive, Legislature and finances, like the Leewards. It is not a personal union of separate colonies under the same Governor like the Windwards, it is not a Confederation of States. If adopted, his proposals can hardly be a permanent solution and I gather that Sir F. Lugard only regards them as temporary – at any rate in part. With one man in practical control of the Executive and Legislative organs of all the parts, the machine may work passably for sufficient time to enable the transition period to be left behind, by which time the answer to the problem – Unitary v. Federal State – will probably have become clear.[130]

Seventy years on, the answer has yet to be made clear.

Egerton's plan to amalgamate Lagos Colony and Southern Nigeria, and Lugard's plan for the new Southern Nigeria and Northern Nigeria, each represented partial fulfilment of policy decided on and recorded in the report of the Niger Committee in August 1898. After considerable modification of Egerton's plan and minor modification of Lugard's, the Colonial Office authorised the implementation of each. Both schemes promised administrative convenience and the improvement of the new entity's financial and economic condition. Neither posed a threat to the authority of the Colonial Office (in the Colonial Empire or in Whitehall) and both were in conformity with policy. Therefore the Colonial Office accepted them. The same could not be said for Lugard's scheme of continuous administration to which we turn now.

LUGARD'S SCHEME OF CONTINUOUS ADMINISTRATION

The story of the permanent officials and Lugard's scheme of continuous administration is instructive; it clearly illustrates that permanent officials perceived themselves as crucial to the Colonial Office administrative system and were quite unwilling to see themselves displaced.

In a Crown Colony all necessary business with the Colonial Office was conducted through the Governor. When he was on leave (six months, non-consecutive, out of every eighteen), or when the colony was between governors, an Acting Governor was appointed from the Governor's staff (usually, but not always, the colony's Colonial Secretary).[131] Lugard, however, believed that the Governor should always be in complete command, whether he was in the colony or away. To this end, in 1905, he presented a scheme of continuous administration to the Colonial Office in a memorandum entitled 'Administration of Tropical Colonies'.[132]

Lugard pointed out two defects, as he saw them, in the existing colonial system: a lack of continuity in administration; and the redundancy of the permanent officials, who acted as intermediaries between a Governor and the Secretary of State. Lugard believed that the Governor, in his person, should provide continuity. Many governors did not serve their full six-year term, due to the effects of the West African climate, and those who did were required to spend one-third of it on leave. Lugard personally found the leaves an annoyance and tried never to go on holiday. However, his wife's poor health did not allow her to live in West Africa and for this reason Lugard's motives in proposing the scheme were partly personal. A Governor on leave was not expected to read the despatches from his Acting Governor to the Colonial Office. During his leave a Governor was out of touch with affairs in his own bailiwick, and the Colonial

Office was deprived of his special knowledge of his colony, or so Lugard claimed.

The fact that a West African Governor was frequently on leave was a defect that could be turned into an asset. This was an opportunity to build into the system direct and regular contact between the Governor and the Secretary of State. Lugard himself, after five years' experience, was very unhappy with the colonial administrative system because it gave him no direct access to the Secretary of State. Everything was filtered through the permanent officials, a process of which he took a dim view. He elaborated thus:

> I trust I am not overstepping the proper limits of this memorandum if I venture to offer some observations. . . . Clearly it is a physical impossibility for the Secretary of State to supervise personally the affairs of some 50 colonies and Protectorates in addition to his Parliamentary and Ministerial duties. As a result important matters are decided in his name by the permanent officials at the Colonial Office. These officials play their difficult part usually with tact, discretion, and great industry. But I venture to think that a system which places great powers in the hands of those who have no responsibility to Parliament or the nation is not in theory a sound one, or in practice a successful one. They can overrule the Governor who is held responsible by the nation, nor is it feasible for the Secretary of State himself (except in rare instances) to reverse the action taken in his name, and recorded over his lithograph signature. The Governor, if he has local experience, cannot but regret that the proposals (which are the result of that experience and of the advice of those best able to form an opinion) over which he has expended much thought have never reached the Secretary of State. The Secretary of State is in touch with the larger issues of the Empire, with the views of the Cabinet and of the heads of the other great Departments of State, and to his decision every Governor defers with absolute loyalty.[133]

Lugard felt he had a scheme which would remedy these defects. What was this scheme and how would it accomplish its purpose? His proposal on continuous administration would require the Governor to spend half of each year working in Africa, the other half in England. The Governor would be on duty and not on leave while in England. He would work in the Colonial Office, and have direct access to the Secretary of State. Wherever he was, the Governor would be the working head of his colonial administration. Continuity would be assured. All correspondence with the Secretary of State would be handled by him; all legislation would be submitted to him, as well as budgets and annual accounts. He would interview private interest groups and be present if they sent a deputation to the Secretary of State.

> He would thus be able to keep in touch not only with the centre of Imperial Administration, but with the Tropical Department of the Imperial Institute and the economic and commercial centres of British trade, on which the development of the country must depend, and with which he is at present almost wholly out of touch.[134]

Some of these suggestions were already in effect, and had been for some time. For example, Governors on leave were always welcome at the Colonial Office to discuss matters relevant to their colonies, and the Colonial Office generally tried to consult with a Governor on leave if problems or crises relating to his colony came up. This was done on an *ad hoc* basis: Lugard obviously wanted to formalise and institutionalise it. The crucial aspect of his plan, however, was the idea of a Governor doing the work of the permanent officials at the Colonial Office, and at the same time being beyond their supervision. The officials understandably took exception to this. Ommanney described any attempt to administer a colony from London as 'the one rank heresy we all shudder at'.[135] Strachey replied to Lugard's criticisms and his plan by saying:

> The permanent officials of the Colonial Office have not, it is true, had experience in governing West African colonies, nor are they directly responsible to Parliament. It is questionable whether they would do their work better if they possessed these qualifications. Their duties are, it must always be remembered, *not* administrative, but supervisory. One can criticise a pudding without being a cook. (And, if we were all made Cabinet Ministers, it would no doubt have a broadening effect on our minds, but, except in this indirect way, there seems no reason to suppose that the consequent responsibility to Parliament would make us more ready to adopt new lines of policy or thought.) Before we can be blamed for unwillingness to depart from 'office tradition' it should be shown that this tradition is a bad thing.

If permanent officials were to be replaced as policy-advisers for half the year, the Secretary of State would find himself 'at some disadvantage in his direct dealings with the Governor' unless he was prepared 'to specialise considerably in West African affairs'.[136] Olivier pointed out that general and personal experience as a colonial administrator in the British West Indies had led him to accept the principle that:

> notwithstanding some disadvantages, it is on the whole expedient, if not essential, that the 'Officer administering the Government' of a Colony shall be an officer in the Colony and fully responsible at all times . . . [and] to treat him [the governor] as administering the government whilst in England would paralyse the local administration.[137]

The simplest argument put forward by the permanent officials against the scheme was that it could not be justified even as an experiment, if it did not have potential general applicability. What they did not know was that Lugard, while bewailing a Governor's lack of access to the Secretary of State, had privately approached Lyttelton on this subject. Before sending his memorandum to the Colonial Office, Lugard had written personally to him:

> I sincerely trust that since the new departure is inaugurated experimentally with myself I may be able to show by results that it is entirely to the public advantage and to the great gain of the administrative territory, and no efforts on my part will be wanting to prove it so.[138]

Two months later, in the face of the permanent officials' unanimous objections, the Secretary of State approved the scheme. Lyttelton's approval has been attributed to personal weakness: that is, he succumbed to a combination of Lady Lugard's charm and Lugard's forcefulness.[139] If so, he was not the first or last to do so.

Lyttelton described the scheme as 'a modest reform', stressing its experimental aspects. It could easily be abandoned, or if successful, 'cautiously developed'. All that would be required was to give Lugard an office and show him the Northern Nigerian correspondence first. In his minute authorising the scheme Lyttelton insisted that:

> The only difference of substance in the present routine would be

that the Acting Governor would initiate and the High Commissioner complete such despatches as arrived during his home
sojourn. These despatches would then go through the Office to
the Secretary of State in the usual way, and I should hope that in
all difficult matters, after free discussion between the High Commissioner and the Department, if any difference of opinion arose,
the Secretary of State would then, as now, have the opportunity of
conference with the Department to which, when he thought fit, he
might summon the High Commissioner.[140]

Lugard had been vague about what the permanent officials would do
while he worked at the Colonial Office. They supposed they would
do nothing. Lyttelton assured them that they could carry on as
before – after Lugard had done his work on the despatches. Lady
Lugard wrote in *The Times* that Lugard's scheme represented 'only
the carrying into application of principles already accepted'.[141]
Finally it was Antrobus who, by detailing what was actually involved,
convinced Lyttelton that his 'modest reform' was a radical innovation. However, during the short time before the Conservative
Government resigned in December 1905 Lyttelton was unable to
reconcile his commitment to Lugard with his belief in Antrobus's
argument, and the problem was passed on, unsolved, to the
Liberals.[142]

Once the Earl of Elgin became the new Secretary of State,
Antrobus began, with strong support from Ommanney and Winston
Churchill, Parliamentary Under Secretary, a campaign against
Lugard's scheme of continuous administration.[143] Antrobus was sure
that the scheme owed more to Lugard's concern for his wife than to
any theory of colonial administration. He gave his version of the
origin of the scheme in late January 1906:

It has been regarded hitherto almost as an axiom that government
from Downing Street is impossible. But neither Sir F. Lugard nor
Mr. Lyttelton have explained how these objections are to be
overcome. They do not even allude to them in what they have
written. Yet, Sir F. Lugard, at any rate, must have been well aware
of them; and, to do him justice, he has never himself shown any
unwillingness to stick to his work in West Africa. Even Lady
Lugard, when they were going to be married, represented the great
benefit which the Protectorate would derive from their both
residing in it, and induced Mr. Chamberlain to sanction the

expenditure required to build and furnish for them at Zungeru on what she considered a suitable scale. It was only when it proved that Lady Lugard's health would not admit of hei iesiding in West Africa that the idea that the High Commissioner of N. Nigeria should spend half his time in England began, about two years ago, to be put forward in the 'Morning Post'. Since then it had been propagated steadily, until last summer Mr. Lyttelton was induced to say that he would like to have the memo, which he understood that Sir F. Lugard had prepared upon the subject.[144]

Churchill noted that 'we shall not simplify the labour of the Colonial Office by converting it into a pantheon of proconsuls on leave'.[145] Ommanney's argument carried more weight, if less alliteration. He pointed out that a colonial Governor in England would be forced to rely on the telegraph for recent information and would find himself no longer in 'continuous' control of the Nigeriam administrative apparatus. Indeed, Ommanney said:

> To secure greater continuity by breaking continuity more fre-quently and more completely, seems to be a curious remedy for what is perhaps the greatest difficulty we have to contend with in W. African service. . . . I think that Sir F. Lugard should be told, as soon as possible, that on further consideration the difficulties of the proposed experiment . . . appear to Lord Elgin to be insuper-able, and he regrets to be unable to give effect to the arrangement which he understands his predecessor to have contemplated.[146]

Ommanney pressed on to compliment the work of the permanent officials at Lugard's expense:

> I am surprised to find such absolute silence on Sir F. Lugard's part as to the admirable service which the W. African Dept. had rendered to N. Nigeria under the able and experienced guidance of Mr. Antrobus. This great ability and accumulated experience which Sir F. Lugard refers to as the 'office tradition' which causes it to look with suspicion on reforms . . . is, on the contrary the greatest safeguard against the adoption of schemes and theories which have failed in the past and I can imagine nothing but disaster as the probable result of an attempt to substitute for it such an arrangement as Sir F. Lugard contemplates.[147]

Lord Elgin was convinced; his own past experience as Viceroy of

India had predisposed him to work within the chain of command. When Lugard was informed officially that Elgin had ruled against his scheme, Antrobus sent him a private conciliatory note in which he said, 'you know that the scheme never seemed to me a sound one, and I was not surprised at Lord Elgin's decision'.[148] His note was a masterpiece of civil service understatement. In any case, permanent officials must have felt relieved to know that their position would not be so peculiarly circumvented or their power undermined.

Feeling that he had been let down by Elgin, Lugard resigned. To his surprise, he was offered the governorship of Hong Kong, which he accepted, believing his career in Africa was over.[149] By 1910 he seems to have thought otherwise. Home on leave, he asked a friend to give the Earl of Crewe, Elgin's successor, memoranda he had prepared on colonial administration in Africa. Their contents were much the same as those submitted to the Colonial Office in 1905. Crewe was interested in continuous administration but realised that it had to be, in theory at least, generally applicable to justify allowing it to be tried in any one place. He wondered if some of the governors might not ask if they would get any vacation at all. When Crewe asked his Permanent Under Secretary, Sir Francis Hopwood, to examine 'Lugard's rather terrifying documents',[150] Hopwood's response was that 'a great deal was then said [in 1905] against Lugard's proposals and it could no doubt be said again if necessary'.[151] If Crewe had planned to explore the scheme, Hopwood's attitude persuaded him not to do so.

When Lewis Harcourt succeeded Crewe he told Lugard that the amalgamation of the two Nigerias was impossible without him.[152] Lugard thus found himself in an excellent bargaining position and agreed to accept the post only if he were allowed his scheme of continuous administration.[153] Hopwood's successor, Sir John Anderson, trying gently to argue Lugard out of the scheme, told him that as 'the driving and controlling force of the administration' he could not be away from Nigeria 'where the unexpected is constantly happening' for six months of the year. But Lugard remained adamant. Anderson and Harcourt were so anxious to secure his acceptance of the governorship that they made a counter-offer of four months at home after eight months in Nigeria. They also promised to provide ample office space at the Colonial Office for dealing with his Nigerian work. In the face of such eagerness to please, Lugard could not refuse.[154] For a year and a half after this, only Harcourt, Anderson, and Lugard himself knew the conditions of his appointment.

Needless to say, as permanent officials gradually learned the truth, their dislike and disapproval increased. One expert in colonial administration, Sir John Kirk, suggested to Lady Lugard that the officials were objecting so strongly because they feared 'effacement when the various governors are at home'.[155] There was certainly something in this, but there were also, as noted above, substantive objections to be made to the scheme of continuous administration. Strachey complained that if the Secretary of State was set on trying the system of 'absentee governors' he should do so with an unimportant colony such as St Helena or Gambia. Fiddes refused to speak well of the scheme to Harcourt:

> Perhaps the worst feature . . . is the possibility that we shall remain unaware of the full extent of the evils which will grow up under it until they have reached a point which brings about the collapse of the system in circumstances of more or less discredit to the dept.[156]

A. J. Harding simply stated that he did not know how the arrangement could possibly work.[157]

It is not quite clear why Harcourt and Anderson considered Lugard indispensable. Lugard's reputation had grown since he left Northern Nigeria; but it did not gain a wider audience until his retirement, and after a generation of journalists, publicists, and academics had created the Lugard legend. In 1911 he was only one of several qualified governors who could have done the job. If a logical candidate existed it was Egerton, who had over thirty years' experience in the colonial service and eight years as Governor of Southern Nigeria. However, in spite of his seemingly excellent record, the permanent officials and the Secretary of State were less satisfied with him than with Lugard.

After Lugard's appointment, Harcourt and Anderson found themselves continually defending continuous administration; in time, Lugard's personality became almost as much an issue and obstacle as the scheme itself. Although Lugard's proposed six months in England had been whittled down to four, he had more power in those four months than he would have had under his original proposal. In Nigeria his deputy and subordinates were unclear regarding their responsibility and uncertain as to what should be referred to Lugard in London. Knowing his propensity to do everything himself, it was a foregone conclusion that they would send practically everything to him.[158] Needless to say, the colony's administration was occasionally paralysed. It was not long before permanent officials discovered that Lugard's presence in the Colonial Office interfered with their usual access to current information. Considering his penchant for withholding information when he was in Nigeria, they should not have been surprised to find he continued the same practice in London. For example, Lugard suppressed for six months information concerning a punitive expedition that had involved seventy-five casualties. He explained later that he was waiting 'til such time as I was able to acquaint myself with all the circumstances of the case'. Anderson, in particular, found this difficult to accept, because Harcourt might have been criticised in Parliament for being uninformed on such an important matter. Lugard was warned to inform the Office immediately if another such incident took place.[159]

But other difficulties arose: an English firm attempting to set up a brewery in Lagos found their representative was shuttled back and forth between London and Lagos (no small trip) only to discover, when he finally caught up with Lugard – the only person who could make a decision – that Lugard had misplaced the relevant documents somewhere between the colony and the Colonial Office.[160] The frequent consultations necessary in a colonial administration were now impossible four months out of the year. For example, while in England, Lugard once wrote three different job descriptions for the same position. Harding felt this illustrated all the disadvantages of a governor trying to evolve detailed proposals without being able to discuss matters with his department heads.[161] Harcourt, finally worn down by it all, decided the continuous administration scheme should be clearly labelled 'experimental'.[162]

In spite of these difficulties, in early 1914 Lugard again asked to be allowed six months away from Nigeria (four-and-a-half months in London, one-and-a-half months in transit) because of the extra work regarding amalgamation. As this arrangement might be necessary for several years, it looked suspiciously like the thin end of the wedge. Harding assumed it would be rejected; Fiddes saw it as a sacrifice of the public interest to Lugard's convenience; and Sir John Anderson suggested that if Lugard continued in this vein he should be sent back to Hong Kong. When Harcourt did agree to Lugard's request, it was with the proviso that the scheme had to stand or fall as it was.[163] Permanent officials could not have been happy but were consoled by the knowledge that no more concessions would be made.

After this, continuous administration died a slow death. Permanent officials had pushed their criticism almost to the point where

Harcourt, had he remained at the Colonial Office, would have had to disown either them or Lugard. Harcourt's successor, Bonar Law, thought the scheme of continuous administration was wrong, but felt honour-bound to support it while Lugard remained Governor. Law's successor, Walter Long, decided the scheme was unworkable and ended it in April 1917.[164] If Lugard had succeeded in imposing his continuous administration scheme on the Colonial Office system, it would have constituted the most radical redefinition of the relationship between the Colonial Office and a colonial government in the British Empire. Administrative chaos would have been the result. Lugard's proposal shows how completely he failed to appreciate that the Colonial Office itself secured continuity in policy.[165]

Although the scheme's origins were primarily to be found in Lugard's private life, it had a superficial and appealing reasonableness. His proposal struck a responsive chord in many governors, and in others who had served in the field. All had, at one time or another, been second-guessed by the Colonial Office, had had some scheme or proposal rejected by the Colonial Office. They were all certain that it had been rejected by permanent officials and not by the Secretary of State. Instinctively they felt that their schemes would have been accepted if the Secretary of State had been able to see them through his own eyes and not through those of the permanent staff. When the scheme of continuous administration was first presented, permanent officials thought that it 'seemed hardly to require serious notice'.[166] But once Lyttelton had taken it seriously they had to also. They attacked the plan and the man: they indicated that Lugard really only wanted it adopted because his wife was not keen to live in West Africa. Even when permanent officials had seemingly lost this administrative struggle – in Lyttelton's and Harcourt's time – they continued a rearguard campaign which was ultimately successful. The reason? The scheme of continuous administration represented a threat to their authority and function in the colonial administrative system. The scheme of continuous administration was probably unworkable. However, permanent staff wanted to make certain that it would be perceived as being more than unworkable; they wanted it seen as potentially destructive of the very effective administrative system alrady in existence. In this they were successful and victorious.

3 Public Expenditure and Development in Southern Nigeria, 1900–12

Joseph Chamberlain startled many in Great Britain in 1895 when he informed Parliament that he 'regarded many of our colonies in the condition of undeveloped estates'. At the same time, he announced the British Government's intention to consider 'the judicious investment of British money' in British Crown Colonies to develop them 'for the benefit of their population and for the benefit of the greater population which is outside'.[1] He thus not only signalled the Government's willingness to attempt alternative methods of development, but specifically proposed a new approach. However, this new approach required a change in attitude by those who supervised the Colonial Empire. The permanent officials at the Colonial Office had to be persuaded to give high priority to colonial economic development, and to be more sympathetic to and co-operative with developmentally oriented colonial governors. The permanent officials were never so persuaded.

Chamberlain's doctrine of development was revolutionary. It suggested the overthrow of a well-established system of financing colonial development that extended back to the middle of the nineteenth century. A description of this system had been given with great clarity by Lord Grey, Colonial Secretary (1846–52) in Lord John Russell's administration. Grey said that, 'The surest test for the soundness of measures for the improvement of an uncivilised people is that they should be self-sufficing.'[2] Grey's view had become policy by the time Joseph Chamberlain became Secretary of State for the Colonies in 1895. In Robinson's and Gallagher's words, such 'inherited notions of policy in mature bureaucracies sometimes carry ministers along with a logic and momentum of their own'.[3]

Chamberlain was extraordinary enough to arrest this momentum occasionally, though not as often as is believed.[4] His successors at the Colonial Office were ordinary men. They believed a colonial government should 'cut its coat according to the cloth of its revenue'.[5] Years later – 1929 and 1940 – qualified and conditional legislation sought to implement Chamberlain's theory of development, but the opportunity for extraordinary efforts had passed.[6] Instead of challenging inherited policy, Secretaries of State for the Colonies who followed Chamberlain accommodated themselves to it. One of the reasons for their accommodation was the work and influence of permanent officials at the Colonial Office.

Historians of the empire have discussed these officials and their work in the area of public finance and colonial development before 1914; however, none has systematically examined a single colony whose 'progress' was overseen by a specific Colonial Office department wherein the permanent officials' influence can be documented and interpreted.[7] The expenditure on a colony, not its revenues, is the best gauge of the degree of the commitment by colonial officials to economic development. This chapter will examine the work of permanent officials on the Southern Nigerian estimates before 1914.[8] Of particular importance are a series of budgets, or estimates, presented by the Governor, Sir Walter Egerton, between 1906 and 1912. The Egerton estimates emphasised colonial development, and are therefore important to the study of the relationship between a progressive Governor and the Colonial Office.

Despite Chamberlain's proposal of imperial assistance, in the years before 1914 permanent officials felt that Earl Grey was right: each colony should arrive at self-sufficiency unaided. They believed this despite evidence that such self-sufficiency was often impossible. In fact, the Colonial Office appears to have been as close with money as the Treasury in approving expenditure for colonial development. The idea that the Treasury was the obstacle to development has become one of the received ideas of British Imperial history.[9] This idea needs revision. It now seems clear that the Colonial Office was as important as the Treasury, or more so, in controlling colonial expenditure. The financial restraint of Edwardian Colonial Office permanent officials is a significant link in the chain that connects the nineteenth century to the underdevelopment of former colonies in the Third World of the twentieth century.

The Protectorate of Southern Nigeria was formally proclaimed and placed under Colonial Office control on 1 January 1900. It was an obligation undertaken rather lightly. 'There was no discussion of long-term goals, and the deeper purposes of British governance were not considered at all.'[10] Because Southern Nigeria was financially self-sufficient it received no Treasury grant-in-aid with which to balance its budget. The Colonial Office was the final authority on the colony's financial matters. Reginald Antrobus, Assistant Under Secretary in charge of Nigeria business, noted with satisfaction, 'We do not have to go to Parliament for any help, and are not subject to Treasury control.'[11] The Colonial Office permanent staff believed it was their responsibility to oversee and ensure continuing financial stability for the colony, and also to advance the colony's development. Unfortunately, in the Nigeria Department, which supervised Southern and Northern Nigeria and Lagos, this responsibility was not accepted with any sense of self-assurance. The Nigeria Department shared with the rest of the Colonial Office an odd attitude toward colonial expenditure: obsessive penny-pinching modified by rare fits of generosity. Their major concern was that Crown Colony budgets should balance.[12] A familiar and oft-repeated cry was that of Charles Strachey, Head of the Nigeria Department, who said in 1905 that 'Estimated expenditure should be brought within estimated revenues.'[13] If an imbalance occurred, it was a sign that the colony's Governor was not estimating properly; an error that was only acceptable if revenue exceeded expenditure.

In principle, deficit financing was frowned upon and generally not allowed. Indeed, Keynes and others had yet to promulgate the theory that a government should spend more than it had to stimulate and develop the economy. There was, however, one Southern Nigerian Governor, Sir Walter Egerton, who believed that deficit financing, under certain conditions, was a necessity on the road to development. In practice some deficits were inevitable and might be made up by grants from another colony, from the Treasury, or more usually from the colony's own surplus reserve. (Northern Nigeria used the first two alternatives during the years before amalgamation with Southern Nigeria in 1914; Southern Nigeria used the third.) Such remedies were never automatic, and always involved protracted negotiations between the Colonial Office and the colony, or the Colonial Office and the Treasury, or both. A Crown Colony such as Southern Nigeria was expected to maintain a balanced budget, zealously supervised by the Colonial Office.

At least three factors explain why permanent officials at the Colonial Office were just as insistent as their colleagues in the

Treasury 'on keeping expenditure down, revenue up and budgets balanced'.[14] The permanent officials believed in the dogmas of Gladstonian finance. Nothing was worse than overspending; and the less spent, the better spent. Second, they were determined, if not actually to cut back a colony's expenditure, then to impose on it a steady, no-growth, rate of spending. The third reason was specifically rooted in West African circumstances: strict vigilance was necessary because there were often large and unforeseen fluctuations in a colony's revenue. There was always a possibility of budget deficits, but this possibility hardly merited the paranoid preparations the Colonial Office sometimes demanded.[15] This attitude conditioned the responses and recommendations the permanent officials gave to the Secretary of State. Frederick Butler, a clerk in the Nigeria Department, frankly admitted that the Colonial Office's responsibility was to throw cold water on development proposals made by the colonial governors. But in fact the permanent officials did more than this – they actively discouraged such proposals.[16] A Governor who proposed to spend money on telegraph lines, harbour facilities, dredgers, roads or bridges, not only had to strongly and convincingly demonstrate his need, but also had to be equally persuasive as to how he intended to cover his expenditure. Sometimes even this was not enough when officials were in a mood of heightened financial restraint.

Sir Walter Egerton was the most developmentally minded Governor in Southern Nigeria during this period. Although he has generally been forgotten by historians of the British Empire and of Nigeria, occasionally Egerton's work on colonial development has been discussed.[17] Egerton had been in the colonial service in the Far East for more than twenty years. When he was appointed Governor of Lagos in 1903 he was a seasoned colonial administrator. In 1904 he was made High Commissioner of Southern Nigeria, then Governor of amalgamated Lagos and Southern Nigeria from 1906 to 1912. He brought with him to Nigeria firm ideas of how a colony should be effectively occupied, administered, and developed. In his younger years Egerton had worked under the well-known colonial Governor Sir Frank Swettenham in the Far East. In some ways a disciple of Swettenham's, he followed Swettenham's philosophy of development. 'Revenue and prosperity,' Swettenham said,

> follow the liberal but prudently directed expenditure of public funds, especially when they are invested in high-class roads, in

railways, telegraphs, waterworks, and everything likely to encourage trade and private enterprise . . . The colonial Government
cannot do the mining and the agriculture, but it can make it
profitable for others to embark on such speculations.[18]

Egerton believed that money properly and generously spent would
generate – though perhaps not immediately – more than enough to
cover itself. If spending money on development meant planning a
deficit for a given year, he was not averse to doing so, as long as he
had sufficient funds in his surplus reserves. Obviously, this financial
doctrine was at odds with inherited policy at the Colonial Office.

Charged with extravagance in 1908, Egerton defended himself in a
despatch to the Colonial Office in which he cited the rapid increase of
trade and government revenue figures over the past few years.

I attribute the rapid development of Southern Nigeria in great part
to the large expenditure on 'extraordinary' works; it is an example
of the old adage 'money makes money.'[19]

During his Governorship, Egerton tackled an impressive list of
developmental projects. Among them were: reclaiming swampland
around Lagos; extending the seawall of Lagos harbour; repairing
roads in Lagos, and building more into the interior of the Western
Province as well as the Central and Eastern Provinces; adding to and
improving telegraph service from Lagos to Calabar, Lagos to
Forcados, and Lagos to the interior.[20]

When Egerton presented his budget for the fiscal year 1905/6 he
was still a relatively unknown quantity to the Nigeria Department,
and they were not overly critical. Strachey did note a considerable
increase in proposed expenditure (from £466,000 in 1904/5 to
£592,000) which Egerton justified by predicting an enormous
increase in revenue (from £473,000 to £579,000). Unfortunately, the
increased revenue did not cover the small deficit. Egerton put great
store by the development potential of extraordinary expenditure
which had leaped in a single year from £52,000 to £112,000. In fact,
he even told the Colonial Office that extraordinary expenditure could
'suitably be designated as developmental expenditure'.[21] Extraordinary expenditure was found in the budget under four headings: Works
and Buildings Extraordinary, Roads and Bridges Extraordinary,
Telegraphs extraordinary, and Marine Extraordinary. Together, they
were called 'Public Works Extraordinary'. Money was spent under

these heads to fund specific projects out of annual revenue for a year or more. Beyond a point, of course, these projects could become too expensive to be financed through regular income and then the money would have to come from loan receipts. Railway projects usually fell into this category. Strachey decided, given the large increase under the Public Works Extraordinary heads, to balance the budget by taking the amount of the deficit (£13,000) from the extraordinary expenditure. He was sure Egerton was trying to do too much in a single year. Egerton may have been annoyed by this action, but he accepted it without question. Strachey's excision might also have been intended to deflate the Governor's pride as well as his budget: when Strachey read Egerton's comments about how satisfactory it was to greatly increase extraordinary expenditure to pay for important public works, he wrote in the margin of Egerton's despatch, 'What would the Treasury say to this way of putting it?'[22]

A crucial difference in attitude and approach between Egerton and permanent officials in London is suggested by the 1905/6 estimates, and the Colonial Office's reaction to them. The Colonial Office believed that while economic development was desirable, financial restraint had a much higher priority. Egerton, however, firmly believed that money spent on development would eventually pay for itself. To permanent officials this attitude seemed extravagant and showed a lack of discipline. These opposing attitudes were brought into high relief in a series of important exchanges between the Colonial Office and Egerton over the estimates he submitted for the years 1907 to 1912. The bureaucratic struggle that developed between London and Lagos focused on the general desire of the Colonial Office to decrease or restrain expenditure and Egerton's desire to increase it. Within this general context we shall look closely at the controversies created and decisions made regarding the amounts budgeted for public works extraordinary.

Egerton's budget for 1907[23] showed a deficit of a little more than £15,000; proposed expenditure was £1,168,202, revenue £1,152,679. His estimates were examined very closely and critically in the Nigeria Department. Charles Strachey confessed that he was 'continually hearing charges of extravagance brought against the administration of S. Nigeria'. The Southern Nigerian Financial Commissioner, Mr C. E. Dale, told Strachey, off the record, that Egerton had a tendency to undertake more than he could properly carry out. With this in mind, Strachey thought the simplest way to remedy the deficit would be to order Egerton to cut £15,000 out of the expenditure side of the budget. Reginald Antrobus, Assistant Under Secretary, agreed, remarking that 'Egerton is inclined to be extravagant.' This word would be applied regularly and, for the most part, inappropriately, to Egerton for the rest of his stay in Southern Nigeria. In any case, the cut was made, and the despatch sanctioning Egerton's estimates was sent out. It emphasised the Secretary of State's belief that, as a matter of policy, estimated expenditure should not exceed estimated revenue. Indeed, the despatch went further – estimated expenditure should, if possible, be less than expected revenue.[24] It is noteworthy that extraordinary expenditure for public works came through this examination unscathed. The Colonial Office even allowed Egerton to increase it from £177,000 to almost £194,000.[25] Although it would seem that, for the moment, permanent officials bought Egerton's development theory, it is more likely that they indulged him while his colony was doing well. If this is so, it explains their rather hard handling of him in the wake of the disastrous deficit of 1909.

As 1907 unfolded, it became clear that revenue would be substantially more than anticipated, and Egerton wished to spend some of it. However, permanent officials were annoyed that he had so underestimated his revenues. They felt that he had put them in a false position when they had analysed the budget. But, as Strachey said, it would be rather 'red-tapey' to refuse.[26] Public works extraordinary expenditure was permitted to rise to £242,065, almost 20 per cent of the general expenditure of £1,217,336. The extra money was spent on bringing even more roads under construction and purchasing another dredger (£49,000) to more quickly make Lagos harbour navigable to ocean-going vessels.[27]

The 1908 estimates were uncontroversial. Egerton estimated a small surplus on expenditure of £1,353,561 and revenue of £1,347,120. Permanent officials were pleased. If all went as anticipated the Colony's total surplus reserve fund would be about £700,000 by the beginning of 1908. John Anderson, Junior Clerk, commented that the estimates were 'very satisfactory'. Antrobus added that they had been carefully prepared by Egerton and carefully examined by the Nigeria Department. Because Southern Nigeria was in such obvious good shape financially, general approval could be given with no hesitation.[28] As it turned out, income of £1,388,000 topped expenditure by almost £30,000. Public works extraordinary expenditure accounted for about £238,000 of the money spent – about 17·5 per cent – a continued demonstration of Egerton's firm belief that public works were the necessary foundation of his development programme.[29]

Egerton's 1908 estimates despatch made an important statement about his approach to development. His programme for the administrative occupation and economic development of Southern Nigeria had six points. It is worth listing these to better understand both the man and his approach.

1. To pacify the country;
2. To establish settled government in the newly won districts;
3. To improve and extend native footpaths throughout the country;
4. To construct properly graded roads in the more populated districts;
5. To clear the numerous rivers in the country and make them suitable for launch and canoe traffic; and
6. To extend the railways.[30]

While not particularly original, they reveal Egerton's attention to detail, his belief in planning, and his determination to direct events.

Although the permanent officials had been uncomfortable with Egerton's estimates, they had made no sustained efforts to halt the rising expenditure of Southern Nigeria, particularly the increased spending on public works extraordinary. This was probably because Egerton was presiding over an administration whose income had been increasing every year at an impressive rate. The 1909 budget, or more precisely the permanent officials' reaction to that budget, was a turning-point. From then on they worked to control Southern Nigeria's spending as never before. What happened? And why?

When they first saw Egerton's 1909 estimates, permanent officials may have grumbled a bit. After all, against a projected expenditure of £1,650,765 he only expected to take in £1,545,700. He planned a deficit of £105,000. Egerton downplayed the significance of this amount in two ways. He suggested first that he might be underestimating his revenues, and therefore the deficit might be diminished accordingly. Second, Southern Nigeria over the years had amassed a huge surplus reserve – from around £100,000 in 1901 to almost £700,000. Some of this could be used to cover the deficit.[31]

Egerton attributed the potential deficit primarily to the need to put in hand 'desirable public works'.[32] These projects were crucial to his programme of progress listed in the budget under Public Works Extraordinary heads and amounted to £345,031. At the time, permanent officials seem to have accepted Egerton's arguments and in fact even increased extraordinary expenditure by £13,500.[33] The upshot of this was to make the total extraordinary expenditure for 1909 over £358,000 – almost 22 per cent of total expenditures. Ironically enough, unofficial members of Egerton's own Legislative Council were more critical of the 1909 estimates than was the Colonial Office. They criticised the Governor by saying that Southern Nigeria should not spend money not covered by current revenue. Egerton responded vigorously, noting that public works extraordinary, 'developmental', expenditure had in the past five years (1904–8) averaged about £200,000 a year (total £997,154).[34] He then went on to say that:

> The Administration of Southern Nigeria has been so prosperous that year after year, although there have been profts, i.e. surpluses, and although generous estimates of expenditure have been approved, yet year by year, our surplus balances have been increased until now. We have about £700,000 in hand and that is the reason, as I have before stated, why I feel able to assent to an estimate of expenditure for next year considerably in excess of the anticipated receipts in 1909.[35]

The Colonial Office was convinced, even if members of Egerton's Legislative Council were not, that the budget, deficit and all, was appropriate and necessary. John Anderson went over the 1909 budget in great detail when it was received at the Colonial Office, and though he expressed concern about the surplus reserves being unduly reduced, he found that the estimates had been very carefully prepared. He even suggested that Egerton should be specially commended. Frederick Butler, Senior Clerk, echoed this praise, saying that the Southern Nigerian estimates were now big business and their preparation difficult.[36] Preparation may have been difficult, but passage through the Colonial Office went easily.

These 1909 estimates represented a great moment for Egerton, practically his last in Southern Nigeria. He had not only persuaded the Colonial Office to accept a budget that increased spending to a record high, he had also gained approval for a large planned deficit, the largest since Southern Nigeria had come under Colonial Office control in 1900. This is especially striking given the often repeated and enforced Colonial maxim regarding colonial public finance, that 'Expenditures should not be allowed to exceed revenues unless to meet emergencies.'[37] Perhaps Egerton's own enthusiastic belief that revenue would continue indefinitely to rise by leaps and bounds had infected London. If so, officials there were rudely shocked by the large and unexpected decrease in 1909 revenue, and the enormous deficit that resulted.

In the last months of 1908, as the 1909 estimates were being submitted and discussed, Southern Nigerian revenue began to decline. John Anderson remarked that although 'Southern Nigeria has just been experiencing a series of very fat years . . . it looks as if a series of lean years might be in store'.[38] It is doubtful that he, or any other permanent official, fully appreciated what was meant by his 'lean year' thesis. 'None of us,' John Anderson would say a year later, 'had the faintest premonition of the extraordinary collapse' that was taking place in the Southern Nigerian revenues. At the close of the fiscal year, only £1,361,891 had been taken in, and expenditure exceeded revenue by £287,000, a record deficit. There was a feeling almost of betrayal in the Colonial Office. Anderson seemed to suggest that Egerton had wilfully ignored the implications of the declining trade at year's end, 1908. According to Anderson, Egerton should have realised that the decline would continue through 1909 and leave Southern Nigerian natives with less money to spend on spirits and tobacco. The import duties on these two items, in any given year from 1908 to 1912, provided from 54 per cent to 57 per cent of the colony's revenue. Therefore, Egerton should have known that revenue would be down, and should have reduced his estimates of expenditure for 1909 accordingly. Anderson called it a 'reckless overestimating' of revenue, and rather stiffly concluded that Southern Nigeria was paying 'the penalty of a somewhat remarkable lapse on the part of those responsible for her finance'.[39]

Egerton tried to play down the significance of the 1909 figures. Attempting to establish a relative context for his situation, he argued that given the general trade depression throughout the world, Southern Nigeria's financial results had not been unsatisfactory.[40] He also tried to put his deficit in a positive light by pointing out that it could still be taken out of the surplus reserve. At the time, October 1909, Egerton projected a deficit of £270,000. Even after covering this there would still be more than £400,000 in reserve – a more-than-ample amount for any contingency.[41] Rather than being persuaded, permanent officials were angered. What Egerton had unwisely forgotten was the permanent officials' irrational attitude toward the surplus reserve fund. As we have seen, it had grown to almost

£700,000 by 1909. But as the surplus grew, so too did a reluctance to use it. It had become sacrosanct in the eyes of permanent officials who worried more about losing it than using it. For example, Butler's reaction to an earlier request of Egerton's to use £13,500 of the fund for telegraph-line construction, was that 'we certainly cannot afford at present to let the balances be diminished by even small driblets'.[42] Since revenue expenditure in West Africa were occasionally subject to wild and unforeseen fluctuations, the purpose of maintaining reserves was obvious and rational. But to be reluctant to use it when the need arose was not rational. Yet this is precisely how the permanent officials felt.

When the permanent officials had to permit £287,000 to be withdrawn from the surplus reserve, Egerton became a marked man. The officials had never felt at ease with Egerton's financial philosophy. They had always wanted to 'apply a little judicious dampening to the constantly expanding expenditure of S. Nigeria'.[43] But prior to 1909 they were unable to argue with Egerton's success. However, once the financial figures for 1909 were in, the permanent officials had literally caught Egerton redhanded – £287,000 in the red.

In late 1908, Butler had hinted to his colleagues that Egerton might endanger the financial security of Southern Nigeria. Butler's analysis of the proper relationship between the Colonial Office and a colonial Governor on the subject of spending and colonial development is a classic statement of the 'official mind':

The comfortable principle that the more you spend the more you will have cannot be applied blindly. It is all to the good that Sir W. Egerton should have such an abounding faith in the future of Southern Nigeria. The responsibility is on him to put forward positive proposals for the development of the country. He discharges his responsibility admirably. The responsibility is on the S. of S. to judge such proposals calmly and dispassionately, and with a long look ahead. If any mistake is to be made in the Colonial Office, it should be that of excessive caution, rather than the opposite. The Governor ought to understand and appreciate our essential function of cautious criticism, just as we appreciate his of enthusiastic development.[44]

In 1909, appreciation was at a minimum on both sides.
In 1910 Egerton argued that the previous year had been an

aberration; the financial truth of Southern Nigeria was that revenue would rise regularly and therefore so could expenditure. Consequently, he budgeted expenditure of £1,569,950 and a revenue of £1,560,331. Once again he built into his estimates a deficit, but this time a small one of less than £10,000. Officials were astonished that he would do this and found his argument for its inclusion 'absurd'. John Anderson saw little likelihood that Egerton's estimates of revenue would be reached. To impose fiscal sanity, and probably drive home the lesson of 1909, he recommended that £50,000 be cut out of public works extraordinary expenditure. Thus a surplus would be assured, or at least, if Egerton had again overestimated, a cushion of £40,000. Perhaps to soften the blow, he suggested that they reconsider the cut after six months if the financial situation of Southern Nigeria had improved. With Anderson's recommendation accepted, the estimates were approved.[45]

In June, Egerton reported that revenue was coming in at a much higher rate than had been expected. He asked permission to go ahead with those parts of the public works extraordinary programme that had been cut. He was rebuffed. The Colonial Office had decided that it could not permit any extra spending until the surplus reserves once again were over £500,000. Lord Crewe, Secretary of State, agreed with the permanent officials, saying that 'the careful policy is the correct one'.[46] Egerton was forced to accept this. However, the final revenue figures were so good that Egerton was allowed to increase expenditure by about £70,000 and so restore the public works extraordinary cuts. Over £1,900,000 had been collected, and Southern Nigeria's surplus for 1910 was £341,000. This meant that the surplus reserve fund was more than £700,000. Out of the total money spent, public works extraordinary totalled £211,087 – a mere 13·5 per cent of all money spent.[47]

In 1911, Egerton wisely estimated a small surplus on expenditure of £1,722,977.[48] Anderson said the estimates were 'not likely to give much trouble. . . . They are straightforward . . . and no doubtful question of policy appears to arise.'[49] The Colonial Office had no difficulty sanctioning them. At the end of the year, revenue had once again risen above the estimates. Almost £2,000,000 had been collected, and so another £239,000 was added to the surplus reserve fund. The amount spent on public works extraordinary relative to total expenditure fell further, to 12·6 per cent. Officials must have seen the financial results of 1911 as the best of all possible worlds – a large surplus for the second straight year and a Governor who no longer insisted upon the right to spend money extravagantly. But by 1912 Egerton's confidence in his financial philosophy was restored sufficiently for him to try again. He had energy and drive enough for one more offensive in his bureaucratic battle with the Colonial Office.

Wearing lightly the lesson of 1909, Egerton recommended that expenditure of £2,016,318 be approved for 1912 against expected revenue of £1,942,210, thus budgeting a deficit of £74,108. He ascribed the deficit mostly to the increase in public works extraordinary expenditure, £266,000.[50] He argued that the enormous surplus reserve fund, now not very much under £1,000,000, could be dipped into to make up the deficit without endangering the financial health of the colony in any conceivable way. Anderson was the first to minute the 1912 estimates and he seems to have been incensed. In the first place the Governor's arithmetic was wrong, the deficit was £100,000 not £74,000. In the second place it seemed to Anderson quite misleading to say the deficit was due to public works extraordinary. He thought the increase came from large increases in the ordinary expenditure as well. In general, the great increase in expenditure – over £2,000,000 for the first time – was the results of 'a deliberately reckless financial policy'. And it was all Egerton's fault. The Colonial Office had urged economy on him year after year, but Egerton had remained unimpressed.[51]

Anderson proposed that the Governor should be ordered in no uncertain terms to reduce his estimates of expenditure by £160,000. A deficit of £100,000 would thereby be converted into a surplus of £60,000. This seemed sensible to Strachey and to Sir George Fiddes, the Assistant Under Secretary in charge of West African business, but a snag emerged when the file reached the Permanent Under Secretary's desk. Sir John Anderson, although a career Colonial Office man, had had first-hand experience of colonial administration, having returned recently from a seven-year stint as Governor of the Straits Settlements and High Commissioner of the Federated Malay States. This background enabled him to respond to Egerton's dilemma much more sympathetically than many others at the Colonial Office. He pointed out that, given the large surplus reserve, it would be more reasonable to reduce expenditure by only £80,000, and allow the Southern Nigerian budget to carry the burden of a modest £20,000 deficit. It was this proposal that the Secretary of State, Lewis Harcourt, approved.[52] Sir John Anderson's suggestion had saved Egerton from a £160,000 spending cut, but Egerton was none the less unhappy. When he was informed of the reduction, he claimed to have been misunderstood and mistreated. Instead of meekly accepting the budget cut, Egerton sent a strongly worded telegram which forcefully expressed his theory of colonial development:

> Strongly deprecate reduction in extraordinary budget and in view of the fact that credit balances exceed amount as laid down by your predecessor as desirable, would ask that surplus funds may be drawn upon as proposed. *Would represent that my eight years insistence on necessity for liberal expenditure if development desired has been amply justified by results.*[53]

Egerton's desire to continue to prime the pump and spend his way to prosperity received no support in the Colonial Office. John Anderson said that 'Sir W. Egerton has been carried away by the prosperity of 1910 just as he was by that of 1907. In the latter case it took two successive deficits to bring him to his senses.'[54] John Anderson seemed determined to teach Egerton a financial lesson and to reduce his expenditures. Permanent officials considered Egerton hard-headed and unreasonable. They did seem to be overreacting.[55] There was one small deficit in 1905 and a much larger one in 1909. Yet a glance at the revenue and expenditure figures for Southern Nigeria from 1900 to 1913 (see Table 3.1) shows clearly that the rule was surpluses and a deficit year the exception.[56]

TABLE 3.1 *Southern Nigeria: revenue and expenditure, 1900–1913 (in £'s)*

Year	Revenue	Expenditure	Surplus/Deficit
1900	535,902	424,257	+111,645
1901	606,431	564,818	+41,613
1902	801,737	619,687	+182,050
1903	760,230	757,953	+2,277
1904	888,136	863,917	+24,219
1905	951,748	998,564	−46,816
1906	1,088,717	1,056,290	+32,427
1907	1,459,554	1,217,336	+242,218
1908	1,387,975	1,357,763	+30,212
1909	1,361,891	1,648,684	−286,793
1910	1,933,235	1,592,282	+340,953
1911	1,956,176	1,717,259	+238,917
1912	2,235,412	2,110,498	+124,914
1913	2,668,198	2,096,311	+571,887

In January 1912, Egerton submitted his proposed reductions totalling £83,371. About £56,000 came from public works extraordinary expenditure. Egerton was later allowed, when more revenue than anticipated came in, to increase public works extraordinary by £36,000. At £246,000 the total still came to only 11·67 per cent of 1912 expenditure. John Anderson, with some condescension, suggested that since the Governor had 'loyally carried out our instruction', the estimates should be approved.[57] This was Egerton's last hurrah. It seems clear from an examination of Egerton's estimates of 1910, 1911 and 1912 that he had lost the initiative to the Colonial Office. By 1910 and 1911 the permanent officials were successfully on the offensive. They blugeoned Egerton with the 1909 deficit. When he finally countered with his 1912 estimates he was defeated.

It should be kept in mind that Egerton saw public works extraordinary as being especially important to development. The money spent on this was to create an infrastructure within which commercial development could take place. It was out of these funds that roads, bridges, harbours and telegraph lines were built and improved. There was a general rise in the money spent on public works extraordinary from 1906 to 1909. Public works extraordinary expenditure peaked during the year of the great deficit, 1909. After that, the percentage of such expenditure went down sharply and rapidly, from a high of almost 22 per cent to under 12 per cent by 1912 (see Table 3.2).[58] This drop shows the declining willingness of

TABLE 3.2 *Public works extraordinary expenditure as a percentage of total expenditure*

Year	Public works extraordinary expenditure (in £'s)	Percentage of public works extraordinary	Total expenditure (in £'s)	Total revenue (in £'s)
1906	171,309	16.9	1,056,290*	1,088,717
1907	242,065	19.9	1,217,336	1,459,554
1908	238,016	17.5	1,357,763	1,387,975
1909	358,453	21.7	1,648,684	1,361,891
1910	211,087	13.3	1,592,282	1,933,235
1911	216,375	12.6	1,717,259	1,956,176
1912	246,355	11.7	2,110,498	2,235,412

* Combined figures for Southern Nigeria and Lagos the year they were amalgamated.

the Colonial Office to give priority to what Egerton had called, many years before, developmental expenditure.

The last word, appropriately enough, belongs to a permanent official. In the despatch approving the 1912 estimates is the quintessential expression of the Colonial Office view of the relationship that should prevail betwen public finance and development in a Crown Colony. To a great extent this view helps to explain why the colonies were as undeveloped as they were when independence came in the 1950s and 1960s, and thus it is an important statement. D. O. Malcolm's draft stated, on behalf of the Secretary of State for the Colonies, that:

> I cannot but fear that there has been a tendency of late years in framing the estimates of expenditure to attach more weight to the rapid development of the country than to caution in the management of its finances, and I feel bound again to insist on the paramount importance of the later consideration.[59]

Chamberlain's view of the colonies as undeveloped estates had not made much of an impression on the key Nigeria Department, where officials remained firmly committed to a pay-as-you-go approach.

Egerton's attitude toward spending to stimulate development made him a Keynesian before Keynes, and he paid for it. He was willing to see his government go temporarily into debt if that was the route to a more sound and secure economic future. However, 1912 was Egerton's last year in Southern Nigeria. He was replaced by Sir Frederick Lugard who was appointed as Governor of both Southern and Northern Nigeria to effect an amalgamation of the two. Egerton was sent away to be Governor of British Guiana, a definite demotion. In retirement, however, he made the unrepentant boast that 'one of the things I am proudest of in West Africa is that I found Southern Nigeria with hardly any debt and I left it with a debt of five millions'.[60]

This story should not be seen merely as that of some arcane bureaucratic struggle. On the contrary, it was an important conflict. Attitudes were formed and patterns set over this several years' process that helped define the future. That the Colonial Office won made a dramatic difference. It meant that Lord Grey's view – that colonial development must be self-supporting, and that budgets should, generally speaking, be balanced – prevailed. Officials' treatment of Sir Walter Egerton's Southern Nigerian estimates revealed three things about their approach to and impact on colonial expenditure and development. First, the officials' position as the final arbiters of self-sufficient (non-Treasury-aided) colony's finances did not make them generous. On the contrary, this responsibility made them even more cautious and suspicious, and their responses were remarkably like those of Treasury officials in similar circumstances. They would have embraced a description of the pre-1914 Treasury's work as an apt characterisation of their own on colonial finance – 'the exceptionally prudent house-keeping appropriate to those who are handling other people's money'.[61] Second, permanent officials frequently interfered with proposals and plans of developmentally minded governors, such as Egerton. Third, if officials had been willing to encourage these men, a more positive tradition of development might have emerged in the last years of British domination and the early years of colonial independence. The economic relationship between Britain and her colonies might have been more fruitful. In retrospect, Sir Walter Egerton seems both admirable and interesting, but we can only speculate on what he might have accomplished had he received the understanding, support and co-operation of permanent officials.

In the final analysis, officials' basic doctrine was that financial restraint was more important than development. This doctrine was not imposed on the Colonial Office by any outside agency such as the Treasury. In fact, this study indicates the need to substantially modify, if not discard, the theory that the Treasury was the main obstacle to colonial development before 1914. From the evidence and analysis presented here it should be clear that the Colonial Office policy toward expenditure and development in the colonies originated with the permanent officials in that office. Therefore, when Ronald Robinson speaks about 'the vaults of the Treasury, locked against colonial expenditure since Gladstone's day' finally opening in the 1940s, or when Anthony Hopkins asserts that Chamberlain's development schemes 'were either blocked or whittled away by the Treasury', we must now realise that another formidable obstacle to development spending existed in the form of the permanent officials at the Colonial Office.[62] These officials did not need Treasury prodding to adopt and implement austere colonial financial policies; they did it very nicely on their own, as the case of Southern Nigeria shows. They felt comfortable with the doctrine of financial restraint, and duty-bound to appy it. It was Colonial Office control of colonial budgets that established the limits of colonial development.

4   Budgetary Conflict over Revenue Estimates in Northern Nigeria, 1899–1913

The nature of the Treasury's influence on Treasury-aided colonies has been long debated.[1] The original assumption was that the Treasury controlled the purse strings and therefore the policy. Ann Burton, in an important article published in 1966, rejected this theory for the mid-Victorian years.[2] However, scholars following her, mostly writing about the late-Victorian and Edwardian eras have tended to ignore her work and restore to the Treasury an unwarranted measure of authority over colonial finance and colonial development policy.[3] This being the case it seems worthwhile, even important, to look anew at the controversy and argue that Burton's thesis is also true about the years 1899–1913, during which, for the most part, the administrative occupation of Africa took place. One way to do this is to look at the Colonial Office and the budgetary process in a Treasury-aided colony during these very important years. The years were especially significant in that they were years when imperial interests and attention shifted to the dependent empire, and politics were put in train which would influence and direct the dependent colonies for decades.[4]

This chapter examines the Northern Nigerian annual estimates during the fiscal years 1899/1900 to 1912/13. In particular it studies the work done by Colonial Office and Treasury officials in a crucial area of colonial public finance: the provision of revenue for Northern Nigeria. Based on the minutes, memoranda, and correspondence of officials and their masters at both departments, this chapter argues that the Colonial Office was the paramount influence on Northern Nigerian financial policy, and that the Treasury did not significantly influence colonial policy, financial or otherwise, contrary to the

118

Colonial Office's desire. Where it was applicable, Treasury control, it seems, meant essentially that spending departments such as the Colonial Office had to appreciate the necessity of justifying both new and existing expenditure, and therefore programmes; it did not mean that control over colonial policy passed to the Treasury. The Colonial Office–Treasury relationship was at base a solid and constructive one. Regular correspondence – formal and informal – and frequent meetings between officials of the two departments were the means by which differences arising over colonial finance and development, where the Treasury had a say, were resolved. It would be very wrong to argue that the Colonial Office–Treasury relationship was anything other than an essentially co-operative one, in which the Colonial Office sought ways to keep afloat their poorest colonies – and so sought Treasury help – and one in which the Treasury did its level best to establish and maintain financial order in the aided colony.

When Sir Frederick Lugard became Northern Nigeria's first High Commissioner in 1900, over nine-tenths of the country was controlled by local Islamic rulers who looked to the Emir of Kano and the Caliph of Sokoto for leadership and guidance. There could hardly have been a less developed 'tropical estate' in the British Empire than Northern Nigeria in 1900. Because the colony was landlocked, its government could not rely on the usual source of colonial revenue – custom duties. Other sources produced only a nominal revenue. For example, local revenue for 1901/2 was £4,424. By 1905/6 this had risen to £110,544, and by 1910/11 to £274,989.[5] However, in the same years, Southern Nigeria's revenue was £361,815, £550,233 and £1,933,235 respectively.[6] The area had been a British sphere of influence since 1885 and was established as a Protectorate of the British Crown on 1 January 1900. Functionally and practically Northern Nigeria was a Crown Colony. It was administered by colonial civil servants whose work was supervised and controlled by the staff of the Colonial Office in London. In London and in Northern Nigeria it was assumed that until the entire country was pacified and a strong government established throughout, a substantial military force, maintained at substantial expense, would be necessary. The colony itself was unable to generate funds for either its civil government or for a military force. During the years 1899–1913 an annual contribution was received from Southern Nigeria. This never exceeded £75,000. Therefore an annual grant-in-aid of revenue from the British Treasury, the major source of income for Northern Nigeria, was necessary. Each year the Colonial Office negotiated with the Treasury for such a grant and also worked together on Northern Nigeria's financial affairs. Therefore, the Colonial Office's work on Northern Nigeria was shared with, and complicated by, the Treasury. Their negotiations form the subject matter of this chapter.

One need go back no further than 1868 to discover the modern foundations of Treasury control generally, and to 1870 to see the particular basis on which the Treasury exercised legal control over a Crown Colony's finances. In April 1868, the Treasury decided that its sanction would be required only in cases which involved:

> any increase of establishment of salary, and of cost of a service or for any additional works or new services which have not been specially provided for in the Grants of Parliament.[7]

Theoretically this was interpreted broadly. Treasury Permanent Secretary Sir Reginald Welby said in 1886 that the Treasury's task, the 'maintenance of financial order' in British Government, required that it assent to every measure that increased or tended to increase public expenditure. He quickly pointed out three practical limitations: (i) the Treasury was just another department of state; (ii) the Treasury, a small department, could only do so much; (iii) any Treasury decision could be overturned in Cabinet.[8]

Until 1870, Treasury control over colonial finance was rooted in haphazard tradition. Because a Crown Colony, by definition, was a possession of the Crown, it followed that its finances should be supervised by the Crown's Treasury. But as time went on, this theory was inconsistently applied. The Treasury supervised the financial accounts of some Crown Colonies while others were supervised by the Colonial Office.[9] Robert Lowe, Gladstone's Chancellor of the Exchequer from 1868 to 1873, felt the Treasury would be better off supervising none.

> Our main object should be to keep ourselves clear of financial entanglements with these remote and needy communities and the best way to do that is to have no responsibility for their acts in this office.

Lowe's Permanent Secretary, G. A. Hamilton, pointed out that colonies in financial difficulty would seek and eventually obtain aid from the Imperial Government. It would be wiser to impose some sense of financial probity on the colonies before, rather than after, they got into difficulty.[10] In March 1870 the Treasury decided that henceforth only those colonies in receipt of a Treasury grant-in-aid would be subject to Treasury control. Furthermore the Treasury would examine and sanction the estimates of expenditure and revenue of those colonies annually for two years after the grant had been made.[11]

This was the basis of the Treasury–Colonial Office relationship concerning Crown Colonies in the late nineteenth and early twentieth centuries. It involved a great deal of to-ing and fro-ing by letter and in person between the two offices. Describing this sort of activity, a senior Colonial Office official, Robert Meade, said in 1888 that:

before any additional expenditures can be approved we are obliged to refer to the Treasury all questions in reference to a colony which receives a grant-in-aid; their estimates have to go to the Treasury for the Treasury approval.[12]

This system was still in effect, and applicable to Northern Nigeria, during the years 1899–1913.

Of course the system was subject to the vagaries of human behaviour. Thus the attitudes of Treasury and Colonial Office staff toward Treasury control are of interest. In the late 1880s, in the face of suggestions that the Treasury had become too powerful, Welby insisted that Treasury control was not, nor was it intended to be, a device for the 'reconstruction of a policy of another department'. Treasury control was simply a method of maintaining financial order in the spending departments of the government, 'and from the moment it interferes in any shape or kind with policy it is departing from its proper sphere'. Welby persistently maintained that although a department wishing to increase expenditure had to first show good prima-facie grounds to the Treasury, this requirement did not imply 'a power in the Treasury to overrule the policy of another Department on the grounds of policy'.[13]

In 1904, the question of undue Treasury influence over the policy of other departments was again raised. Roland Wilkins, another Treasury official, gave the Treasury view:

The merit of the present system [Treasury control] is, in fact, this: that no Department may incur increased expenditure until it has formulated a statement of the reasons for it which will satisfy 'the man in the street', the intelligent layman – represented in this case by the Treasury. If the statement is not accepted, the chances are that either the case is a bad one, or it is incompletely put. The actual criticisms of the Treasury may not be a great value, but the existence of the Treasury, and the need for making out a case which will satisfy them, undoubtedly are.[14]

From this reasonable position, though it did not always seem reasonable to those in other departments, the Treasury did not budge.

What about the view from the other side of the fence? How did officials at other departments look at Treasury control and Treasury officials? The answer is, with jaundiced eyes. For example, the Assistant Under Secretary at the Colonial Office, Reginald Antrobus, in 1899 characterised Treasury control as being minutely detailed, and then went on to point out that:

the process of explaining to them [Treasury officials] the needs of a Colony involves endless correspondence and practically transfers the responsibility for the affairs of the Colony from the Colonial Office to the Treasury.[15]

This last remark was due more to exasperation with the seemingly 'endless correspondence' than to genuine fear of policy interference. In fact, the Colonial Office was rarely disappointed in its negotiations with the Treasury. What did irritate officials in the spending department was the hectoring and didactic way in which the Treasury approached its work of financial control. From retirement, an ex-official, Sir William Baillie Hamilton of the Colonial Office, spoke bitterly of Treasury officials. His career had spanned the years 1864 to 1908 and he had been Head of the Nigeria Department from 1901 to 1906. It was particularly galling to Hamilton that when the Secretary of State for the Colonies needed funds that could not be raised in a colony he was 'expected to go on his knees to another department', the Treasury, for the money. Hamilton believed the Treasury knew nothing about a colony's requirements, and complained that the Colonial Office had to work up cases that were 'best calculated to explain the situation and secure a favourable hearing'.[16] This, of course, was exactly what the Treasury wanted. In fact, George Goschen, Chancellor of the Exchequer (1887–92) insisted that:

The first object of the Treasury must be to throw the Departments on their defence, and to compel them to give strong reasons for any increased expenditure, and to explain how they have come to demand it. This control alone contributes to make the Departments careful in what they put forward.[17]

Exercising this responsibility did not make the Treasury popular. Welby warned his colleagues that they 'must not mind very often the form in which their suggestions or remonstrances are received'.[18] In actuality the Treasury did the Colonial Office and other spending departments a service by putting its financial expertise to work for them. It was done, however, with a very heavy hand.

The Treasury had no monopoly on the desire for economy. The Colonial Office, too, was intent on enforcing fiscal restraint in Crown Colony expenditure; its officials subscribed to, and were influenced by, notions of Gladstonian finance which permeated the Civil Service from the 1860s on. At the same time, they realised that some colonies had been incorporated into the British Empire for policy reasons. Financial assistance was necessary to help these colonies, if they were not self-supporting, to eventually become so. In such cases, the Colonial Office had to take the long, as well as the financial, view. Northern Nigeria was one of these revenue-starved colonies that needed the long view. Each year Northern Nigeria would submit its annual estimates to the Colonial Office for examination. The geographical department responsible for the business of Northern Nigeria then determined how large a grant was necessary to keep the colony financially afloat for the coming year. The estimates and grant request were then sent to the Treasury for approval.

The first negotiations between the Colonial Office and the Treasury over Northern Nigerian budgets set a pattern: we shall examine that pattern and its evolution during fiscal years 1899/1900 to 1912/13. (The fiscal year ran from 1 April to 31 March.) In February 1899, Lugard submittd estimates for 1899/1900; they showed he had his own ideas about how Northern Nigeria should be administratively occupied and economically developed. Sir Edward Wingfield, Permanent Under Secretary, felt that Lugard's ideas were 'much too exalted and contemplated a more complete administration than will be possible for some time to come'. W. H. Mercer, Head of the Nigeria Department, noted the Colonial Office was in no hurry to see this 'more complete administration' established: it would cost too much money. His view was that new expenditure had to be justified by new revenue.[19]

Lugard wanted to spend £130,000. This sum is not large by late-twentieth-century standards, nor was it, in the larger scheme of things, a great deal of money in 1899. However, as we shall presently see, it was a shockingly large sum to the Secretary of State, Joseph Chamberlain, and to high officials in the Colonial Office. One of their fundamental financial principles was 'Empire on the cheap'. Most of this £130,000 was for an extensive administrative staff which would take over and begin the onerous task of organising the nine-tenths of Northern Nigeria that was British in name only. Mercer thought Lugard should at first confine himself 'to maintaining amicable relations with the chiefs and encouraging trade to come through our territories'. For the moment the government should remain in the area under British control, and only gradually move beyond. At the Colonial Office, officials had no idea how quickly Lugard would move to pacify the rest of the territory. Wingfield and Antrobus proposed to reduce Lugard's budget by about £54,000 to just under £76,000. However, Chamberlain upset the smooth progress towards an office consensus. Alarmed by this 'impossible' amount, he wanted more information: how much had the Royal Niger Company (the organisation that had ruled much of Northern and Southern Nigeria before the Crown took over) spent on administering the territory? When received, the information persuaded Chamberlain that Lugard's expenditure should total no more than £70,000.[20] Lugard resubmitted the estimates in April, having made, he said, every effort to reduce the figure to the smallest amount compatible with efficient administration. This strenuous effort produced a budget figure of £92,000. Meanwhile Chamberlain had been brooding over the Royal Niger Company figures. Since the Niger Company had spent only £57,000 on the same area of Nigeria that Lugard was now administering,

> Why are we to spend so much more than the Company? . . . My strong feeling is the £70,000 is too high until experience and events – and the development of the country – justify a larger expenditure . . . I think £50,000 enough and to £60,000 maximum.[21]

At the Colonial Office's insistence Lugard again submitted the Northern Nigeria estimates. Disregarding the Colonial Office's order about reducing the amount to £60,000, he brought in a revised estimate of £86,000. Mercer, Antrobus, and Wingfield, key permanent officials, reviewed the figures with Lugard and grudgingly admitted that this figure was most probably the irreducible minimum. They recommended that the Colonial Office request Treasury approval to spend £86,000 in Northern Nigeria during 1899/1900. Chamberlain accepted this unanimous recommendation from senior staff and authorised its presentation to the Treasury.[22] Although the new fiscal year had begun in April, the Colonial Office was not able to send the Northern Nigeria estimates to the Treasury until 27 June. Wingfield gloomily predicted that 'the Treasury will demur', adding, 'but I don't see where the pruning knife is to be applied'. Earlier the Colonial Office had advised the Treasury to expect estimates of £60,000 or less. The Colonial Office now explained to the Treasury that the £60,000 maximum had been abandoned – 'with due regard to the economy and to the legitimate requirements of the territory to be administered it is not possible to reduce the total amount to a lower figure than £86,132'.[23]

We should realise that in this first year, consideration of the grants-in-aid was separate from discussion of the estimates. A grant of £75,000 had alrady been approved months before in a meeting between senior officials of the Colonial Office and the Treasury. Ordinarily the grant depended on the size of the estimates, but that first year Northern Nigeria needed money immediately, to cover the expense of taking over from the Royal Niger Company, and could not wait for approval of the estimates.[24] Thereafter, as the routine developed, the grant was an integral and indeed central part of the negotiations over estimates.

Treasury approval of the estimates was slow in coming, and did not occur until mid-November. Northern Nigerian salary rates were a major concern – Treasury officials thought them too high. More to the point, they felt that once set the rates would be difficult to change, and although applicable only to a small group the first year, would eventually apply to a much larger group as the Northern Nigerian government grew. While the Treasury deliberated, the Colonial Office became more and more impatient. Treasury officials finally concluded that the salaries Lugard proposed were higher than those in colonies administered by the Foreign Office and should be reduced.[25]

While Colonial Office officials were considering a suitable reply to this suggestion, the Office received a second Treasury letter. The Treasury now objected to Lugard's salary of £3,500 a year, saying they would agree to nothing over £2,500 a year. Antrobus was very annoyed, and told his colleagues, rather fiercely, that:

If the Treasury are going to insist upon Nigeria being administered in accordance with the methods of the F.O. [in East Africa], and refuse to listen to what we recommend as the result of our experience in *West* Africa. it would be better that Nigeria should be placed under the F.O.

Comparing salaries in the colonies under Colonial and Foreign Office supervision seemed the sort of common-sense control advocated by Welby; to Antrobus, however, this was Treasury nit-picking which was seriously undermining the work of the Colonial Office in Northern Nigeria.

We are having great difficulty with the Treasury. They have given notice to the Company that the Administration will be taken over on the 1st of January; but after having led me to believe that they would sanction the Estimates which we submitted to them on the 27th of June, they began in September a correspondence which is still in October going on, with the result that we have not yet been able to select the officials – European and native – who ought to be on the spot ready for work on the 1st of January.[26]

A private conference with senior Treasury officials seemed a good way to cut through this difficulty. So Antrobus, with strong backing from Chamberlain, met with Robert Chalmers, a Principal Clerk at the Treasury, on 10 October 1899. They worked out an agreement whereby the Colonial Office secured almost if not all that it had wanted. The Treasury agreed to, with only a few minor deductions, the salary scales proposed by the Colonial Office.[27] Regarding the High Commissioner's salary, his base pay would remain at £2,500 a year but he would get an annual duty allowance of £500. Now the Treasury felt that it could approve the estimates. Expenditure at the rate of £84,638 annually was to be allowed, and the Colonial Office was so informed on 17 November 1899.[28] Treasury officials seemed relieved when it was all over. T. L. Heath said 'we have taken much trouble and done our best'.[29]

In light of these negotiations, the questions may be asked: did the Treasury try to influence policy in Nigeria?; and if so, did they succeed?; did they extract concessions from the Colonial Office regarding Northern Nigeria? The answer in each case is, no. Although the Treasury desired to lower authorised expenditure in Northern Nigeria, it abandoned its demands for further reductions once the Colonial Office staff made it clear that in its experience good salaries meant good civil servants. Treasury officials had little interest *per se* in the policy of administratively occupying this new colony. What did interest them was the principle of justifying new expenditure. In fact, the Colonial Office received Treasury authorisation to spend about 98 per cent of the money it had asked for. What is significant is not that Treasury objections served to reduce the estimates by only £1,300, but that earlier efforts by the Colonial staff had resulted in reductions of £44,000. This might appear to be due to the Colonial Office's reading of what the Treasury would allow, thereby creating a case for indirect influence. But the evidence – from the Treasury and the Colonial Office – does not support this. It was the Colonial Office's insistence – from the Secretary of State and the permanent staff – that brought about the basic reduction. Once the budget was reduced to what Colonial Office officials thought was proper and necessary, they forcefully persuaded the Treasury not to attempt further reductions.

Approval for the 1900/1 estimates of £85,278 and for the grant-in-aid of £87,800 was easily gained.[30] An amount of £44,000 from the grant was earmarked for special projects – river steamers, new buildings and the like – just as a portion of the 1899/1900 grant had been.[31] However, after this fiscal year, such extraordinary expenditure was incorporated into the regular estimates. in 1901 the Treasury accepted the Colonial Office's figures for 1901/2 without question. The amounts were much larger for this year – £314,000 expenditure against a grant of £280,000;[32] and they would continue to increase each year. This was not simply because there had been an increase in spending, but because estimates for the West African Frontier Force were henceforth combined with the civil estimates of Northern Nigeria.

After several years (1899–1903) of overseeing Northern Nigerian finances and dealing with the Treasury concerning these finances, Colonial Office staff felt sufficiently confident to take the initiative when necessary. An example of this occurred during deliberations over the estimates and grant for 1903/4. In August 1902, Lugard notified the Colonial Office that more money would be needed to expand the West African Frontier Force. Maintaining a military establishment might be expensive but a native rebellion or a long-drawn-out native war in Nigeria would cost much more – psychologically as well as financially. When Great Britain took over Northern Nigeria in 1900, both politicians and officials assumed that

control of the country would come gradually, and therefore
expenditure would increase gradually. In fact, what happened was that
Lugard's expeditions against unconquered native states suddenly and
dramatically expanded the area under British control, and more
soldiers were needed. Colonial Office staff found his argument
compelling. Lugard requested authorisation and funds to increase his
force by 750 men. Antrobus went further, and argued that Lugard's
proposal was inadequate, suggesting that the number of men be
nearly doubled. Sir Montagu Ommanney, Permanent Under Secretary since Wingfield's retirement in 1900, felt his staff had made 'a
strong case for the increased expenditure'.[33] The Treasury, without
much enthusiasm, eventually agreed that the case had been made: it
not only allowed £50,000 for 1,400 men, but also sanctioned the
largest grant-in-aid ever – £405,000.[34] Not surprisingly, Treasury
approval was accompanied by some reluctance and grumbling over
'these heavy hinterland charges'.[35] Speaking for the Treasury, W. H.
Fisher told the Colonial Office of the Treasury's earnest hope that:

> no further extension of the area of effective administration will be
> sanctioned until a substantial decrease is shown in the demands
> made by the Protectorate on the British taxpayer.[36]

In general, officials at the Colonial Office could not have agreed
more; however, the strategic military situation was, and might
continue to be, a higher priority. As Ommanney pointed out:

> future extensions of administration cannot be regulated by
> financial considerations solely. They are forced upon us by the
> conduct of the Emirs which we cannot with safety allow to pass
> unnoticed.[37]

In this instance, the Colonial Office felt that inadequate military
funding was no ecomony. The Treasury seemed perfectly willing to
see the reasonableness of this proposal and allow it to go through.
    Indeed, throughout all these years one never encounters the
'Treasury beast' of legend and myth. What shows up in Treasury
minutes is a marked willingness to listen to, be persuaded by, and
co-operate with, the Colonial Office. True, there was occasional
irritation, petulance, and perhaps a general weariness over Colonial
Office requests for money,[38] but this should not hide the generally
good and productive relationship that existed between the two
departments.

The Colonial Office usually made a case for expenditure to the satisfaction of most, if not all, Treasury clerks. For example, in 1908 the Colonial Office requested Treasury authorisation to spend £530,000 in Northern Nigeria during the coming year. Lugard's successor, Sir Percy Girouard, estimated that on the revenue side he could count on £120,000 locally – £50,000 from reserves, and £70,000 from Southern Nigeria – which left a balance of £290,000 to be provided from the Imperial Treasury. Treasury clerk Malcolm Ramsay suggested that the grant could be reduced by £10,000 or even £15,000. Northern Nigeria still had almost £10,000 in reserves, and the government there had been underestimating its local revenue every year since 1903/4. Local revenues would probably exceed £120,000. His superior, E. G. Herman, agreed that a £10,000 reduction was reasonable. However, when the file reached Sir George Murray, the Permanent Secretary, he ignored the suggestions of his subordinates and accepted the Colonial Office proposal of £290,000.[39] Clearly, senior Treasury officials had come to rely on the Colonial Office. In fact, when the Colonial Office submitted estimates of £515,000 for the next year (1909/10) and requested a grant-in-aid of £237,000, a Treasury clerk passed them, saying, 'I submit that these proposals of the CO – who have scrutinised the Governor's estimates with evident care . . . may be accepted en bloc.'[40] The request was approved, and in a letter of 3 February 1909 the Treasury acknowledged the 'care with which these estimates have been prepared'.[41]

After 1904/5 the grant began dropping, and continued to do so until fiscal year 1901/11. Table 4.1 shows this.[42]

The decreasing grants did not indicate any less need in Northern Nigeria, for expenditures tended to rise. However, local revenues

TABLE 4.1 *Grants-in-aid of revenue from Imperial Treasury to Northern Nigeria, 1904/5–1911/12*

Year	Amount of Grant-in-aid of revenue (in £'s)
1904–5	405,000
1905–6	320,000
1906–7	315,000
1907–8	295,000
1908–9	290,000
1909–10	237,000
1910–11	275,000

increased annually, and the annual contribution from Southern Nigeria continued to rise until it levelled off at around £70,000. These factors allowed the Treasury grant to decrease, and all assumed that eventually the grant would be unnecessary and Northern Nigeria would stand on its own.

The good relationship that had developed was strained and almost disrupted while the 1911/12 and 1912/13 estimates were being considered – from December 1910 to October 1912. During this period the end of the grant system was negotiated and the whole question of Northern Nigerian finances was combined with Southern Nigeria's finances, and with the question of amalgamation of the two colonies. The Northern Nigerian local revenue had risen rapidly, but so had expenditure. This was especially so during 1911/12 (see Table 4.2).[43]

TABLE 4.2 *Northern Nigerian revenue (local) and expenditure 1907/8–1911/12*

Year	Local revenue (in £'s)	Expenditure (in £'s)
1907–8	143,005	498,302
1908–9	178,444	540,644
1909–10	213,436	566,843
1910–11	274,989	565,760
1911–12	348,366	827,939

Even Colonial Office officials who anticipated an unusually large grant for 1911/12 were surprised by the amount that would have to be requested from the Treasury – £365,000. This included the ordinary part of the grant – £286,158; interest on the railway loan – £50,600; and payment of Northern Nigeria's outstanding liability – £29,000. This last was later reduced to about £10,000, making the total grant request about £347,000.[44] George Fiddes, Antrobus's successor as Assistant Under Secretary since 1909, said the Treasury would be 'sick' when they saw the figure. He warned that the Treasury would again propose the amalgamation of Northern and Southern Nigeria.[45]

Some background on the amalgamation issue is necessary here. As early as 1898 the Colonial Office had decided that its objective was to create a single British colony from the Niger Territories (Northern and Southern Nigeria, and Lagos).[46] Its achievement was contingent upon several conditions: an expanded transport and communication system, pacification of the quasi-independent states in the North, improved public health, and financial stability. The Treasury felt that the financial burdens carried by the Imperial Exchequer could be shouldered by Southern Nigeria and had over the years urged the Colonial Office to begin amalgamation.[47] The Colonial Office wished to delay amalgamation, because officials feared that the amalgamated colony, instead of just poorer Northern Nigeria, might come under Treasury financial supervision. This was to be avoided if possible.

The substantial grant requested for Northern Nigeria for 1911/12 seemed to tip the balance in favour of amalgamation. In turn, Fiddes, thinking to take the initiative, began to make preparations. In January 1911 he ordered an internal examination of the question, and told the Secretary of State, Lewis Harcourt, that if, after analysing the question, 'the project seems now to be feasible from our viewpoint, we should make it the subject of a deal with the Treasury'.[48] Within the Colonial Office there was a difference of opinion as to how and when they should proceed. As a result it took a long time to develop a position. Regarding the 1911/12 grant, the Treasury rather surprisingly gave its consent with little fuss.[49] Perhaps hints of amalgamation in the near future softened the Treasury.

However, in November 1911 Charles Strachey, Head of the Nigeria Department, wrote a deeply pessimistic memorandum in which he strongly recommended against amalgamation, at least for the present. Surveying Northern Nigeria's past three fiscal years he concluded that, 'it is quite evident . . . that the amalgamated Nigeria would require, for a good many years to come, a grant-in-aid in order to make ends meet. The minimum, to begin with, might be £250,000.' He went on to note that:

> The public have just been subscribing to the Southern Nigerian Loan [for various important public works projects] on the strength of figures showing the past prosperity and probable future prosperity of Southern Nigeria. Any amalgamation which had the effect of making it appear that this prosperity was jeopardised would probably be resisted by investors.

They should do no more than appoint a single Governor for Northern and Southern Nigeria whose charge would be to devise a plan for amalgamation. Using Strachey's memorandums, Colonial Office officials arrived at a tentative grant figure for Northern Nigeria for 1912/13 as £229,000. A note of frustration entered Harcourt's comments when he saw Strachey's figures: 'I have nothing to bargain with if I say to the Treasury "the grant-in-aid required next year for Northern Nigeria is £229,000 but if you let me amalgamate it with the rich Southern Nigeria I shall want £250,000" '[50]

Top officials at the Colonial Office, Fiddes, Sir John Anderson (the Permanent Under Secretary), Lord Emmot (the Parliamentary Under Secretary), and Harcourt, found it impossible to accept Strachey's figures or his analysis. Fiddes, saying that Strachey's conclusions were 'much too pessimistic', ignored them. They should operate on 'the reasonable assumption that if we bring together the prosperous Southern and the struggling Northern Protectorate, the result will be to diminish the burden on the Treasury'. An effort should be made to delay the amalgamation for a short while until a deal had been made concerning the length of time, if any, that the amalgamated colony would be subject to Treasury control. Although amalgamation might cost the Treasury a good deal in the short run, it would be cheaper than continuing to provide, indefinitely, an annual grant.[51]

Meanwhile, the grant for fiscal year 1912/13 – recalculated to be £156,000 – was again agreed to with surprisingly little trouble.[52] The problem of how to achieve amalgamation with Treasury assistance but without Treasury control continued to be discussed in the Colonial Office for the next several months. On this issue Fiddes said that the Treasury's assistance was 'fundamental'. He realised they were skating on thin ice and that the Treasury might well refuse to pay more unless an excellent case was made. Fiddes, Sir John Anderson, and Harcourt discussed the situation and decided to ask the Treasury for a fixed annual grant (£100,000 a year) for the next five years, beginning 1 April 1913. During these years the Treasury would have no authority over the Nigerian estimates. After that, the Colonial Office would request no more money from the Treasury for Northern Nigeria. The Permanent Under Secretary ordered that a letter be drafted which would 'enlarge on the immense relief that will thus be given to the Treasury'.[53] That letter, dated 27 June 1912, said that:

The secretary of state is aware that with assistance limited to £100,000 it can hardly be expected that the expenditure can be kept within the revenue for the first two or three years . . . From the point of view of the Nigerian Administration it might, therefore, have been preferable to defer amalgamation until the development of the resources of Northern Nigeria had reduced the gap between its revenue and expenditure. But Mr. Harcourt is anxious to relieve the Treasury, at the earliest possible date, of a portion of the burden which it assumes in connection with that Protectorate; and, in view of the steady increase in the local receipts of Northern Nigeria he considers that it should be possible to meet the requirements of the amalgamated administration with the limited grant-in-aid suggested, supplemented, during the first years of amalgamation, by recourse to the surplus balances of Southern Nigeria.

The Treasury was convinced. Treasury clerk N. E. Behrens wrote that 'on the whole it seems to be a fair bargain', and that 'it is greatly to the benefit of the Exchequer that it [amalgamation] should take place and the proposed bargain is, I submit, one that we may readily accept'. The Treasury provisionally approved this scheme on 23 July 1912. The Colonial Office had to agree that no new permanently recurring charges against revenue would be allowed in Northern Nigeria during the five years of the agreement, unless offset by an equivalent increase in revenue.[54]

Colonial Office officials, generally pleased, found this condition unacceptable. Behrens defended the idea when the Colonial Office objected: the Treasury needed some protection against a failure on the part of the amalgamated colony to make ends meet during the first five years. 'If she does fail', Behrens continued,

we should have to continue the policy of grants-in-aid and it was to ensure that at any rate we should not have to find more than £100,000 per annum that the condition was suggested. . . . I think it is a small condition to attach to a subsidy of £100,000 for five years.

Behrens was overruled. His superior, L. J. Hewby, did not want Treasury control, after amalgamation, to extend to the Southern Province as well. 'It would be a decided mistake,' he said, 'if the Treasury were to use the new financial arrangement for meddling with Southern Nigerian finances.' They would have to be satisfied with the Colonial Office's promise to do all that could be done to secure the financial stability of the amalgamated Nigeria.[55] The Treasury's unconditional acceptance of the Colonial Office proposal came on 12 October 1912. This marked the end of the negotiations between the Colonial Office and the Treasury over Nigeria [56] Northern Nigeria's budgets were no longer subject to Treasury scrutiny; the annual negotiations over estimates and grants-in-aid were a thing of the past.

With few exceptions generalisations about the nature of Treasury control and its effect on colonial policy have in the past been made without reference to much detail. The necessary detail can only come from monographic case studies such as this one. With such an examination in hand, we can return to the chapter's theme and look anew at the question of Treasury control over colonial policy. We should realise that for the period of the administrative occupation of British Africa we can now bring the question of Treasury control and colonial policy into much sharper focus. From this new angle of vision four important generalisations can be made. They are germane to the Colonial Office–Treasury relationship *vis-à-vis* Treasury control, and – coming out of this – are comments on the very limited role the Treasury played in imperial policy in British tropical Africa.

First, the Colonial Office, and not the Treasury or any other department of state, was clearly in charge of the formation of colonial policy and day-to-day overseeing of that policy's implementation. Second, Treasury control imposed on the Treasury an obligation to maintain financial order in the spending departments subject to Treasury control. This obligation did not extend to, nor did the Treasury want it to extend to, the making of policy. Third, while there might be some difference as to the means by which policy goals were achieved, there was no great divergence of views as to what these goals were – in this case that a certain colony should be developed into and administered as a self-sufficient colony. Fourth, differences between the two departments were generally settled by co-operative negotiation and not by antagonistic confrontation. Occasional irritations which surfaced should not obscure this important point. We should also realise that the Colonial Office, more often than not, got its own way. In the final analysis, however, the defining characteristics of the relationship between the Colonial Office and the Treasury, over Treasury control and Colonial policy in the 'undeveloped estates', were flexibility, pragmatism, and co-operation.

5 The Creation of the Lagos Railway, 1895–1911

In the late Victorian and Edwardian eras, colonial railways became distinguishing marks of British colonial development policy. A basic assumption of British officials concerned with colonial development was that rapid, efficient, and inexpensive transportation was necessary if economic progress was to be made in the 'undeveloped estates'. This was true when Joseph Chamberlain was Secretary of State and still true when Lewis W. Harcourt became Secretary of State in 1910. It was felt that railways were essential for the development and integration of a colonial hinterland into the greater international economy of the British Empire. In this context the economic and developmental mission of the Colonial Office was to oversee – in Africa at least – the building of a transportation infrastructure of railways and harbours in each British colony, thereby linking the coastal areas to the interior. In this way, Nigerian colonial railways and British shipping systems linked Lagos, Ibadan, Zaria, and Kano to London, Manchester, Liverpool, and Glasgow.

Permanent officials at the Colonial Office were expected to recognise the value of public works projects such as railways, understand their ramifications, and supervise their organisation. The purpose of this chapter and the next is to describe what actually happened when officials were given this opportunity. The argument presented here is that these officials had a substantial and positive impact on the development and implementation of railway policy in Nigeria in three crucial areas: planning the railways; funding their construction; and selecting construction methods.

Although in the past scholars have commented on the role of Colonial Office officials in the development of railways this role has never been the central or even major focus of scholarly analysis.[1] This case study of Nigeria's Lagos Railway describes the work of a single Colonial Office department, supervising a single cohesive geographic area in which colonial railways were planned, financed, and constructed. The influence of permanent officials in the Nigeria Department is analysed here in relation to the development and implementation of railway policy in Nigeria. Also examined as a part of the general discussion will be the extent to which the Colonial Office's reliance on and co-operation with other departments – namely the Crown Agents Office and the Treasury – affected official work. Between 1896 and 1912 two major railways were begun and completed in British Nigeria: the Lagos Railway (1896–1911) and the Baro–Kano Railway (1907–11). The planning, financing, and method of construction of these lines form the basis of the next two chapters.

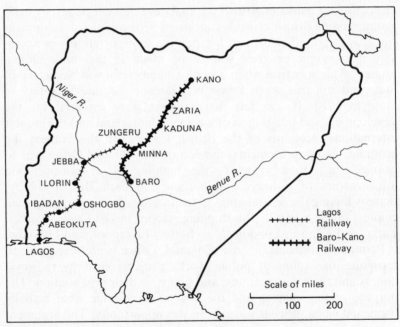

MAP 5 *Routes of the Lagos Railway and Baro–Kano Railway, 1895–1911*

GETTING THE LAGOS RAILWAY GOING

By the 1890s, tribal warfare, the salient characteristic of the Lagos hinterland for decades, had been brought under control. It would, now be possible to open up and exploit the Lagos Colony hinterland.[2]

In response to a variety of pressures the Colonial Office began to give serious consideration to the idea of building a railway in Lagos Colony.[3] One of the first problems to be resolved was funding. Where should the money come from? Should a railway be built with private funds or through government financing? In 1893 the Colonial Office solicited the advice of the Crown Agents for the Colonies. The three Crown Agents who headed this office were appointed by the Secretary of State for the Colonies and were the chief source of advice on colonial public works projects and matters of colonial finance. Sir Montagu Ommanney, Senior Crown Agent, opposed privately funded railways. He argued that private sources required guaranteed profits, which meant 'in plain English . . . the use of the Government's credit for the enrichment of promoters and . . . troubles and losses for the Government'.[4] Ommanney's opinion was accepted, but the discussion signified a new level of seriousness in the Lagos Government and at the Colonial Office. The Colonial Office did authorise the Crown Agents to gather information about routes and costs. This they did through their own Consulting Engineers.* In 1984 the Crown Agents sent Mr W. Shelford as Consulting Engineer to survey Lagos Colony and the Yorubaland Protectorate and develop possible routes to exploit the territory.

By the time Shelford presented his report in late 1895, Lord Rosebery's Liberals had been replaced by the Unionist Government of Lord Salisbury. The consequences were to prove significant for British Africa. Joseph Chamberlain became Secretary of State for the Colonies. He brought to this post all the reforming fervour that he had once expended on Birmingham. In a well-known speech, delivered shortly after assuming office, Chamberlain said:

> I regard many of our colonies as being in the condition of undeveloped estates . . . estates which can never be developed without Imperial assistance. . . .
> I shall be prepared to consider very carefully myself, and then, if I am satisfied, to confidently submit to the House, any case which may occur in which, by the judicious investment of British money, those estates which belong to the British Crown may be developed for the benefit of their population and for the benefit of the greater population which is outside.

---

* The Crown Agents regularly appointed Consulting Engineers – usually a highly respected engineering firm – to give professional advice on, and sometimes to provide personnel for, various public works projects in the Colonial Empire.

Less well known is another part of this speech in which Chamberlain spoke specifically about building railways in British West African possessions.

> I can say at once that the [British] Government are of the opinion that, wherever it is possible, it is better that railways in these circumstances should be made either by the colony or by Imperial Government, rather than handed over to speculators. In these cases there is more probability of an economical progress of the work if it is taken up by the Government instead of private speculators.[5]

Thus when the Crown Agents sent Shelford's report to the Colonial Office on 31 October 1895, a new, highly enthusiastic, and developmentally oriented Colonial Secretary was there to receive it.

Shelford had looked at eight possible routes. In a covering letter Ommanney advised that the route chosen should include the two major towns of the interior, Abeokuta and Ibadan, if the railway was to pay for itself and return a profit. The probable cost of a line from Lagos to Ibadan would be between £800,000 and £1,250,000. A final decision could not be taken lightly, yet the Colonial Office was anxious to begin work. As a compromise, Shelford and Ommanney suggested that the Colonial Office approve immediate construction of a twenty-mile line from Lagos to Otta. Ommanney saw this as something of a test case and an ideal learning experience. 'Railway construction in Lagos,' he said,

> as elsewhere on the West Coast of Africa, will be attended with exceptional difficulties, towards the solution of which the experience gained on a short tentative section, such as that to Otta, will greatly contribute. It will enable us to deal, with some confidence, with the serious question of the necessity of a large importation of alien labour; it will show how far it is possible to carry on railway construction continuously throughout the change of seasons and under the condition of frequent leave of absence to members of the staff which is inevitable; it will test the possibility of working with some measure of economy and it will open up a district from which stone can be readily supplied to Lagos, where the prosecution of public works of the first importance has had to be abandoned owing to the entire absence of this material.

Ommanney also pointed out that, should Lagos be chosen as a southern terminus, the Lagos–Otta section would have the additional virtue of initiating a system which could effectively serve the commercial needs and development of Abeokuta and perhaps Ibadan. Regarding the costs of such a short line (a little over £7,000 a year in debt charges) and the expected returns, Ommanney felt the advantages he had outlined 'would not be too dearly purchased at the price'.[6] The Colonial Office found Ommanney's arguments compelling and the Governor of Lagos was authorised to proceed with construction to Otta.[7]

In this way the first railway in British West Africa was proposed and accepted, and construction began in March 1896. Given the preceding, a few concluding points should be made. First, the Colonial Office relied on the expertise of the Crown Agents and Consulting Engineers; second, the Lagos Railway was initially conceived as a local line to serve Lagos Colony; third, the Lagos to Otta section was experimental; and fourth, the choice of Lagos as a coastal terminus for this short line did not necessarily mean that Lagos would also be the terminus for the proposed larger system.

PLANNING AND CONSTRUCTING THE LAGOS RAILWAY

Opinions concerning the route of the Lagos Railway and its purpose began to change in the decade after 1895. This change occurred in three stages. First, the railway was seen as a short experimental line. Then, without real discussion or disagreement, it began to be seen as the means of opening up the hinterland of Lagos Colony, the Yorubaland Protectorate. And finally, after much discussion and some disagreement among the Colonial Office staff, the Crown Agents, the Consulting Engineers and the governments of Lagos and Southern Nigeria, a new consensus emerged – the Lagos Railway should be a Nigerian railway, a means of opening up not simply Lagos Colony but most of western Nigeria as well.

By the end of 1896, as construction proceeded, the Colonial Office became convinced that the Lagos–Otta line was no longer experimental and could become a 'necessary link' in a larger scheme. It was decided to advance the line another forty miles to Abeokuta.[8] The Governor of Lagos, Sir Henry McCallum, recommended that the line continue to Ibadan: the Colonial Office approved this in June 1898.[9] Otta had been reached in September 1897, and the line

reached Abeokuta in April 1899. Ommanney's original observation
that the most advantageous route was through Abeokuta was
realised.

However, despite all this construction on the Lagos line, the most
elementary question about a major Nigerian railway had yet to be
answered – where should it begin and end? This problem was
addressed by the Niger Committee, set up in July 1898 by
Chamberlain to discuss and give advice on arrangements for the
future administration of the Niger Territories. The Committee had
six members, four of whom were associated with the Colonial Office
or were colonial governors: Lord Selborne, Chairman and Parliamentary under Secretary of State for the Colonies; Reginald
Antrobus, Assistant Under Secretary of State in charge of West
African business at the Colonial Office; Sir Ralph Moor, Commissioner and consul-General of the Niger Coast Protectorate; and Sir
Henry McCallum, Governor of Lagos Colony. The remaining two
members were Sir Clement Hill, representing the Foreign Office, and
Sir George Goldie, head of the Royal Niger Company.[10] All the
members agreed that a railway to the far north of Nigeria should be
built; they further agreed that the northern terminus should be the
commercial city of Kano; and finally they agreed that the southern
terminus should be a port on the coast that could handle ocean-going
steamers. However, beyond this point, all agreement ended. Moor
and McCallum each argued for their territory's interests almost as if
they were heads of foreign states instead of governors of contiguous
colonies within the same Empire. McCallum insisted that the existing
line should simply be continued north to Kano. He reminded the
Committee that a new proposal to remove the sand-bar from the
Lagos Harbour entrance would make Lagos an excellent port. Moor
and Goldie, on the other hand, thought the railway should begin at
either Warri or Sapele on the Benin River. Both these ports were
already open to ocean-going steamers. McCallum did not accept this;
Hill and Lord Selborne sided with Moor and Goldie; and Antrobus
'reserved' his opinion. In spite of its disagreement on a southern
terminus the Committee was at least clear on one thing: whether or
not the Lagos Railway was selected as the major line to the north, it
was still valuable locally in opening up the districts around Lagos
City.[11]

The Crown Agents supported McCallum's view that the Lagos
Railway should be continued to Kano. Ommanney told the Colonial
Office in 1898 that:

To approach the problem from any other direction, as, for instance, by means of a railway from Forcados [yet another suggested port] would be to sacrifice the enormous advantage of the heavy expenditure which will have been incurred by the time the Lagos Railway reaches Ibadan, and it seems as though the necessity of serving the rich and populous districts through which the Lagos Railway will pass has already determined the line of future railway development and the destiny of Lagos as the port at which the great bulk of the trade of Nigeria will have to be dealt with.[12]

At the Colonial Office, Antrobus was inclined to agree, but stopped short of actually endorsing Ommanney's position. He knew that before a Lagos–Kano route could be approved, nearly £1,000,000 of work had to be done on Lagos Harbour. The Colonial Office needed more information on the points raised by the Niger Committee – i.e., could a paying railway be built from a port on the coast to the Niger? If so, what work would be required on those ports? Or alternatively, how far north could the Niger be made navigable and could a line be built from that point on the Niger north to Kano? Antrobus recommended that they discover the views of the Governor of Lagos and the High Commissioners of Northern and Southern Nigeria before making any decision.[13] His caution here was typical of permanent officials; but given their ignorance of the matter at hand, caution was a virtue. Nevertheless, discussions on railway routes advanced no further for some time.

In June 1899, as construction moved on toward Ibadan, the Crown Agents urged the Colonial Office to approve a survey beyond Ibadan to Jebba. Percy Ezechiel's reaction was to reject this idea because Lagos Colony could not afford a survey. William Mercer, Head of the Nigeria Department from 1898 to 1900, agreed, adding that as yet there was no guarantee that the line would show a profit. It was still unclear how far the Lagos line would be extended. Sir Edward Wingfield, Permanent Under Secretary, did not consider that extending the Lagos Railway was 'the most pressing of railway schemes', and Chamberlain agreed.[14] In spite of the urgings of the Crown Agents, the Colonial Office refused to be pressured into further surveys until they could obtain more information about the territory and its commercial prospects. The Crown Agents were influential, as the work of R. E. Dumett, Richard Kesner, and Robert Kubicek can testify.[15] But it is noteworthy that there were limits to their influence. The Colonial Office staff was willing and able to evaluate and choose among Crown Agent recommendations; decision-making was the prerogative of the Colonial Office itself.

The fate of the Lagos Railway remained uncertain as 1899 became 1900. The only thing everyone agreed on was that Kano, in Northern Nigeria, was the ultimate goal. But no one could agree on how to get there.[16] In April 1900 the Colonial Office asked the Crown Agents to instruct W. Shelford to prepare 'a general scheme for railway extension and other works dependent upon that extension' in Lagos Colony and the rest of British West Africa. Shelford's report, based on available information without any new surveys, was submitted in July. He argued against using Lagos as the southern terminus of a major line to the north: first, because it would take years before the city of Lagos could develop as the principal port and commercial centre of Nigeria; second, because it would be too difficult and expensive to make Lagos Harbour suitable for ocean-going vessels; and third, Lagos was just too far to the west.[17] The Lagos Railway should be extended only as far as to make it self-supporting within Lagos Colony.

Meanwhile there had been an important personnel change at the Colonial Office. Sir Montagu Ommanney, after twenty-three years in the Crown Agents Office, had succeeded Sir Edward Wingfield as Permanent Under Secretary at the Colonial Office. As a young man, Ommanney studied at the Royal Military Academy at Woolwich and for ten years served as a military engineer. He became Lord Carnarvon's private secretary, and after three years, in 1877, Carnarvon appointed him a Crown Agent. From 1877 to 1900 he advised on colonial public works and colonial finance throughout the Empire. Thus a person of great experience and expertise could now affect decision-making about colonial railways in Nigeria.

But before six months had passed the Consulting Engineer had retreated from his earlier conclusion regarding Lagos as the principal port of Nigeria. Shelford had originally felt that Sir Frederick Lugard, High Commissioner of Northern Nigeria, and the British shipowners were not interested in developing Lagos Harbour and advancing the Lagos railway. Now he believed otherwise and said so. The Crown Agents promptly passed his letter on to the Colonial Office, saying:

> We entirely concur in the advantage of starting a railway from a great trade centre like Lagos, and in the practical importance of the fact that the line is now all but complete to Ibadan, from which

place we understand that it may be profitably extended to Ilorin. From this point we have sufficient information to justify the opinion that the line can be carried across the Niger, and up the Kaduna valley . . . [northward].[18]

The Lagos Railway reached Ibadan in December 1900 and was opened to traffic in March 1901. No more work was done on the Lagos Railway for almost five years. The lack of a fixed destination, and underlying that, uncertainty about the actual purpose of the line, were the major reasons for the delay. However, there were financial problems as well: the shaky financial situation of the Lagos Government, the nervous condition of the London money market, and the negative impact of the South African war.

In the absence of any general policy, opinions began to proliferate. For example, the Governor of Lagos, Sir William MacGregor (1899–1904) urged that the Lagos Railway should continue eventually 'to Kano, perhaps someday to the Nile'.[19] Later he was willing to settle for a line that simply reached past the Niger; and Ommanney agreed that this more-reasonable goal was 'deserving of consideration'.[20] In Lugard's opinion, what was needed was 'a general railway policy'. He told the Colonial Office staff that such a policy statement would be a considerable boon to Nigerian administrators' local development plans.[21] By the middle of 1901 much heat had been generated but little light had been shed on the two crucial questions. First, where was the Lagos Railway going?; and second, if another line, perhaps to be the major line, was built, where would it start? Ezechiel raised these questions when Sir Ralph Moor, now High Commissioner of Southern Nigeria, presented a new and elaborate railway scheme for eastern Nigeria. Ezechiel now seconded Lugard's request for a general railway policy. He believed such a policy had to be based on the assumption that Nigeria could not be developed by a single railway starting from Lagos.* He thought that an eastern system could be started from Old Calabar.[22] Essentially, however, Ezechiel's main argument was that a general policy was necessary to provide direction and incentive for progress and to put an end to aimless discussions of alternatives.

But before the Colonial Office could arrive at definite conclusions, Ezechiel suggested a final survey for the Ilorin-to-the-Niger section.

---

* Because: Lagos had no pure drinking water and was unhealthy for Europeans; it would be very expensive to improve Lagos Harbour; and strategic considerations necessitated major railways along both the eastern and western frontiers of Nigeria.

The Consulting Engineers wished to find the ideal crossing-point on the Niger and then survey back from there. They estimated that the survey would cost £5,628. How was this to be paid for? The Ibadan–Ilorin section had been surveyed in November 1900 and had been paid for by Lagos Colony and Northern Nigeria. Northern Nigeria's share had come from the Treasury because Northern Nigeria had no revenue of its own. Would the Treasury provide Northern Nigeria's share a second time? Ezechiel was not sanguine, but the new Head of the Nigeria Department, Sir William Baillie Hamilton, thought a good argument could be made for Treasury assistance:

> We should now be justified in bringing before them the vast imperial interests involved in a railway to the interior, not only as regards its intrinsic importance, but in view of the ceaseless activity of the French.

The amount involved was not great, and postponing the survey might damage the future prospects of the railway. However, he agreed to go along with whatever decision the Consulting Engineers made. Ezechiel and Baillie Hamilton seem to have lost sight of the wider goal of determining a general railway policy – the initial purpose of the survey. Ommanney helped reset their sights. He insisted that they should not allow the survey to be put off; it should begin immediately because:

(1) It was essential that the general direction of the Lagos Railway be settled so that other public works projects in Northern Nigeria could be co-ordinated with it;
(2) determining the crossing-point on the Niger would obviously influence the general direction taken;
(3) the extension beyond Ibadan would not become a paying proposition until the Niger was reached and the wealth of the Hausa Lands tapped;
(4) the Consulting Engineers currently had ready a team of survey engineers with Nigerian experience – if the survey was postponed these men might not be available at a later date; and
(5) if they planned to resume construction in 1902, the survey should start in October to be completed during the dry season.

Since the railway survey would take place entirely in Northern Nigeria, Ommanney felt the Treasury should provide Northern

Nigeria's share of the costs. Indeed, if Lagos couldn't pay its share, the Treasury should be pressed to finance it all. Finally, Ommanney solemnly warned that 'the Railway policy of these great territories cannot stand still for want of this insignificant sum'. When Chamberlain agreed, the Crown Agents authorised the survey and the Treasury did promise to cover Northern Nigeria's half of the survey cost.[23] The surveying team went out under an engineer named W. Gee.

The decision to proceed with the survey from Ilorin to the Niger is significant on two counts. The first was the Treasury's willingness to co-operate. This should be noted, if the image of the Treasury as a parsimonious bogeyman is to be modified; the Treasury was amenable to reasoned argument, and was willing to approve justifiable expenditures. The second is Ommanney's role. His background and experience, so different from the rest of the permanent officials, gave great weight to his recommendations in their eyes. Also, he seemed possessed of a genuine imperialist ethos and was fond of references to 'vast imperial interests' and 'imperial purposes' of expansion. Permanent officials, on the other hand, seemed mainly moved by an administrative ethos.

In the early spring of 1902, the Colonial Office decided to hold a full-scale review of the Nigerian railway situation and establish the general policy which Ezechiel, Ommanney and Lugard had been advocating. On the basis of correspondence from Gee, the Chief Survey Engineer, whose formal report had not yet been submitted, it was already clear that Jebba was the most suitable if not the only place to cross the Niger without heavy expenditure.[24]

At the request of the Colonial Office, the Crown Agents and Consulting Engineers presented a paper containing their views and recommendations on a general policy, on possible route surveys to implement such a policy, and on actual extension of the Lagos Railway. The first minute on the paper, by Ezechiel, reminded the rest of the Colonial Office staff that the point of trying to define a general policy was 'to enable the three Governors [of Lagos, Southern Nigeria and Northern Nigeria] to proceed with the work of development and administration with due regard to the future course of the railways'. He also warned that it would be pointless, given their present dearth of information, to attempt a definite plan, but insisted that even a very general policy would aid the governors considerably. The discussions that followed made it clear that Nigeria should be developed by two trunklines: the western line – the Lagos Railway –

should ultimately cross the Niger, probably at Jebba, and extend northward towards Kano; an eastern line might start from Old Calabar and move northwards beyond the Cross and Benin Rivers to Lake Chad or Kano. There was hardly any disagreement in the Colonial Office regarding these two points. Serious differences, if they existed, would only emerge when the time came to develop specific projects.[25]

Although they agreed in principle on the need for two lines, financial considerations and the fact that the Lagos Railway was already in existence to Ibadan predisposed the Colonial Office staff to focus on the western line. For example, when Sir Ralph Moor proposed an elaborate £15,000,000 railway scheme for Southern Nigeria Ezechiel objected because it might divert revenue from the Lagos Railway. They should proceed cautiously on plans for an eastern line. Charles Strachey, Senior Clerk, even suggested it was 'extremely doubtful that the railway will be wanted at all within the near future'.[26] Therefore, if they approved the Consulting Engineers' proposal to survey an eastern route they would be in danger of having a survey before they were even sure they wanted a railway there.[27] This attitude prevailed; the eastern railway was not seriously considered again for another ten years.

The paper submitted by the Consulting Engineers and Crown Agents had also recommended extending the Lagos Railway from Ibadan to Oshogbo. Ezechiel initially believed such an extension was totally out of the question because the colony could not afford it and the British Government would not consider helping as long as the South African War continued. (He was more correct than he knew about the lack of funds. Even when the South African War ended a few weeks later, no money was forthcoming.) However, Ommanney reminded the permanent officials that the Lagos line should be continued to Oshogbo or 'to the full extent which the traffic prospects justify'. He still had doubts about taking the Lagos line across the Niger, though, and urged that discussions on this point remain open.[28] Strachey argued that Jebba was on the direct line between Ilorin and Kano, and the Niger should be bridged there.[29] But it was agreed that no decision on the crossing would be made until Gee sent in his formal report.

As part of the general review, the Colonial Office had to deal with still another problem. The Consulting Engineers, perhaps in an effort to force the pace and generate more business for themselves, had proposed three more surveys: one in Southern Nigeria, north of Old

Calabar; and two in Northern Nigeria – from Jebba north to Sokoto, and from the Kaduna Valley north to Kano. In fact, the route from Old Calabar (discussed above) had already been rejected, and Sokoto, a religious but not a commercial centre, had never been seriously considered. Kano still appeared to be the natural railway terminus. Ezechiel and Strachey doubted the value of the northern surveys, and felt that only one was really needed, but this would have to wait until the decision on where to bridge the Niger had been made. Antrobus felt that the Consulting Engineers had not developed a convincing case. His view was that:

> at present . . . we want to get what Sir F. Lugard calls a general conception of the country, by collecting and putting together the reports . . . of various officers, rather than to have particular routes surveyed by trained engineers.

Ommanney, not surprisingly, supported the need for surveys and thought even one survey would assist them. If a northern railway scheme proved workable, it might, he said 'simplify the problem of the Lagos Railway and the bridging of the Niger', i.e., the Lagos Railway would become a local line with no need to cross the Niger.[30] Eventually the permanent officials decided that such an important survey shouldn't be rushed into, and it was put off until money and more information were available.[31]

By August the policy review was completed. What had been accomplished? A decision had been made to build two railways in Nigeria, one in the east and one in the west. However, Colonial Office attention was focused on the western line. In short, what had been practised before was now policy. Three decisions had been made regarding the western line: (i) that the Lagos Railway could be extended as finances allowed; (ii) that the extension would reach at least to Ilorin; and (iii) construction was authorised for the first step of that extension, from Ibadan to Oshogbo, contingent upon the availability of funds.

One important question remained unanswered: where to cross the Niger. Gee, the Chief Survey Engineer, reported that a crossing site had to be governed by natural adaptability, inexpensiveness of construction, and suitability of foundations and approaches. There also had to be building material of adequate quantity and quality nearby. Then Gee said that '*downstream of Jebba there is no place that fulfils, or even approaches, the above necessary conditions*'; Gee believed Jebba met his conditions and was *'the binding point of the railway from Ilorin to the North'* (Gee's emphasis). The Consulting Engineers added, 'the superiority of Jebba is indisputable'. The Crown Agents supported this but felt a final decision must wait until the country north of the Niger had been examined.[32] Jebba seemed to be the preferred point of crossing, but it took many more years and discussions before it was officially approved.

As noted, there had been no further construction after the Lagos line had reached Ibadan. Throughout 1902 and 1903 the finances of the Lagos Colony were not sufficient to resume work on the railway. The Colony could not borrow money at reasonable rates on its own security and Chamberlain was not prepared to ask Parliament for another loan or guarantee on a loan. Nevertheless in early 1904 Sir William MacGregor, Governor of Lagos, argued that the time had come to start construction on the Ibadan–Oshogbo section. Ezechiel agreed, noting that it was 'clearer than ever that the railway will not pay before it gets to Oshogbo'. The British Cotton Growers Association was also anxious for construction to begin because it believed Nigeria had great potential for cotton production. Of all the available sources of funding, the Treasury seemed the most logical. When the Colonial Office decided to appeal to the Treasury, however,[33] the Treasury refused to help[34] (for a full discussion of this see pages 162–5). Fortunately, just at that point, it became clear that the amalgamation of Lagos Colony with the prosperous Protectorate of Southern Nigeria would create not only a new colony, but a more appealing borrower, one that could raise money in the City at reasonable rates. The new Governor of Lagos, Sir Walter Egerton (shortly afterwards to be High Commissioner of Southern Nigeria also), enthusiastically endorsed the Ibadan–Oshogbo extension, and it was sanctioned in November 1904. Actual construction began in January 1905, and Oshogbo, sixty-two miles away, was reached in April 1907.

While this construction was under way, Egerton urged the Colonial Office to continue past Oshogbo to Ilorin. Ommanney and Sydney Olivier, the new Head of the Nigeria Department, agreed, because things were going so well from both the financial and construction point of view.[35] By December 1906 Egerton had been given the go-ahead to Ilorin.[36] This would put the Lagos Railway about 125 miles beyond Ibadan.

Reaching Ilorin represented an important point in the development of the railway. At the suggestion of a Junior Clerk, Frederick

Butler, the Colonial Office agreed to review the question of Nigerian railways when construction reached Ilorin.[37] This review took place in July and August of 1907 while Egerton was in England.[38] The review began with Sir Percy Girouard's report on transport policy in Nigeria. Girouard had just been appointed High Commissioner of Northern Nigeria, particularly to advise on railways. He opposed the extension of the Lagos Railway beyond Ilorin because this sparsely populated territory would produce little commercial traffic. Girouard was a railway construction engineer and an administrator who had made his name building railways in Africa. He was a knowledgeable but not objective critic. In 1907 he had his own plans for an independent 400-mile railway from Baro to Kano and was anxious to forestall competition in his own territory. He insisted that taking the Lagos Railway beyond Ilorin was 'ill-advised and unnecessary':

> The Lagos Railway may form the backbone of a considerable system for the southwestern portion of Nigeria, but it is my firm conviction that in the economical development of Northern Nigeria we may place our reliance upon the existing water ways, supplemented by railway systems based upon them.[39]

Girouard's concept captured the admiration of Winston Churchill, then Parliamentary Under Secretary, and he wrote that Egerton must be told that the Lagos Railway, as such, could not be extended. Colonial Secretary Lord Elgin rejected Churchill's approach, saying that 'the time had not come for pre-emptory orders'.[40] However, Girouard and Churchill were supported by Butler, who felt that if a Baro–Kano Railway was to be built, then an extension of the Lagos Railway from Ilorin would be too much too soon. Furthermore:

> It would mean spending . . . just the sum that is wanted for constructing the whole line from Baro to Kano. . . . [The Lagos Railway] as far as Ilorin will be remunerative even if it goes not a mile further. Every mile of extension up to Zungeru will be unremunerative and will impose a burden on the prosperous section of the line between the coast and Ilorin.
> If then, the Baro line is built, the plain policy seems to be to refuse to advance the Southern Nigeria railway beyond Ilorin within any time that can now be determined. That extension will take place ultimately there can be little doubt, since it is only by way of Jebba that Nigeria can secure its alternative outlet to the sea when the

state of its trade demands the double exit. But that is a question of many years hence.[41]

This was a sensible argument but essentially an administrative one and was overtaken by a more political approach. Negotiations within the upper echelons of the Colonial Office with Egerton and probably Girouard changed the framework of discussion completely. An agreement was reached whereby Egerton allowed Northern Nigeria to raise railway construction capital on Southern Nigeria's credit. In return Egerton could continue the Lagos Railway towards the Niger and beyond to Zungeru.[42] No clear economic principle was involved. Egerton had simply realised that the easiest way to advance the Lagos line was by assisting the Baro–Kano line. The 1907 review resolved most of the Lagos Railway's problems: the line would extend beyond Ilorin, cross the Niger at Jebba, with Zungeru as its northern destination. Furthermore, it was agreed that the Lagos Railway would link up with the Baro line at Minna,[43] and through this connection, reach Kano.

Two problems remained: how to cross the Niger River – by bridge or ferry? And how to build the Lagos Railway extension – use pioneer standard with no frills, or continue with the higher standard currently in use? Egerton proposed a ferry crossing in late 1906 and again in 1907, claiming that a ferry could handle all traffic for years to come and would be more economical than a bridge.[44] The Colonial Office ignored his suggestions, perhaps considering them premature, since the crossing site had not yet been chosen.[45] Once Jebba was fixed as the crossing-point, however, Egerton changed his mind. Southern Nigeria's financial situation had improved – why not build a bridge? But now Elgin was in favour of beginning with a ferry service and was not at all sure that Southern Nigeria should spend its money on a bridge. To spend £90,000 on a bridge while the economic and political future of the colony was still uncertain smacked of extravagance to Elgin.[46] Egerton responded with a unique compromise. He proposed taking the railway across the Niger by bridge *and* ferry. There was an island in mid-river where the planned crossing would take place. Egerton suggested that a bridge span the distance from the northern bank to the island in mid-stream, and that a ferry operate in the wider distance between the island and the southern shore.[47] The Colonial Office was sufficiently intrigued to ask the Crown Agents for their opinion. Instead of simply commenting on the bridge–ferry idea the Crown Agents instructed the Consulting

Engineers to reconsider the whole question of how to cross the Niger. This irritated Butler, who said, 'I do not know by what authority the C.A. have raised the question again. If we are to go back to that point, the delay and discussion of the last few months go for nothing.'[48] But Antrobus defended the Crown Agents: given the practical difficulties which they saw in a ferry system they were right to conduct a second review. Rather than discuss whether or not the Crown Agents had exceeded their brief, the Colonial Office should neither rule out nor accept any particular solution to the problem of crossing the Niger until they received the Consulting Engineers' report.[49] The Consulting Engineers' recommendation was that the Colonial Office accept Egerton's bridge–ferry proposal. When they realised the railway would reach Jebba before a bridge could be built, but not before a combination bridge–ferry could be set up, the permanent officials approved the plan.[50] By 1909 this had been done, and trains on the Lagos Railway regularly crossed the Niger. The system functioned well enough. Later, when traffic increased, a southern portion of the crossing was bridged.

The question of the type of line to be built beyond Ilorin was also being discussed. In August 1907, believing the agreement with Egerton did not commit the Colonial Office to immediate construction, Strachey proposed that they consider using the pioneer standard beyond Jebba. This would save a substantial amount of money – current estimates for the Lagos standard were £5,867 a mile, but pioneer standard could be built for £3,000 or £4,000 a mile. Elgin requested a comparison study of the savings involved if the entire extension to Zungeru was built to a pioneer standard, or if only the Jebba–Zungeru section was.[51]

While this file was making its way through the Colonial Office corridors, Egerton was becoming impatient. Why couldn't he begin construction? All Egerton knew was that his agreement with the Colonial Office was not being kept. The Colonial Office, waiting for the Crown Agents' report, felt the delay made perfect sense. After all, how could construction begin if the standard of construction had not been decided? Egerton sent a rather stiff private letter to Elgin:

I do not understand the delay. . . . I understand from the correspondence upon which the financial assistance of Southern Nigeria towards the construction of the Baro–Kano line was promised that formal sanction would be at once given to the construction of the Ilorin–Zungeru section to link up Lagos with Kano. It was only on that understanding that I was able to conscientiously give my support to the proposal. The early completion of this line is being delayed by the absence of the necessary sanction for the commencement of the work. If I cannot return to Southern Nigeria next month able to say that the Ilorin–Zungeru is sanctioned and to be pushed to completion as rapidly as possible I know that I can only get the assent to our raising the loan required for Southern Nigeria in the teeth of the opposition of all the unofficial members [of the Legislative Council]. I should be very sorry to have to do that.[52]

Egerton had reason to be impatient. The railway was expected to reach Ilorin in October 1907, and if the work was to continue without a break ('as in justice to Sir W. Egerton it must', said Butler) the choice between Lagos and pioneer standard had to be made quickly. Materials must be ordered and the engagement of the construction crew and staff continued. Antrobus sympathised with Egerton and argued that under the terms of the agreement he should be allowed to continue the work without further delay, building the railway to the standard he chose. Elgin was reluctant to leave things in Egerton's hands. After all, he said, 'Southern Nigeria is a Crown Colony and we have the right to supervise its proceedings'. He thought Egerton could hardly object to ascertaining the cost differences between the two standards, and wrote assuring him that he (Elgin) adhered absolutely to the Colonial Office–Southern Nigerian understanding, and felt bound 'personally and officially . . . to see that you have fair play'. But surely, he continued, it was within the bounds of fair play, common sense and practicality to get these new estimates, especially since they could be prepared before Egerton returned to Southern Nigeria.[53]

The Crown Agents' study recommended: (i) that Lagos standard be used from Ilorin to Jebba, and (ii) that pioneer standard be used from Jebba to Zungeru. Southern Nigeria would thus save about £250,000. Elgin was pleased, and at a meeting with Egerton and Lugard persuaded them that the railways north of the Niger should be built to similar standards so as to put them on equal footing. This was made formal in correspondence between the Secretary of State and the Governor on 22 October 1907.[54] By early November the Consulting Engineers had the preliminary work in hand.[55] It should be noted that the idea of saving money with a pioneer standard had first been raised by a member of the permanent staff, Strachey. Treasury men were not the only ones interested in economy.

Now construction of the Lagos Railway proceeded without a hitch. Ilorin was reached in August 1908, Jebba in January 1909, and Zungeru in March 1911. Although the railway had reached its northern destination, it still needed to connect with the Baro line and secure enough traffic to justify the Jebba–Zungeru section. The branch line from Zungeru to Minna on the Baro–Kano Railway and the Baro–Kano Railway itself were completed in 1911. Therefore, by the end of that year the Lagos Railway was complete and functioning on its own as far as Zungeru, and through the Baro–Kano line, all the way to Kano.

The planning and building of the line had been a long and arduous task. It had involved a variety of individuals in the Colonial Office from the Secretary of State for the Colonies to the permanent staff, and Crown Agents, Consulting Engineers and the Governors of Lagos and Southern Nigeria. It represented an impressive accomplishment, though not a perfect one. A railway now ran 467 miles through some of the most populous portions of British West Africa, and through difficult terrain into relatively unknown country. It had great potential not only for aiding development but for turning a profit as well. The Colonial Office had been understandably cautious in supervising this task. Its officials had no previous experience of railway planning and construction, although they received advice from the Crown Agents and Consulting Engineers. The permanent officials had a special supervisory and co-ordinating function *vis-à-vis* planning and construction. They showed themselves able to deal with conflicting opinions, and perhaps more important, realised that co-operation, flexibility, and teamwork were essential. The Colonial Office staff, when necessary, deferred to the Crown Agents and Consulting Engineers without being dominated by them. Especially important to this success was Sir Montagu Ommanney. As Crown Agent and as Permanent Under Secretary he showed a striking perspicacity and shrewdness in carrying out his job. Also important was the permanent officials' understanding of the need to proceed cautiously. One might say that they raised this to the level of doctrine; and it was this that prevented the development of any real bold or imaginative plans. Ommanney seemed to realise this in 1903 when he wrote:

If it were settled that the railway to Kano is to be an extension of the Lagos Line and we were in a position to form an estimate of the cost, it might be possible to treat the whole line as one great scheme of development. . . . But we have certainly not reached that stage.[56]

However, their decision to progress slowly and as funds permitted was not entirely bad. As Chamberlain pointed out, they had to avoid 'overloading these undeveloped provinces with unproductive lines'.[57]

THE LAGOS RAILWAY AND THE DEPARTMENTAL SYSTEM OF CONSTRUCTION

There were two systems of railway construction in use in the mid-1890s: construction by private contractors, and the departmental method. Examining the way the first was rejected and the second chosen reveals some interesting power relationships in the Colonial Office and gives some insight into how the Office really worked.

Between 1893 and 1904 at least three attempts were made to put the construction of the Lagos Railway into private hands. The first two attempts were rejected because of the influence of Sir Montagu Ommanney. The last attempt was not even taken seriously and may simply have been an effort to satisfy interest groups.

In 1893 a private company, the Western Syndicate, requested special privileges and concessions in return for conducting a survey in Lagos Colony. Ommanney, as mentioned earlier, was adamantly against private business involvement in West African railway construction. He strongly recommended that the Colonial Office have nothing to do with the Western Syndicate. Chamberlain seems to have followed Ommanney's advice when he decided late in 1895 that British West African railways would be built by colonial governments under the direction of the Crown Agents. No one seriously questioned the Crown Agents' methods – the departmental system – until mid-1903. This is not to say, however, that everyone wholeheartedly supported it. In 1899 Sir Robert Herbert had announced, 'I shudder at the thought of a "Crown Agents" Railway, i.e., the most expensive that can be made – in Nigeria.'[58]

In 1903 when work on the Lagos Railway had been suspended for over two years the Manchester Chamber of Commerce urged that the work be turned over to private contractors. Antrobus used this opportunity to reopen Office debate on the matter. He felt the departmental system was best, but none the less suggested that:

> now that we know what it costs to build lines departmentally we are better able to judge at what price the work could be done by contractors, and it would be useful to know whether any contractors would be willing to undertake the work, subject to the conditions which would be necessary to impose upon them, at a reasonable price.[59]

Ommanney, chief upholder and protector of the departmental system of construction, rather than condemning the contract system as he had in 1893, now damned it with faint praise. There was, he noted, much to be said for the contract approach if time admitted the full preliminaries and if conditions did not involve indefinite risks which 'a contractor must allow for fully whether they prove to be real or not'.[60] As the Colonial Office's resident engineering expert, Ommanney's authority enabled him to sound objective when he was in fact establishing the criteria by which the Office would eventually have to reject the contract system.

Meanwhile, the Manchester Chamber of Commerce withdrew its recommendation because it feared that experimenting with the contract system would mean further delay in the construction. For expediency's sake, it preferred that the Colonial Office continue with the departmental system. No doubt this is precisely the attitude Ommanney had hoped to inspire. But Antrobus felt that at the very least they could request private bids for the extension beyond Ibadan and thus obtain some idea of the comparative costs. Calling this a 'worthwhile experiment' Ommanney nevertheless managed to hint at obstacles that would make it difficult if not impossible. He stressed the problems of obtaining a valid cost comparison, saying the Consulting Engineers would have to do 'a sufficiently detailed survey' over the same route to develop standards of comparison. All this would take time and cause delay. Chamberlain made an effort here to stem the tide of bureaucratic objections. His analysis and prescription were typically forceful and to the point:

> The system of departmental construction has been tried and the result is that the estimates are always exceeded – in this case by 40%. We get a good line but it is very expensive and outsiders maintain that they could make it more cheaply and quicker. This

may be . . . wrong but we have no answer until we have tried.
Let this line be put up for tender and do not make the conditions
extravagant.

Unfortunately there are objections in every case and unless I
overrule them we shall never try the desired experiment.[61]

Despite overruling objections, Chamberlain was never to see the
contract system given a chance. Under his direct order the Colonial
Office did require the Consulting Engineers to specify what was
needed to judge bids from private contractors. But by the time their
report was submitted in early 1904, Chamberlain had resigned and
Alfred Lyttelton had succeeded him. The Consulting Engineers were
not about to make it easy for private contractors to take over. They
reinforced all of Ommanney's arguments. They said they would first
have to make a series of preliminary surveys and ascertain other
technical information before they could knowledgeably compare and
evaluate bids. This they noted would cost £19,000 and would take two
years. Obviously, this was impossible. There was an urgent need to
start construction. The textile mills of Lancashire needed British
West African cotton and a good transportation system was crucial.
Ezechiel pointed out that 'if Lagos [Colony] is not to be left out of the
race in spite of its advantages of soil and irrigation, the line should be
built at once'. The points the Consulting Engineers made in their
report were clearly self-serving. They were certainly not going to
advertise the advantages of a system which directly competed with
their own. At the same time, simply by virtue of their tropical
experience, they could present themselves as uniquely qualified to
organise and carry off railway construction. To be fair, they never
presented themselves as inexpensive. Their argument, as Richard
Kesner has pointed out, was that:

> where much of the land was unsurveyed, raw materials hard to
> come by, and labour scarce . . . contracts opened to tender were
> potentially dangerous because they encouraged contractors to
> under-bid each other without any appreciation of the actual costs
> of the proposed project. . . . [If] a colonial government neverthe-
> less accepted the lowest bid, it might quite reasonably end up with
> a bankrupt contractor, a great deal of money spent, and no public
> works to show for it.[62]

The Head of the Nigeria Department, Sir William Baillie Hamilton, then said that only 'endless delays and problematical advantages' would result if they experimented with private contractors. They were better off not getting involved.[63] Not surprisingly, Ommanney, who had been working the debate towards this point all along, promptly agreed, and lost no time in confirming that the Lagos Railway must therefore continue to be built departmentally. The objection Chamberlain had overruled prevailed in the end.

The debate over the contract system is instructive as a reminder that the Secretary of State, no matter how powerful, was temporary. In the middle of his efforts to enable private enterprise to build railways in West Africa, Chamberlain left the Colonial Office. The situation suggests the accidental quality of history. Alfred Lyttelton was not as forceful as Chamberlain, nor did he have the same concerns. Ommanney's expertise in the area of public works carried considerable weight, and in fact he simply outmanoeuvred the rest of the staff. Clearly, when Ommanney first proposed various controls, he knew the Consulting Engineers would be asked to submit a report, and after twenty-three years as Crown Agent, working with them, he doubtless had a very good notion of what such a report would say.

The question of private contracts was raised one last time in June 1904 in the House of Lords by the Earl of Portsmouth. No one was interested and the idea sank without a ripple.[64]

If the departmental method was preferable to private contracts, what exactly was the departmental method and how did it work? When a colonial railway was perceived as necessary for commercial development, or for administrative or strategic purposes, or some combination of the three, the Colonial Office first approved the idea in principle, and then instructed the Crown Agents to initiate practical arrangements. They in turn would order their Consulting Engineers (in the case of West African railways, the firm of Shelford and Sons) to dispatch a surveying party. The surveyors traced, between two indicated points, the route or routes that went through the most populated areas and took best advantage of the terrain. The Crown Agents forwarded the surveys and reports with their own recommendations to the Colonial Office. This information was discussed by the Secretary of State and the permanent staff. Sometimes the recommendations would also be shown to the colonial Governor for his comments. Once a route was chosen the Consulting Engineers would be authorised to appoint a Chief Resident Engineer to head the project in the colony. This man would be responsible for deciding what was needed in the way of men, money, and material. Native labour was provided through the local government and European labour through the Crown Agents; money came from the colony, was borrowed on credit, or came from the British Treasury; and material would come through the Crown Agents. It was a system in which the specialists did the work and were supervised by the Colonial Office staff.[65]

Although private contracts had been discussed at great length, the departmental method was adopted for the Lagos Railway without much discussion. However, it was a traditional system with which the Colonial Office felt comfortable. The Consulting Engineers were experts with unrivalled experience in Britain's tropical empire. They had had for many years a contractual relationship with the Crown Agents, and their reputation and livelihood depended on building good railways. The Colonial Office had good reason to rely on and trust them. The Crown Agents provided the Colonial Office with second opinions by evaluating the recommendations and work of the Engineers, and also served as purchasing agents. The Colonial Office felt the Crown Agents had such wide knowledge of the English commercial world and railway construction needs that quality control and economy in procurement would be maintained. Large sums of money were involved in public works projects, so a reputation for integrity was essential.[66] The Colonial Office staff believed the Crown Agents and Consulting Engineers were responsible and accountable. It is no wonder that they favoured the departmental method – at once familiar and controllable – over private contracting. Ommanney's role in this should be emphasised. His authority as a former Crown Agent and his close contacts in the London financial world, made him a pivotal figure in all colonial public works projects. It is no coincidence that the departmental system of construction was the only one used until his retirement.

In discussing the departmental system there has been little mention of the colonial Governor. This is no oversight. Even though the railway was being built and paid for by his colony, the Governor had no important role to play in its construction. On one occasion Egerton questioned the propriety of the Consulting Engineers evaluating their own work and suggested that an obvious conflict of interest was involved. But the Colonial Office staff, while admitting the possibility that this was so, were unwilling to forgo the many advantages of such a comfortable arrangement. Antrobus did suggest that the Colonial Office should do its best to see that the Engineers did not abuse their authority.[67] Ommanney, appropriately enough, had the last word. He was confident that they would not abuse their position and pointed out that:

> it would be unwise to cut ourselves off from a source of information which has been in the past most useful to us. The Consulting Engineers . . . are much in touch with the railway world and have opportunities of ascertaining the latest practice in such matters which are not open to us or the Crown Agents.[68]

The Colonial Office was satisfied that whatever privilege and protection the Consulting Engineers received, they were worth it.

In a larger sense this could also be said about the departmental system. Whatever may be said about its general applicability, the departmental system was entirely appropriate for the Lagos Railway. At that time, the Colonial Office, unused to supervising railway construction, needed the assurance that came from experience. And this could and did come from the Crown Agents and the Consulting Engineers. The Lagos line might have been expensive, but it was soundly built and would play a central role in the development of Northern and Southern Nigeria.

FINANCING THE LAGOS RAILWAY, 1895–1905

When Chamberlain decided to experiment with the first section of the Lagos Railway, no system of financing railways existed in Crown Colonies. Chamberlain, like Mr Micawber, seems to have acted on the assumption that something would turn up. This is not to say that he did not have ideas on how to finance the railways, and indeed other public works programmes like it; in his early and middle years at the Colonial Office he came up with some original and intriguing plans. One idea was a developmental fund based upon 'Colonial Consols'; another involved siphoning off profits from British shares in the Suez Canal Company. Both required Treasury participation and approval. Neither was adopted, because the Treasury refused to participate or approve.[69] In fact, the Treasury had its own plan to provide money for public works and development projects. The Treasury was responsible for investing and paying interest on Post Office savings accounts. By the mid-1890s these accounts contained more money than the Treasury could profitably invest. Casting about for new remunerative investments, they hit upon the Crown Colonies. As this idea took shape and was discussed by the Treasury, the Colonial Office, and the Crown Agents, it seemed that a permanent development fund (to be called the Colonial Loan Fund) might be set up. However, when negotiations clarified positions on each side it became clear that an agreement would be difficult, if not impossible, to reach. Chamberlain insisted on the Colonial Office's right to use the Treasury-administered funds as it saw fit, while the Treasury insisted that all spending be subject to regular Treasury control.[70] After several years both sides abandoned the scheme. (The excess money in the savings bank accounts was soon to be absorbed by financial demands made on the government by the South African War, and imperial economic development in large measure became a casualty of that war.)

All this affected the Lagos Railway. It meant that there was no system of financing being created to develop railways, although construction on the Lagos line had already begun. How then was the railway to be paid for? Initially it was done through Chamberlain's willingness to adopt unorthodox financial approaches suggested by the Crown Agents. Colonial Office staff had little contact with or knowledge of the London financial world. Various ways to finance the railway, including three loans obtained, respectively, in 1900, 1905 and 1908, were used (the 1908 loan, whereby the Baro–Kano Railway was also financed, will be discussed in the next chapter). With each new loan and each new phase of construction the Colonial Nigeria staff took a larger and more confident part in the proceedings. What follows is a description and analysis of how the Lagos Railway was financed, with special emphasis on the interaction of the Colonial Office, the Crown Agents, and the Treasury.

R. E. Dumett has called Chamberlain a 'consummate improviser'.[71] This was especially so in late 1895 when he authorised McCallum to approve a Crown Agent's issue of Lagos Colony inscribed stock on the London money market.[72] Without waiting to see how the stock moved, Chamberlain, at Ommanney's suggestion, further authorised the Crown Agents to spent £50,000 of Lagos's surplus funds to begin railway construction.[73] However, West African railways did not appeal to investors and the inscribed stock went unsold. Money was needed; therefore, while negotiations over a colonial loan fund were proceeding with the Treasury, the Crown Agents persuaded the Bank of England to advance £288,524. This was highly unusual, as were the conditions under which the advances were made. The Crown Agents did not specify the purpose of or authority for the advances; they merely assured the Bank of England that colonial legislative authority for the money was forthcoming. That such a venerable institution would accept this indicates either great foolishness or great trust. It seems clear that the Bank of England trusted the Crown Agents and in particular their Senior Agent, Sir Montagu Ommanney.[74] Ommanney had been responsible for integrating the Crown Agents into the City of London as respected members of the financial community in the 1880s.[75] His personal connections with influential men in the City – including those who ran the Bank of England – were exceptional. Thus it is not surprising that the Bank advanced the money. As improvisation it was inspired, but it was only a stopgap measure.

By 1899 it was clear that much more money would be needed. The Colonial Loan Fund was in a shambles. However, the Colonial Office and the Treasury managed to salvage something from the ruins. The Treasury agreed to provide money for all the projects connected with the proposed Loan Fund. This would be a once-only effort to bail Chamberlain out because, anticipating the permanent loan fund, he had already gone ahead with a number of colonial development projects.[76] When passed by Parliament, the Colonial Loans Act of 1899 seemed just what was needed – enough money (at a reasonable rate) to pay off the Bank of England's advances and to continue the Lagos Railway.

However, on closer examination, the Crown Agents concluded that the Colonial Loans Act should not be used by Lagos. The Treasury had insisted that money borrowed under the Act be a first charge on the revenue and assets of the colony and therefore take precedence over any future loans. This meant that future efforts to borrow would be circumscribed; potential investors would be reluctant to lend if they knew previous creditors had to be paid back first.[77] As if these problems weren't enough, in August 1899 the Treasury announced that colonial loans would now have to pay interest as high as $3\frac{3}{4}$ per cent instead of the previously announced figure of $2\frac{3}{4}$ per cent.[78] This was the straw that broke the camel's back. The Crown Agents were now absolutely opposed to a Treasury loan. Ommanney told the Colonial Office staff they would be much better off issuing a loan as inscribed stock, although he never explained why he thought this would do well when the earlier issue had failed.[79] Nevertheless, the Colonial Office accepted Ommanney's advice and authorised the Crown Agents to place a loan on the open market for £792,500 (the amount needed to repay the Bank of England and advance the railway as far as Ibadan.) After several months, the Crown Agents had to admit that it was simply impossible to place the Lagos loan in a market unsettled by the South African War. This meant that the Colonial Office had no recourse but the Colonial Loans Act. Ommanney, now Permanent Under Secretary, still viewed this as an unwholesome alternative. Originally he had felt that money could be raised on the open market at about 3 per cent interest despite the War. But then events more local to West Africa – the Ashanti War and the consequent halt in gold-mining operations on the Gold Coast – destroyed any such hopes. He now claimed he had foreseen this situation for some time. 'I am regretfully driven to the conclusion that there is no [other] alternative', he said. Chamberlain agreed: 'luck has been against us and we are driven into the arms of the Treasury'. Antrobus blamed the Treasury for:

> leading us to suppose for two years that they would not only agree to but wished to get the Colonial Loans Fund Bill passed, [and for] . . . their more recent action in refusing to allow the Crown Agents to issue West African loans when it would have been possible to do so.[80]

Everyone in the Colonial Office realised that doing this would make future loans much more difficult to come by, but they could not wait. The request was sent to the Treasury in June 1900 and approved before a week had gone by.[81] As a result, the Lagos Colony received £792,500 at 3¼ per cent interest.[82]

As noted earlier, once the Lagos Railway reached Ibadan in 1900, it was another four years before construction was resumed. Initially, this delay was due to combined problems regarding financing, routing, and construction methods. But by early 1904 financing was the main obstacle. Chamberlain, after several attempts, finally succeeded in arranging early repayment of the Treasury loan, thus enabling Lagos to borrow 'unencumbered on the open market'.[83] However, the Colonial Office staff believed that they could only attract underwriters and investors with some sort of Treasury assistance. Ezechiel suggested that an imperial guarantee would make a loan very attractive on the open market and enable Lagos to obtain money at a reasonable rate of interest. It was felt that the Treasury might be reminded of the present Government's commitment to cotton-growers in the Empire, and told that it 'could hardly do better' than to help advance the railway to Oshogbo, thus helping to supply Lancashire with cotton from the Nigerian interior. Although a loan guarantee of this magnitude would have to be presented to and approved by Parliament, Ommanney thought the Colonial Office could 'make a strong case'! 'It is quite clear that this extension cannot be built so as to serve the Imperial purpose of increasing our cotton supply without an Imperial guarantee.' On 15 March 1904 the Colonial Office requested a £1,000,000 loan guarantee from the Treasury for the Lagos Colony. Half this sum would be used to extend the railway to Oshogbo; the remainder would repay advances from the Bank of England and replace money taken from the Lagos Government's surplus reserves fund.[84]

The Treasury, with little tact or diplomacy, simply said no. An indignant Ommanney informed the Secretary of State that they had written:

a carefully reasoned letter to the Treasury explaining the grounds upon which, as a matter of Imperial as well as Colonial policy you think a guarantee might be given to the Loan of a million required to build this extension and to repay advances for the construction of the present line.

The Treasury replies by this short letter in which, without attempting to answer any of our arguments, they favour us with the expression of their opinion as to the policy of building the extension, as to which you are in a far better position to judge than they can be, and volunteer their advice as to the general policy of raising colonial loans, a subject on which they certainly cannot claim to be experts.

I think you have a right to expect more serious consideration than this . . . [and since] the object we have in view is of really imperial importance, you may think it worth while to discuss it personally with the Chancellor of the Exchequer.

Lyttelton agreed with Ommanney, 'I am not,' he said,

disposed to acquiesce in the commentary of [Treasury] officials entirely without knowledge of the subject that the considered policy of this department is 'very doubtful' when no reason is given for such a commentary.[85]

Lyttelton had a conference with the Chancellor of the Exchequer,

Sir Michael Hicks Beach, in May 1904, but Hicks Beach merely confirmed the contents of the Treasury letter. Not only would the Treasury not go to Parliament, but no more loans would be permitted under the Colonial Loans Act of 1899. He also hinted that if the Colonial Office really had the nation's best interests at heart they would avoid the open market because of the 'large demands the Treasury has to make on the market this year'. This was being rather petty, for, as Ommanney observed, 'Our small Crown Colony loans do not usually affect such a question and they [Treasury loans] appeal to a different market.' Of course, the Chancellor did recognise the imperial interest involved in the extension of the Lagos Railway, and did want to help. Unfortunately, what he had to offer did not help much. If the Colonial Office insisted on going to the open market, he offered to pay three years' interest and the sinking-fund charges on any loan they could obtain. Although this sounded generous it was only a gesture. As Ommanney realised, with his long experience of the City, three years guaranteed on what might be a thirty-to-fifty-year loan 'would not induce an otherwise shy market to take up a Lagos loan, even if the Crown Agents were allowed to refer to this small measure of Treasury support in their prospectus'. The offer of Treasury assistance seemed worse than no offer at all, and the Colonial Office turned it down. Ommanney then recommended that the Crown Agents investigate the cost of a loan without a Treasury guarantee. Recently, Sierra Leone had borrowed money for railway construction and Ommanney described the terms as 'more unfavourable than I ever expected to see in the case of a Crown Colony loan'. Still, the cost of such a loan might be covered by revenue from the Lagos Railway.[86]

The Crown Agents replied that a loan could be placed without too much difficulty. But they also pointed out that as it would not have a Treasury guarantee, investors would demand exorbitant interest rates. In order to avoid this, the Colonial Office would have to assure potential investors that no previous lenders had prior claims. The Crown Agents therefore proposed that the Colonial Office borrow not £1,000,000 but £2,000,000 as a consolidation loan. This larger sum would pay for the railway extension and cover all their outstanding debts – to the Lagos Government, the Bank of England, and the Treasury (under the Colonial Loans Act).[87] The money market had been improving over the past couple of years and by the time the loan was floated in March 1905, it was well known that Lagos would soon be amalgamated with the Protectorate of Southern

Nigeria, a larger and richer colony. This promise of prosperity convinced investors to back the loan.

By now the permanent officials at the Colonial Office had learned a great deal about financing railways. The lack of a permanent colonial development fund for larger colonial projects was both a hindrance and a help to them. A permanent fund would have encouraged long-range development planning. On the other hand, its lack forced the Colonial Office staff to learn perhaps more than they had ever wanted to know about finance – not only did they develop a railway, they developed the judgement necessary to assess financial needs and to find alternative financial resources. After the South African War there was less enthusiasm for the Empire, and this affected the financing of colonial public works projects. Nevertheless, they found the money to build the Lagos Railway.

The main financial lessons learned by the Colonial Office in the decade after 1895 seem to have been that while they could always rely on the Crown Agents, they could not always rely on the Treasury. The Treasury would not automatically provide grants, loans, or guarantees for projects beyond the capacity of a Crown Colony's revenue. When the Treasury did not live up to Colonial Office expectations, the staff discovered they could obtain funding from the open market even when the Treasury disapproved. (Of course, Treasury money and Treasury guarantees would always be preferable.) With the assistance and expertise of Sir Montagu Ommanney, the Colonial Office staff gained financial judgement and greater confidence in their ability to obtain funds for Nigerian railway projects.

6 The Creation of the Baro–Kano Railway, 1897–1911

The Baro-Kano Railway was conceived and approved as a single line that began at Baro on the Niger and ended at Kano in the north. It was funded in one lump sum. The Colonial Office staff approached this railway project with considerable assurance and aplomb. They had learned the value of flexibility and adaptability. Few of the fits and starts seen in planning, building, and financing the Lagos Railway were in evidence. The Colonial Office staff had reason to be more confident. When construction began in 1907 they already had more than a decade's experience in dealing with railway problems on the Lagos line.

The purpose of a Northern Nigerian railway was to reach 'into the heart of the Hausa States' – a region previously accessible only by footpaths and caravan trails.[1] Almost from the start, the Colonial Office considered Kano, the commercial centre of the interior, to be the natural terminus of any Northern Nigerian railway. Spending money to build a line into Northern Nigeria would save money. Secretary of State Lord Elgin believed that with a railway:

Considerable economies in civil and military expenditure, together with greater security and efficiency, can therefore be confidently anticipated, resulting, first, from increased mobility and accessibility enabling fewer men (whether soldiers or civilians) to do more work; secondly, from the reduced expense of maintaining and supplying troops in garrison or in the field; and thirdly, from the improvement in the conditions of service of Europeans (food and housing) and consequently in their health. These reasons may be regarded as sufficient in themselves to justify a considerable amount of not directly remunerative expenditure on railway construction, but additional to them is the prospect of the speedier

166

development of local trade, upon which ultimately the capacity of the country to yield revenue depends. . . .

But even more important from a commercial point of view is the prospect which the construction of a railway opens up of a great development in the cultivation and export of cotton. The Chambers of Commerce in this country and the British Cotton Growing Association strongly advocate railway construction. The latter see in Northern Nigeria the most fruitful field for their labours, and a railway would enable them to open up areas of production which otherwise the lack of transport would compel them to leave untouched.[2]

Northern Nigeria was obviously one of Chamberlain's 'undeveloped estates' and clearly a railway was necessary and justifiable. It was less clear why it had to be a second railway linked to the Niger River and the ocean – a transportation system completely distinct from the Lagos Railway – particularly since the Lagos line had recently reached Northern Nigeria. The idea of a second railway originated with Sir Frederick Lugard, the first Northern Nigerian High Commissioner. Like most colonial governors, Lugard wanted a self-sufficient colony; unlike them, however, he was extraordinarily intense about it. He saw Southern Nigeria more 'as a hostile or rival community' than a sister state. He intensely resented the fact that Northern Nigeria's only access to the sea was through Southern Nigeria.[3] Lugard's greatest wish was to obtain an independent route to the sea. The only way this could be accomplished was by a second system – a rail–river system.

When Lugard first proposed this rail–river combination in 1903, the Colonial Office staff was quick to point out that the Niger was a difficult river to navigate at the best of times, and that most of the time it was so shallow it only could accommodate the smallest crafts. This made it an unlikely route. However, Antrobus suggested that the Colonial Office compare the cost of improving the Niger's navigability and building a new railway line to the cost of improving Lagos Harbour and simply extending the existing railway from there into Kano in Northern Nigeria. Ommanney seized upon this point as a means of killing the rail–river idea:

The improvement of the Niger navigation would be a work requiring . . . years of careful investigation, certain to be extremely costly. On the other hand we have reason to believe that for an expenditure which has been carefully estimated by the best authorities, ocean steamers can be brought alongside at Lagos and a railway from Kano, via Jebba to Lagos, offers a mode of dealing with the trade of Nigeria and Lagos on the basis of a greatly shorter mileage, fewer risks . . . and one transhipment instead of two.[4]

As the resident railway expert, Ommanney's authoritative minute convinced Chamberlain and the rest of the Colonial Office. Although they did not carry out Lugard's proposal, the Colonial Office did accomplish something important as a result of that proposal. They asked the Consulting Engineers to survey a route from Baro on the Niger northwards to Kano. Several years later, these surveys enabled Sir Percy Girouard – without further surveying and with a minimum of fuss – to choose the route for the Baro–Kano Railway. However, the idea of a rail–river route was not resurrected and accepted until four years later. Why? Primarily because by then Ommanney had left the Colonial Office and Girouard had replaced Lugard as High Commissioner in Northern Nigeria. Girouard was now the reigning railway expert. The letter offering him the post of High Commissioner had been most explicit:

In deciding to offer you this employment Lord Elgin has been influenced by the consideration that your experience of railway construction would assist him in arriving at a conclusion with regard to the project for a light railway from Baro on the Niger which has been put forward by Sir F. Lugard.[5]

Like Lugard, Girouard wanted to keep control of the Northern Nigerian transport system. Like most people at the time, he believed there could never be too many colonial railways. He was willing to agree that 'the Lagos Railway may form the backbone of a considerable system for the southwestern portion of Nigeria', but, he continued, 'it is my firm contention that in the economical development of Northern Nigeria we must place our reliance upon the existing railways supplemented by railway systems based upon them'.[6] When Girouard advised in favour of a rail–river combination, there was no one at the Colonial Office who felt strongly enough about it, now that Ommanney had retired, or who carried enough political weight, to oppose the idea. The Colonial Office sanctioned the proposal to make the Niger navigable and to build a railway from Baro on the Niger to Kano. At the same time, they agreed that the

Lagos Railway should continue north to, and then cross the Niger at, Jebba. This was not necessarily the cheapest or the best way to develop and exploit Northern Nigeria. Elgin approved both routes, according to Ronald Hyam in his *Elgin and Churchill at the Colonial Office*, because he did not want to disappoint anyone. Rather than choose between the two routes, he decided to have both.[7]

Sir Walter Egerton, Governor of Southern Nigeria, had told his Legislative Council that he looked upon the proposed line from Baro to Zaria as being merely 'temporary'. Nothing, he said, could prevent the Lagos Railway from ultimately becoming the main line from the interior to the seacoast. 'It is all very well,' he said, 'to talk of water transport being cheaper. Water transport on a river such as the Niger will never beat a railway.'[8] In 1908 he attempted to persuade Elgin's successor, Lord Crewe, to reconsider the situation, by pointing out that if the Lagos Railway was extended to Kano via Zaria, the whole idea of a rail–river route would be unnecessary. Antrobus agreed with Egerton and admitted that the rail–river line was due 'to the divergence of opinion at the Colonial Office'. But Crewe refused to reopen the discussion. It was too late to alter the track of the Baro–Kano line and he told the officials that they must all learn to live with the decision taken in 1907.[9]

The authorisation of a second railway required a separate set of decisions concerning how it should be built and financed. The route itself, the one the Consulting Engineers had devised between 1903 and 1905, and which Girouard had incorporated into his own proposal, posed no problems. In accepting the idea of the railway – which the Crown Agents said could be built 'with confidence as a remunerative undertaking' – the route from Baro to Kano was also accepted.[10] It is to a discussion of the method of construction used and the difficulties of financing the railway that we now turn.

Although the Colonial Office had accepted the Consulting Engineers' choice of route between Baro and Kano (with some modifications), this was not the case with regard to the method of construction. No one doubted that the Crown Agents and Consulting Engineers built good railways. But their system (the departmental system discussed in the previous chapter) was sometimes slow, cumbersome, and expensive. The Consulting Engineers insisted on building only top-quality railways. This was commendable; however, if such a line was the only option available, a poor colony simply couldn't afford a railway. Most Colonial Office officials, though admitting the expense, thought a departmentally built railway worth

the cost, and of course, Ommanney, out of loyalty to the Crown
Agents, and out of a firmly held conviction that their method was
best, made certain that the Colonial Office used the departmental
method until he retired.

The local method of construction was developed by Lugard and
John Eaglesome, the Northern Nigerian Director of Public Works,
between 1900 and 1906.[11] What was this method? It was one in
which, Lugard said, a railway could be constructed by:

> the local staff, asssisted by all the existing machinery of the
> Government; labour to be largely recruited by the Political Staff;
> transport by the Government vessels, and so on. All would work
> with an enthusiasm which it would be impossible and impracticable
> to expect from contractors and their agents, while the system of
> leave and pay given to the latter is more costly than that of the
> Government.[12]

Eaglesome's expertise made this method especially attractive. He
was by profession a railway engineer, having worked many years on
Indian railways. He had already directed construction of a short
tramway in Northern Nigeria and was familiar with the availability of
local labour, difficulties of river transport, and local conditions.
Eaglesome would have his own reputation at stake if the local
method was tried, and would therefore be particularly anxious to
succeed.

At first the Colonial Office rejected this system. In 1903, when
Lugard proposed to build a line from Baro to Zaria by the local
method, Antrobus said, 'although Mr. Eaglesome is a very good man
in his way, we are not prepared to rely upon him in a matter of this
magnitude'.[13] Ommanney doubted that the Public Works Department of a Colony, even one headed by a trained railway engineer,
could build a proper railway; there was 'nothing more certain', he
said, 'to end in disaster'.[14] Not surprisingly, the Crown Agents and
Consulting Engineers supported Ommanney, saying that building a
railway was a major project that could not be undertaken by anyone
with other duties such as Eaglesome had as Director of Public Works.
They suggested that if Lugard and the Colonial Office were
disenchanted with the departmental method, they might try to create
a Railway Department in Northern Nigeria under the direction of an
experienced Railway Engineer. In any event, they refused to
recommend the local method.[15] The Colonial Office accepted this

advice until Ommanney resigned and Girouard became High Commissioner of Northern Nigeria. Girouard came to the job with a high reputation for building good railways, inexpensively, under difficult conditions, and when he endorsed the local method, the Colonial Office agreed.[16] After all, Girouard had been appointed to give expert advice; it would have been surprising if it had not been taken.

In accepting Girouard's opinion, and adapting the local method for the Baro–Kano Railway, Colonial Office officials showed that they were open to new approaches. At the same time, while being co-operative, they also wished to protect themselves. In August 1907, Butler said that:

> We at the Colonial Office must be prepared to comply with all his demands for materials or staff, without criticism and without demur, unless there is anything patently unreasonable or impossible in what he asks . . . There must be no room for him to say that we have refused to give him what he asked for.[17]

The line was laid between 1908 and 1911. Girouard made good his promise to build a 'no frills' pioneer railway quickly: 99 miles were laid in 1908–9; 151 miles in 1910–11 (including the Zungeru to Minna section); and 144 miles in 1910–11.[18] The local method had turned out to be a successful method. The product was an adequate railway, inexpensively built. By the mid-1920s the local method was accepted as the standard procedure for building railways in British West Africa.[19]

Finding the money to build the Baro–Kano Railway was essentially a Colonial Office task; in fact, it was the greatest challenge permanent officials faced in their work on the Northern Nigeria railway. Northern Nigeria could not support its own colonial government, much less pay for expensive development projects. It was a Treasury-aided colony; indeed most of its revenues came from the Imperial Treasury. In addition to the purely budgetary function of making up the difference between Northern Nigerian revenue and expenditure, the Treasury decided whether a proposed project was financially justified, and, if so, might well assist in its financing. The discussion and exchanges of correspondence on these issues provide a valuable opportunity to observe the Colonial Office and Treasury at work and the operation of the principle of Treasury control.

For a variety of reasons the decision to build a railway in Northern Nigeria had not been made until 1907. The main reason was money – or rather the lack of it. Lugard had been urging Colonial Office approval of a railway scheme for many years. His endeavours were important because they resulted in route surveys which were eventually used to build the Baro–Kano Railway. Furthermore, Lugard's insistence forced the Colonial Office staff and the Crown Agents to begin thinking seriously about railway funding. A construction budget was created by determining the cost of an average mile of construction and the length of the proposed route, and then multiplying the former by the latter. In Northern Nigeria this was especially difficult because so little was known about the terrain. Lugard had at one time supplied estimates of about £1,400 per mile, a sharp contrast to 'the Consulting Engineers' initial estimate of £5,200 a mile.[20] However, by 1907 the two sets of estimates had somehow been refigured until they more or less agreed. Lugard, Girouard, and the Consulting Engineers all separately concluded that a light railway of 3ft. 6in. gauge could be built, using the local method of construction, for £3,000 a mile.[21] Once the experts had agreed, the permanent officials were able to draw up a sensible proposal for financing and constructing a railway. All that remained was to decide upon a terminus north of the Niger.

Although the logical and eventual goal was Kano, the Colonial Office staff doubted the Treasury would be willing to fund the entire project. They reluctantly admitted to themselves that Northern Nigeria could also benefit economically and commercially from a line that only went as far as Zungeru – roughly a third of the way to Kano. At this point the Colonial Office seemed to be approaching the problem of the Baro–Kano line construction with the same old attitude and answers they had used on the Lagos line. Once again, it seemed, instead of determining their goal and requirements, and then seeking funds to accomplish their task, they had anticipated possible financial constraints and decided to limit their objectives to fit the resources on hand. But the Colonial Office, after years of delay, now believed that Northern Nigeria could not afford to wait any longer, and thus initiated financial negotiations on this basis. It turned out to be a false start. On 28 February 1907 the Colonial Office asked the Treasury to provide a grant of £375,000 (£3,000 a mile for 125 miles) to build a railway from Baro to Zungeru, emphasising the administrative, strategic, and commercial advantages that would accrue to Northern Nigeria.[22]

Elgin, hoping that a personal plea would make the proposal more acceptable, added a note to the Chancellor of the Exchequer, H. H. Asquith. Elgin admitted having squelched earlier Northern Nigeria railway projects because they 'had no scientific foundations' ('I could not,' he said, 'bring myself to send them to you – and that was my real motive in employing Girouard.') The current proposal was the work of experts, a 'no frills' railway at a bargain price. He hoped the Treasury would provide the money immediately so that construction could begin right away. In conclusion he said:

> There is a good deal that I should be glad to explain of my views regarding railway progress if you cared to talk of it. . . . I will merely say that if I am right there would not be further demands on the Treasury [from Northern Nigeria] for some time.[23]

At the Treasury, Sir George Murray, Permanent Secretary, was dubious about the way the scheme had been developed. For example, the Colonial Office had described the Niger River as Northern Nigeria's proper outlet to the sea, without mentioning the problem of its navigability.* The Colonial Office had also neglected to consider the operating expenses of the railway. But Murray objected most of all to the unexplained estimate of £3,000 a mile. Murray felt that the only estimate that had been 'carefully worked out' was the one given by the Consulting Engineers. (Their original figure of £5,200 a mile, it should be noted, raised the estimated cost to about £600,000.) How had the Colonial Office hit upon the £3,000-a-mile estimate? Murray suggested that it was by a miraculous process through which 'some remarkable discrepancies . . . ultimately became still more remarkable coincidences'. 'We have ample experiences,' he continued. 'of this tendency to cut down estimates at the beginning, with the consequent discovery after the work has been in progress that the cost must be doubled or trebled.'Even worse, Murray thought the proposal was written as if the Colonial Office was going into the business of company-promoting; he said it read very much like a prospectus promoting a new 'Nigerian Railways Limited'. The Colonial Office wanted to begin at once, but Murray felt this was hardly possible, and suggested that the Treasury might not be able to obtain Parliament's approval for several months.[24] The project could only be improved if it was re-thought and re-written. Therefore,

---

* The Niger's maximum draught, on the average, was 12 feet for 2 months of the year, 3 feet 6 inches for 8 months, and only 1 foot 3 inches for the other 2 months.

Murray suggested that the proposal be returned to the Colonial Office with a long list of questions. When satisfactory answers were available the discussion could continue.

Although Asquith accepted Murray's recommendation, he also responded to Elgin's personal plea for a prompt response by scheduling a conference to be attended by Colonial Office and Treasury representatives. The Treasury had been the object of such a piecemeal approach before, and suspected that financing a railway to Zungeru would eventually lead to financing it well beyond. Consequently they were reluctant to get started until a definite end was in sight. A memorandum to this effect was sent to the Colonial Office prior to the meeting, ending – in true Treasury spirit – as follows:

> All the circumstances appear to make a start this year pretty much of a risk – which may lead not only to a much heavier expenditure than you contemplate but may because of insufficient information lead to mistakes large and small.[25]

The memorandum contained sound advice, but Treasury analysis and advice was easier to take than the tone in which it was given.

At the conference the Colonial Office representatives were no more convincing in person than on paper. Asquith had to inform Elgin that he could not, even after the 'fullest consideration', approve the request. He reiterated some of the Treasury's major objections: i.e., the discrepancies in the cost-per-mile estimates, the lack of evidence to support Girouard's low estimate, and the indisputable fact that the railway, once started, would really have to go to Kano. Warming to this theme, Asquith said:

> It was conceded yesterday by the representatives of the Colonial Office that the 'pioneer' line of 125 miles from Baro to Zungeru is intended as the first link in a system which is to be in time extended to Zaria and Kano – a further distance of about 270 miles.
>
> Assuming the estimated cost of construction (£3,000 per mile) not to be exceeded, either in the pioneer line or in the extension, the scheme involves a minimum capital expenditure approaching £1,200,000. But past experience and the obvious necessities of the case, combine to show that we shall have to spend a vast deal more before we get to the end of the business . . . I cannot doubt that the ultimate capital expenditure will not be far short of, even if it does not exceed, £2,000,000.

I am bound to consider the present proposal in the light of these further developments, and, if I were to assent to it, the Treasury would be left without any logical *locus obstandi* when its sanction was asked to the construction of the later links in the chain.

I cannot, possibly, in the present state of national finances, commit myself – at any rate upon the materials now before me – to such a scheme.[26]

This being the case, the Colonial Office then suggested that the Treasury should take advantage of Girouard's impending departure for Northern Nigeria. He could personally investigate the situation, and then prepare what might well be a sounder proposal. Thus in the Spring of 1907 the Treasury rejected the Colonial Office request,[27] and agreed that Girouard would be directed to assess the situation in Nigeria and report back.[28]

Treasury officials still seriously doubted the possibility of a good railway being built for £3,000 a mile,[29] but the matter rested until Girouard's report arrived at the Colonial Office in late June. The report was long, but its conclusions and recommendations were concise. He proposed that Northern Nigeria's outlet to the sea should be the Niger River, not the Lagos Railway. A new line should be constructed from Baro on the Niger to Kano, a distance of about 400 miles. A pioneer 'no frills' line, Girouard emphatically stated, could be built for £3,000 a mile. The total amount needed would be £1,230,000 (the additional £30,000 for a dredger to keep the Niger River open all year round). Strachey thought Girouard's plans and proposal were:

calculated to carry conviction. I hope we shall back up Sir P. Girouard's views as strongly as possible in writing to the Treasury, frankly recognising that the scheme is for a railway to Kano, and not to Zungeru.[30]

Girouard's report seems to have given the Colonial Office staff a shot in the arm, providing them with courage as well as conviction. They were now ready and willing to abandon the piecemeal approach and aim directly for Kano. When the Colonial Office sent the report to the Treasury, Treasury clerk Malcolm Ramsay called it 'the artillery preparation for the infantry attack'.[31]

In early July the Colonial Office and Treasury resumed their discussions. This was done through informal meetings and through formal and informal correspondence. It was obvious that the Treasury would not fund the railway by an outright grant. This being the case, the next best thing was a Treasury guaranteed loan. The Colonial Office wanted a loan of £1,230,000 to be provided in three instalments over a period of four years: £500,000 to the end of 1909 (for the Baro–Zungeru section); £430,000 to the end of 1910 (for the Zungeru to Zaria section and the dredger); and £300,000 to the end of 1911 (for the Zaria to Kano section). In negotiation with the Treasury, the Colonial Office's Parliamentary Under Secretary, Winston Churchill, suggested that Southern Nigeria pay the interest on the loan, so as to make it more palatable to the Treasury. This suggestion was made on the assumption that the money would be borrowed on the credit of the British Government. The Treasury responded that it had 'the strongest possible objection' to borrowing in this manner, no matter who paid the interest, in part because there were already other, higher, claims on that credit. A specific colonial public finance aspect also influenced Treasury thinking. Just a few years earlier, the Treasury had allowed to be borrowed, on government credit, a huge sum to build the Uganda Railway. In consequence the Government had been saddled with a substantial and much-larger-than-anticipated debt. As a result, Treasury staff had begun to feel that they should guard against, or at least be very careful in, allowing 'proconsuls' power to draw on the public purse'. Instead, Treasury officials suggested that the loan be raised on the credit of Southern Nigeria. Churchill admitted that this was certainly feasible. However, if Southern Nigeria was to risk its high credit rating, the loan should be made as painless as possible. If the Treasury permitted funds to be raised in this way, Churchill proposed that the arrangement be sweetened by an offer from the Treasury to pay the annual interest and sinking-fund charges on the loan. As Churchill pungently put it, 'If she [Southern Nigeria] is mulct in credit, she should not be mulct in cash.'[32]

This was discussed at the Treasury, where Robert Chalmers, an Assistant Secretary, pointed out that since they were convinced the project was necessary, but could neither provide a grant nor permit Northern Nigeria to borrow on its own or on Treasury credit, the only alternative was to allow the money to be raised on Southern Nigeria credit with the Treasury paying the interest. However, there was no reason why the Treasury should pay the sinking-fund charges. Finally, said Chalmers, if the Treasury were to help Southern Nigeria by paying the interest, then Southern Nigeria could help the Treasury by borrowing from one of the Treasury-administered funds, the Local Loans Fund of the Public Works Loan Commission.[33] William Blain, another Assistant Secretary and colleagues of Chalmers, carefully noted that such a loan for colonial purposes violated the spirit of the law and worked against the public interest of those who had a first claim on the money – the local British authorities. However, more practically, he also noted that if 'the line must be built, and built at once in spite of adverse financial conditions, I agree that the objections to any other course of action may be considered to outweigh these'.[34] On 1 August the Treasury officially notified the Colonial Office that they believed the railway project was important and would give the proposal sympathetic consideration if the Colonial Office agreed to raise the money on Southern Nigerian credit.[35] Financial Secretary to the Treasury, Walter Runciman, intimated that the Treasury would approve such a proposal if the Colonial Office agreed to pay the sinking-fund charges. 'I can see no justification', he said, 'for asking the Exchequer of the United Kingdom to find the sinking fund. Surely it is enough that we find the whole of the interest charges.'[36] The Colonial Office accepted this view – whether from conviction that the Treasury was correct or because it was politic to do so, is not clear. In any case the Treasury did approve the proposal to borrow on Southern Nigerian credit for the Northern Nigerian railway and so informed the Colonial Office on 8 August 1907.[37]

However, the Crown Agents were trying to dissuade the Colonial Office from raising money through the Local Loans Fund; such a loan would be a first charge on Southern Nigerian revenues and assets and would have priority over subsequent borrowing. Several years earlier Southern Nigeria had borrowed £2,000,000 and now was planning to borrow again – specifically for harbour works, roads, and the extention of Lagos Railway. If funds were obtained for the Baro–Kano Railway through the Local Loans Fund, on Southern Nigerian credit, the loan planned for Southern Nigeria's own public works could only be obtained at a very high rate of interest. In the Crown Agents' view, Southern Nigeria should have nothing to do with the Local Loans Fund, and any money required for Southern or Northern Nigerian public works should be raised without Treasury assistance.[38] On 12 August 1907 a high-level Colonial Office–Treasury conference was held to try to resolve this situation.

The Chancellor of the Exchequer, the Financial and Permanent Secretaries to the Treasury (Runciman and Sir Edward Hamilton, respectively), and four other Treasury clerks attended. The Colonial Office was represented by its Parliamentary Under Secretary (Churchill), the Permanent Under Secretary (Sir Francis Hopwood), and the Senior Crown Agent (Sir Ernest Blake) who came as financial adviser to the Colonial Office. It became obvious that the Treasury was unaware of Southern Nigeria's other loan schemes. After some discussion it was decided, though 'not without some hesitation on the part of the Chancellor of the Exchequer', that the situation was serious enough to justify some concession on the Treasury's part. Consequently, the Treasury was willing to allow Southern Nigeria to borrow up to £2,000,000 through the Local Loans Fund to finance not only the public works projects mentioned above, but also the Baro to Kano Railway. It would be repayable at any time on terms agreed on by the Colonial Office and the Treasury. If market conditions improved they could borrow again on Southern Nigeria's credit in order to pay off the Treasury and thereby clear the way for future loans.[39] As the Colonial Office understood the situation, the Treasury was being most co-operative and accommodating.

Unfortunately, Treasury and Colonial Office officials left the conference with very different understandings of what had been agreed on. Treasury notes on the meeting indicated that 'S. Nigeria is to undertake to spend the necessary money (£1,230,000) out of the 2 million loan on the Kano line in Northern Nigeria.'[40] However, Churchill's Colonial Office minute on the meeting made no mention of any specific amount having been earmarked for the Baro–Kano line. Churchill told the Colonial Office staff that the crucial condition of the loan, as far as the Treasury was concerned, was that construction on the Baro–Kano Railway begin without delay and continue to a speedy conclusion. To the Colonial Office, the loan's purpose was to get the Baro–Kano line started and to keep several Southern Nigerian projects going at the same time. They anticipated using £800,000 for Southern Nigerian public works, £700,000 for the Lagos Railway and £500,000 for the Baro–Kano in 1908/9.[41] (This was in keeping with their scheduled estimated costs of £500,000 for the first year, £430,000 for the second, and £300,000 for the third.) Other money would be obtained when needed and when the market improved.

To the Colonial Office this posed a problem of financial management: how to continue existing projects from the proposed loan funds until Southern Nigeria could go to the money market and secure another loan at a reasonable rate. To deal successfully with this, the Colonial Office would have to regulate the rate of expenditure on their various projects and the Crown Agents would have to carefully monitor the money market. Co-ordination was important, Butler pointed out:

> So long as . . . [the Crown Agents are] unable to give any sort of date at which So. Nig. can go to the market, so long must loan expenditure proceed with extreme caution. Otherwise we may find ourselves, two or three years hence, with the Baro–Kano line and the Ilorin–Zungeru connection partially finished, the Treasury loan exhausted and the Colony in the predicament of having to go *at any cost* [Butler's emphasis] to the market for a very large loan.

Regulating expenditure, though difficult, would not be impossible. Both Nigerian Governors, Girouard and Egerton, would be 'very pressing in trying to get what they want'. However, until the permanent officials knew where they were with regard to the money market they would have to go slowly, even at the risk of causing the Governors some disappointment. Secretary of State Lord Elgin commented that 'Mr. Butler quite rightly dwells on the necessity of very careful management of the finances', but he agreed that if they were careful all would be well.[42] On 22 August Elgin authorised acceptance of the Treasury offer as reported and interpreted by Churchill.

But when the Treasury received the Colonial Office letter, Treasury officials were quick to point out that these were not the terms that had been agreed on. They had understood that £1,230,000 of the loan had to be used on the Northern Nigerian railway and only £770,000 should be used for other purposes, and so informed the Colonial Office on 12 September.[43] The Colonial Office was taken aback by this message. 'If money can be got from Local Loans Funds only on this condition,' said Butler, 'the situation is an impossible one for So. Nig.' Obviously, Southern Nigeria would not be willing to lend its credit to Northern Nigeria if this meant jeopardising Southern Nigeria's own development projects. Butler was sure the Treasury had simply misunderstood, and urged quick action to clear the matter up. Elgin concurred, saying that he could not see why the Treasury had raised this obstacle.[44]

Despite their concern, no quick action was taken; it was almost six months before the Colonial Office responded to the Treasury. Why this delay? Strachey informed the Colonial Office in October that 'the condition of the money market is improving'.[45] At the same time, Southern Nigerian revenues had increased dramatically. This meant that that Colony was in extraordinarily good financial shape and could continue to finance the Baro–Kano and its own public works on a temporary basis until a favourable loan could be arranged on the money market. At the beginning of 1908 another factor had to be taken into account. The Southern Nigerian public works projects – those already approved and new ones being proposed – exceeded the original estimates by £1,000,000, and Governor Egerton requested permission to raise additional funds. This helped to crystallise discussion in the Colonial Office and they began to consider withdrawing from the Treasury deal altogether.[46] Churchill, always impetuous, wanted to immediately demand a release from the commitment to borrow from the Local Loans Fund. Butler suggested that before doing so they needed specific information from the Crown Agents comparing the expense of the Treasury loan as opposed to an open-market loan. However, the direction of the Colonial Office opinion was already apparent and clearly expressed by Elgin when he said, 'I do not see any reason why we should take money from the Treasury if we can raise it better otherwise.'[47]

On 11 February 1908 the Crown Agents conveyed two main points to the Colonial Office: first, a £3,000,000 loan, the sum now needed, could be raised on the open market at an interest rate slightly lower than the 3¾ per cent the Treasury would probably charge; second, a Treasury loan could not be more than the £2,000,000 recorded in the Public Works Loan Act of 1907. To ask for an additional £1,000,000 would require an act of Parliament, which neither the Colonial Office nor the Treasury was willing to request. If they accepted the Treasury offer of £2,000,000, Southern Nigeria would then have to obtain the additional £1,000,000 on the open market. In such a case the interest rate on the latter sum would be excessive, because the Treasury loan would constitute a prior charge on the assets and revenues of the Colony. There seemed to be no doubt they should back out of the Treasury deal. Butler drafted a letter sent 26 February 1908 replying, at long last, to the Treasury letter of 12 September. Churchill called the letter 'an excellent statement of a complicated but perfectly reasonable position'. It stated that the Treasury understanding of how the £2,000,000 would be spent 'was not understood precisely in this sense' by the Colonial Office, and that it did not now appear to be in Southern Nigeria's interest to borrow through the Local Loans

Fund. But before definitely rejecting the Treasury offer the Colonial Office wanted to know exactly what interest rate they would charge. And finally, to leave no stone unturned, and perhaps to defuse possible criticism, the Colonial Office asked the Treasury if they could suggest any other method of borrowing the money in the open market which would be more advantageous than borrowing through the Crown Agents.[48]

The Treasury promptly reminded the Colonial Office that its (the Colonial Office's) first request 'as the official records clearly show' had been for £1,230,000 to build the Baro–Kano Railway. The amount was increased to £2,000,000 to cover Southern Nigeria's public works projects. Ordinarily this was not the kind of loan the Treasury considered and it had done so as a special concession to Colonial Office needs. The Treasury further noted that its interest rate was 3¾ per cent and it could not suggest any new method of raising money. With this in hand, only one decision made sense. And so on 10 April the Colonial Office formally withdrew their request for a loan and informed the Treasury that Southern Nigeria would be authorised to raise money in the open market.[49]

The Crown Agents were given authority to raise a loan of £3,000,000 for Southern Nigeria 'at such time and on such terms' that seemed most favourable.[50] Everything after this was simple, straightforward, and anti-climactic. A prospectus was issued by the Crown Agents and by 8 May the loan had been successfully floated. The interest rate was just under 3¾ per cent.[51] Sufficient funds were now available to continue the Lagos Railway and to create a rail–river route to Kano – going up the Niger River and thence by rail from Baro, on the river, to Kano.

In 1895 Chamberlain said that it was the task of the colonising government in new countries to build railways, and until this was acknowledged and achieved, Britain would 'not have fulfilled her obligation to the Dependencies . . . under her rule'.[52] Clearly, the Colonial Office and its officials fulfilled this obligation by planning and overseeing the construction of the Nigerian railways, choosing a method of construction, and financing the railways.

These metropolitan officials, it should be remembered, were supervisors or controllers of colonial administration. They had no direct knowledge of the area in which the railways were to be built. Consequently, they had to rely on the colonial governments for information about the country, and on the Crown Agents and Consulting Engineers for advice on the actual business of creating railways. Therefore it is not surprising that they were at first careful and cautious. Throughout the first several years of the railway work, officials insisted at every juncture on knowing almost everything about any proposed step and on considering all possible alternatives. The comment, 'we must have more information', appeared in their minutes and draft dispatches with monotonous regularity. But no one at the Colonial Office had any experience of railway work in a tropical dependency. However, this began to change in 1898 when Charles Strachey, and in 1900 when Montagu Ommanney, came to the Colonial Office. Ommanney's influence, as I have tried to indicate in these two chapters, was felt practically in every aspect of railway planning, financing, and building. By the time he retired, the Colonial Office had been involved in West African railway work for more than a decade, and other Colonial Office officials were almost as experienced, knowledgeable and confident as Ommanney. This is borne out by the work they did on the completion of the Lagos Railway extension as well as the Baro–Kano Railway between 1907 and 1911. The completion and amalgamation of these two lines, on 1 January 1912, signalled a great accomplishment and should be recognised as such. The Nigerian railways made Britain's control of the Nigerias more effective – administratively and militarily – and also facilitated commercial development. The railways were part of Britain's imperial policy which aimed at, in Robinson's and Gallagher's words, 'integrating new regions into the expanding economy' of Great Britain.[53] As any Colonial Office administrator or colonial civil servant would have confirmed, these railways were built to benefit the Empire, and they did. Moreover, the permanent officials at the Colonial Office also believed in what would later be called the dual mandate, i.e., Britain must develop Nigeria not only for the benefit of the metropolis, but in the interests of the indigenous people. What was good for Europe in Africa, must be good, they believed, for Africans in Africa as well.

Two other points should be made: one about the Colonial Office and its railway work *vis-à-vis* the Treasury and the Crown Agents; and the other about the Colonial Office's standing in the process through which the Nigerian railways were conceived and built. What the Treasury attempted to do, in context, did not constitute an attempt to influence colonial policy so much as it represented the Treasury's desire to impose its own financial system. When the Colonial Office found it inconvenient to conform to this system, they simply avoided it. The Treasury had influence in that it could deny the Colonial Office access to British Government financing. But this is not as significant as it sounds, because another option existed – the open market. On the occasions that the Colonial Office exercised this option for Southern and Northern Nigeria in 1905 and 1908, the money was obtained freely and without onerous conditions attached. Going to the open market greatly pleased the Crown Agents because they realised that, in the long run, Treasury funding cost more and often made other borrowing more difficult. The Crown Agents played an influential and important role as advisers, but it is important to understand that they were only advisers – decisions were made by the Colonial Office.

This leads to a more general point. The locus of decision-making was the Colonial Office. Officials there dealt with railway matters initially with some diffidence, but eventually with great confidence. They successfully argued and negotiated – by formal and informal correspondence, and through formal and informal meetings – with the Treasury, the Crown Agents, the Consulting Engineers, and the colonial governors. The result was that by 1912 there was a railway system connecting the coast to the far north. Goods and passengers could now make the trip from Lagos to Kano in a matter of days rather than weeks. This was no small accomplishment, and indeed was of enormous economic, administrative and political significance. The work done was not always done perfectly and the decisions taken were not always the best. But over the long term most of what they did was efficient, competent and occasionally wise. Through the agency of the Colonial Office and its staff the task that Chamberlain had set for Britain *vis-à-vis* railways was accomplished. If railways were the most obvious symbol of and witness to nineteenth- and early-twentieth-century British power, commerce, and civilisation, then the Colonial Office and its staff must be given a great deal of credit for their being built.[54]

7 The Search for Petroleum in Southern Nigeria, 1906–14

The early twentieth century was a great age of oil exploration; major strikes were made all over the world and oil was seen as the fuel of the future. In these years, the British Royal Navy began its changeover from coal to oil fuel. In the monthly review, *The Nineteenth Century,* Sydney Brooks wrote that 'there is no bigger and no more obvious gap in our . . . Imperial equipment than the paucity of our supplies of oil'.[1] British oil companies began oil exploration in Trinidad, the East Indies, Burma, Persia, and elsewhere. The Persian fields, though not in British territory, seemed the best source of oil. These fields were already in production; and they had known reserves that would last for the foreseeable future. Additionally, Persian oil was closer to the surface and thus required no new technology; and the area surrounding the fields admitted fairly easy access to this inexpensive oil. There was only one major disadvantage. Potentially, the involvement necessary to assure Britain a secure supply might lead to political and strategic complications. Obviously a similar source of oil within the British Empire – if discovered – would be ideal.

In 1906, John Simon Bergheim, a British businessman, convinced the Colonial Office and the Government of Southern Nigeria that petroleum existed in Southern Nigeria and that his company, the Nigeria Bitumen Corporation, could find it. For the next six years, permanent officials at the Colonial Office protected Bergheim's virtual monopoly of prospecting rights, rewrote mining legislation at his request, and provided the Nigeria Bitumen Corporation with a loan to support an eventually fruitless search for petroleum. How did this happen?

The relationship between businessmen and permanent officials at

184

the Edwardian Colonial Office is an aspect of British imperial history that rewards the researcher. It offers the opportunity to investigate and assess the role of private enterprise in the development of a colonial economy, and to analyse the degree to which permanent officials in London and the colonial governor in Southern Nigeria helped, or hindered, this process. This is especially so during the period of administrative occupation of British tropical Africa. Permanent officials at the Colonial Office received a steady stream of business deputations – from Liverpool, Birmingham, Manchester, and London – bearing plans for the construction of railways, bridges and harbours in the colonies. Such projects required government funding, or government loans, or government loan guarantees. Many of these negotiations were carried on through an exchange of prepared statements. In these instances there was no dialogue or exchange of views. Often these statements were reported in newspapers and generated publicity but no action. Of course, some businessmen furthered their particular interests more directly – through correspondence and personal visits to the Colonial Office. These methods of approach had the advantage of creating one-to-one relationships where personalities and persuasion had more impact. Several personal relationships – of mutual benefit – were established between individuals at the Colonial Office interested in colonial development, and businessmen interested in colonial profits.

An example of this sort of relationship was the one which developed between Reginald Antrobus and John Holt.* The positive elements of a government–business relationship can be pinpointed in letters exchanged between Holt and Antrobus. In 1898 Holt wrote to Antrobus saying that he should regard him (Holt):

> as part of your industrial department, working with your other departments to develop the resources of a new and vast region of the globe – one with a great future before it if worked with prudence, economy, enterprise, and ability.[2]

Ten years later, when Antrobus transferred to the Crown Agents' Office, Holt wrote congratulating him on his promotion and on the work he had done in the Colonial Office over the years. In reply, Antrobus expressed pleasure at hearing this praise, and added: 'It has always been a pleasure to me to meet you and the conversations which we have had [at the Colonial Office] have been very useful as

* A merchant prominent in British–West African trade from the late nineteenth century until his death in 1915.

well as pleasant.'[3] There was no rule that said officials and entrepreneurs had to get along. Sometimes they didn't. Permanent officials were concerned with development that would create revenue and a self-supporting colony. Entrepreneurs were concerned with development only in so far as it created profits. Conflicts and disagreements arose inevitably. The mechanics of these relationships have not been fully sorted out and documented, but the case of J. S. Bergheim and the Colonial Office staff provides an excellent opportunity to investigate such a relationship.

The principals in this story are Bergheim, several permanent officials, and Sir Walter Egerton. There is very little information available about Bergheim, the Chairman of the Nigeria Bitumen Corporation. By profession he was an engineer, and at the time of his death, in 1912, he had been in the oil business – exploring, drilling, producing and refining – since the early 1880s. He took part in opening up various oil fields in Central and Eastern Europe,[4] and at one time formed a company to manufacture oil-drilling equipment, a venture that proved very successful. During the period of his involvement with Nigeria, he was also chairman of several other oil companies. One of them, the Anglo-Mexican Oilfields Limited, struck oil in 1912. Two years earlier that company had paid up capital of £205,197 in shares plus £16,800 in bonds.[5] Bergheim must have been an exceptional man. He persuaded officials at the Colonial Office to accept ideas they would have normally rejected, and lured them into activities they would ordinarily have refused to consider. Given that the permanent officials were generally sceptical of businessmen and their schemes, Bergheim's effect on them is all the more extraordinary.

The three members of the permanent staff most involved with Nigerian oil exploration between 1906 and 1914 were Frederick Butler, Charles Strachey, and George Fiddes: the former as clerks in the Nigeria Department, the latter as Assistant Under Secretary in charge of West African business. Although a Junior Clerk in the Nigeria Department, Butler soon became the Colonial Office resource person regarding oil, and remained so until he was transferred to the East African Department in 1909. His recommendations carried great weight. Strachey, as Senior Clerk in the Nigeria Department from 1900 to 1907, and then as Principal Clerk in charge of the Department until 1924, is the only one who was involved in the Nigerian oil question from beginning to end. He was cautious about innovation and strict about colonial finance. Fiddes, we should recall, was unusual in that he was an imperialist. In fact, one Colonial Office official believed Fiddes had single-handedly brought about the South African War.[6] Two other men should be mentioned: Reginald Antrobus and Sydney Olivier – Antrobus as Assistant Under Secretary in 1909, and Olivier as Head of the Office's Nigeria Department in 1906.

Sir Walter Egerton, then Governor of Southern Nigeria, as has been discussed earlier, should be remembered for his firm ideas on how a colony should be developed. He believed that colonial development would not take place unless the government was willing to spend money – to build a transportation and communication infrastructure, to create or develop a trade product. Spending government money was the route to colonial prosperity.

In the official records of the Colonial Office, the search for oil started with a letter from Bergheim on 1 August 1906.[7] This letter began a close relationship between himself and the staff concerned with Nigeria that continued until Bergheim's untimely death in 1912. Bergheim informed the Colonial Office that, based on his knowledge of Southern Nigerian geology, he was certain considerable quantities of oil existed in Southern Nigeria. He believed that those who assisted in the discovery of oil would raise the colony to a 'very high position', and create a new industry in Southern Nigeria that would provide revenue for the colonial government and fuel for British ships.[8] Bergheim had expertise and some money, but he wanted financial assistance and special legislation. He had already achieved a monopoly on prospecting rights in Nigeria through the simple expedient of buying up all the other drilling licences. However, he wanted to make his monopoly permanent and proposed a special agreement with the Southern Nigerian Government. As the first to minute Bergheim's letter Butler disapproved of the idea of a special agreement with a private firm. He felt that Southern Nigeria should reject Bergheim's request for financial assistance, but leave open the possibility for assistance at a later date. He recommended that the Company make the initial exploratory efforts unaided and continue under the current licences, which would be extended when they expired. However, no licences would be issued to any one else, thus assuring Bergheim of at least a temporary monopoly. Butler noted that it was important to prevent 'a mad rush of concession mongers'. If there were a large proportion of failures and a resulting loss of confidence among investors, the opportunity to properly develop the oil field might be lost. Lord Elgin, Secretary of State, said that 'Mr.

Butler's excellent minute sums up [the situation], I think, correctly throughout.' Elgin was very clear on one thing: 'If oil exists,' he wrote, 'this is a very important matter for Nigeria.'[9]

Although the Colonial Office had rejected Bergheim's request for financial aid, he did convince permanent officials that existing mining regulations were not suitable, and that oil should be treated separately.[10] Antrobus told the staff:

> All that we need do for him [Bergheim], or for any company which is really prepared to spend money on boring operations, is to afford them security that their operations will not be interfered with by others; this can be done, *inter alia,* by the general regulations it is proposed to make.[11]

Antrobus was very anxious to make it clear that their willingness to write new legislation did not imply favouritism. At Butler's suggestion a committee was formed, made up of himself, Strachey, and one of the Office's legal advisers. They composed a draft ordinance and sent it to Bergheim, who was not happy with it. In mid-November 1906 he appeared in person at the Colonial Office to point out that the committee had not addressed itself to the major issue – that drilling for oil was very different from traditional mining. Under the present Southern Nigerian mining law, mineral prospecting required no great expenditure. But exploring for oil involved very expensive drilling. An oil strike made further exploration practically unnecessary for those who came after the pioneer driller, whereas a mineral strike gave no guarantee that there were any other veins in the area.

Bergheim, a single-minded and tenacious man, proposed instead that the Governor of Southern Nigeria give the Nigeria Bitumen Corporation an exclusive four-year licence to explore for oil. Once again, the Colonial Office rejected the idea of special arrangements. They were interested in Bergheim's ideas but were obligated to provide regulations that would be applicable to all who wished to drill for oil. They repeatedly impressed this on Bergheim. He conceded the point but argued that special inducements for pioneers should be incorporated into the general regulations. Largely because of the objection made by Bergheim, the committee then discarded its first draft. Butler presented another a few days later. As Bergheim had requested, it made a sharp distinction between those who explored for oil and those who came after a strike had been made. Pioneer drillers would pay a 7½ per cent. royalty, while those who drilled after a strike would pay more according to a sliding scale of increased royalties. It was also decided that applicants could obtain licences to explore as much as one thousand square miles, but once oil was struck, leases to drill would only cover forty square miles.[12] Bergheim, however, wanted the right to lease the same one thousand square miles for drilling. Not surprisingly, he objected strongly to the forty-square-mile limit. He appeared at the Office again, and complained, as Olivier said, 'very pathetically of the bitterness of seeing others come in and share the advantages of profitable districts which he might have discovered'. But the officials stuck to their mileage: forty square miles was generous, but one thousand would be ridiculous.[13] Butler's second draft of the legislation was approved by Antrobus and the Secretary of State.[14]

However, Bergheim was still not satisfied. During a third visit to the Office he met with Olivier, Strachey, and Butler, and described the great profits Southern Nigeria would reap if he were given special assistance. Officials were well aware that Bergheim's company had made real beginnings toward the exploration for oil. However, Butler noted:

We have gone very far out of our way in trying to give him . . . consideration. A new draft law which had been prepared . . . was cancelled in order to meet various points raised by him, and the whole scheme of the present law is that which he himself suggested as a possible basis of agreement satisfactory to all concerned . . . the draft law represents our attempt to give Mr. Bergheim equitable consideration.

Butler decided that Bergheim should be reminded 'clearly and forcibly' of a few home truths. If Bergheim struck oil, he could not work the field commercially without a lease. His existing licences would end in the early part of 1907. After that point, he would have no legal rights. He could only apply for oil rights along with everyone else under the new legislation. As Butler pointed out, Bergheim could find himself 'in a very sorry plight'.[15]

At the next meeting, a few days after Christmas 1906, when Antrobus outlined the situation, Bergheim was forced to acknowledge his position. Officials then generously agreed to several of his suggested amendments to the draft legislation, only one of which involved substantial departure from previously approved policy. This was a lowering of the royalty scale of 7½ per cent to 15 per cent, down to 5 per cent to 12½ per cent. The results of this meeting illustrate the growing sense of informal partnership and the first signs of flexibility on the part of Colonial Office staff. Butler spoke for the Office when he said:

> We do not want to cut our throats by making it difficult or impossible to work oil in Southern Nigeria at a profit, and from this point of view, I think the proposed reduction of royalty is quite justified.

Butler felt he and permanent officials were holding their own rather well in these dealings. He noted:

> Bergheim had asked for more than he really thought he would get or ought to have. This can hardly be called an unwarrantable assumption in dealing with a successful promoter of companies.

To prevent further personal appearances by Bergheim, and additional amendments (against which they might no longer be able to hold their own), Butler asked that Bergheim be sent a memorandum recording the results of their most recent conference.[16] When everyone seemed satisfied, this third and final draft of the oil regulations became the Southern Nigerian Mining Regulation (Oil) Ordinance of 1907.[17]

What had transpired was rather unusual. Bergheim had presented the permanent officials with a situation they were aware of – the need for separate oil regulations. They had responded by drafting legislation based largely on Bergheim's ideas. Bergheim had, practically speaking, become a member of the committee, and during the drafting process had constantly and forcefully pushed his point of view. His success with the Colonial Office staff was due in part to his great tenacity. But it was his vision, not his persistence, that had somehow galvanised officials out of their usual routines and convinced them to rely on his ideas. Bergheim and the Colonial Office were establishing exactly the sort of relationship John Holt had described to Antrobus as the ideal in 1899. In the face of Bergheim's demands, officials had responded cautiously, but for the most part co-operatively. Butler, Olivier, and Strachey felt they had protected and enhanced Southern Nigeria's economic interests by giving private enterprise sufficient incentive to invest. As Antrobus reminded everyone, if oil was found, the revenue would not only pay for the administration of Southern Nigeria, but for its poor relation, Northern Nigeria, as well.[18]

By late 1907, after drilling for a year, the Nigeria Bitumen Corporation had still not struck oil. Bergheim maintained that there were excellent signs and believed that the more wells the Company sunk, the more likely it was that oil would be found. Therefore he soon reappeared at the Colonial Office seeking financial assistance. Antrobus, who was by now convinced that the Company was 'a genuine enterprise', went so far as to encourage him to approach the Government of Southern Nigeria.[19] Butler also felt that Southern Nigeria should offer assistance, saying that if they abandoned the Company at this point it would mean 'the neglect of the possibilities of the oil fields for a generation'.[20] Bolstered by this support Bergheim asked for a loan of £25,000 for new rigs, to be repaid when oil was struck. To make the loan more appealing, once it was repaid, royalties would be increased by 2½ per cent.[21] Bergheim received an enthusiastic response from the Governor of Southern Nigeria, Sir Walter Egerton. Not only was Egerton interested, he proposed that instead of a loan, Southern Nigeria should purchase a 20 per cent interest in the Nigeria Bitumen Corporation. It was not unheard of for the British government to purchase interest in a private company. The most striking example from the late nineteenth century was Disraeli's purchase of the Suez Canal Company's shares. And in 1912 the Post Office bought out the main telephone company.

However, permanent officials were taken aback by the idea, and together condemned it. Butler spoke for them all when he said that it would be:

an invidious thing for Government to hold shares in an industrial undertaking. There would always be an inclination to view the affairs of such an undertaking too favourably, and, if that inclination never had a tangible result, there would always be room for competing concerns to raise vexatious and embarrassing cries of favouritism.

To the officials, Bergheim's proposal was 'somewhat novel',[22] the Governor's unthinkable. And so a loan was what he got. Again, the permanent officials' flexibility can be seen, but this time, with clearly defined limits. To permit a colonial government to purchase shares in a private company was outside all their experience. Ordinarily they would have left such a company to fend for itself. But Bergheim had stretched their horizons. They had been brought to a point where they were willing to break with the doctrine of *laissez-faire* (if only temporarily) and provide government funds to assist a speculative venture. There can be few other occasions before 1914 where the Colonial Office approved such a loan. But a loan was as far as they would go.

With Colonial Office approval, the first instalment of the colonial government's loan to the Nigeria Bitumen Corporation was paid in February 1908. Later in the year several firms and individuals applied for drilling licences but were rejected. The Nigeria Bitumen Corporation was still alone in the field. Butler gave voice to the question that was in everyone's mind:

> Can the Government of Southern Nigeria legitimately persist in the refusal to grant further licences to drill for oil, except to the Nigeria Bitumen Company until that Corporation has thoroughly explored the areas over which it holds, or may be granted, licences?[23]

When asked for his opinion, the Governor expressed satisfaction with the status quo. He did not want any other licences issued. He urged the Colonial Office to view the Nigeria Bitumen Corporation as a partner with the colonial government in the search for oil, rather than as a 'mere mercantile company'. Butler realised that Egerton was reluctant to issue licenses because he was afraid that a speculator's market might build up around Nigerian oil. However, Butler pointed out that the more firms drilling in an area the sooner oil would be found. The Colonial Office could not protect Bergheim's monopoly any longer. Butler proposed that henceforth all applications should be considered on their own merits, and licences granted to all applicants possessing working capital equal to the Nigeria Bitumen Corporation's (about £55,000 to £65,000). Butler also added certain other technical requirements to make certain that the oil fields would have to be worked if licenses were taken out, and not simply held onto by speculators. Butler's analysis and prescription were accepted by his superiors,[24] and by the Governor of Southern Nigeria, who incorporated Butler's guidelines for granting licences into the Oil Ordinance of 1908.[25]

By clearly stating the conditions under which new applications would be approved, Butler anticipated and defused the possibility of everyone accusing the Colonial Office of protecting a monopoly. However there is little doubt that the Office had been playing favourites. The officials had been so impressed by Bergheim and the real effort his company was making that they had paved the way for him, while leaving rocky the path of potential competitors. Bergheim's willingness to devote long hours at the Colonial Office discussing the oil question and helping draft legislation had paid off. The diligent and persuasive promoter of industrial ventures in the Crown Colonies could obviously make a difference in the tone and achievement of a private-enterprise–government relationship. Permanent officials appeared to have been willing, and perhaps eager, to provide (for a few years at least) a monopoly of drilling licenses, a special oil ordinance, and financial assistance for Bergheim's company. Now, by making conditions difficult but reasonable, Butler and his colleagues had made certain that it would be possible for qualified competitors to enter the field.

While all this paperwork was being done at the Colonial Office in London, what progress, if any, was the Nigeria Bitumen Corporation making in Nigeria? And how did this progress, or lack of it, affect the permanent officials' attitude toward the Nigerian oil question? In November 1908 an excited Bergheim telegraphed that his crew had struck oil. Butler was impressed, but warned that they might wait a little longer before they plumed themselves on the success of their policy.[26] They waited almost a year. In September 1909 Bergheim told the officials that his crew was getting oil at the rate of two thousand barrels a day. Strachey, now head of the Nigeria Department, said he hoped this would 'do more than merely raise the prices of the Corporation's shares'.[27] However, everyone was encouraged.

Increasingly though, it became clear that if anything was going to come of the drilling more money would be needed. By 1912 the Nigeria Bitumen Corporation had sunk about fifteen wells in Southern Nigeria, eastwards from the Lekki Lagoon towards the Niger Delta. One of the last wells was only about fifty miles from the oil fields in operation today. The Company had already spent £143,000. It had capital to keep operations going for approximately six more months. Bergheim applied for a new loan. In a long letter to the Governor of Southern Nigeria, Bergheim said that when the drilling began:

Only experienced oil men were sent out to carry on the work; engineers and actual drillers, most of them personally known to me, men who had been drilling for oil practically all of their lives. They found and reported on the outcrops of bituminous substances which went to prove that the territory is oil bearing. These indications are distributed over a very large area, but they could not in the nature of things tell where would be the exact place to drill nor at what depths the oil would be encountered, nor indeed what formations would have to be gone through.

We have been at work continuously for nearly six years, and although we have not struck large oil strata nothing has taken place to prove that our surmises were wrong, on the contrary, we are more and more of the opinion that oil strata are there.

Judging by the history of all the large oil fields of the world, six years is not a long time to open out an absolutely new territory on which no drilling had ever been done and where the depth of the oil strata is unknown. California . . . was supposed 30 years ago to be an oil country. Company after company drilled but none of them deep enough and it is only in the last few years that the sources were discoverd by deeper drilling, and now California is one of the largest producing countries in the world. I have myself drilled a number of wells there with good indications but with no practical results, until this year, when by adopting methods suitable for the formation, and getting down to a greater depth I have struck a splendid flowing well.[28]

The future of oil in Nigeria looked good. The Company had acquired new drilling equipment – a Parker rotary drill specially constructed for the company, which could drill faster and deeper than the old equipment.[29] This drill had been responsible for bringing in the great Spindletop field in Texas, and with improvements, eventually became, and still is today, the basic drill for the industry.

Bergheim wanted to drill in the deep strata, where he was convinced there were large oil deposits.[30] But he could not do it without money. He appealed to the permanent officials' and the Southern Nigerian Governor's patriotism. Britain could not rule the waves, defend the empire, or maintain its strategic independence if it did not have a modern navy fuelled by oil. Therefore, it was important to obtain a reliable and secure supply. Sir Francis Hopwood, now a senior official at the Admiralty, supported Bergheim's plea. 'You can well imagine,' he wrote to the Colonial Office, 'how satisfactory it will be to secure a good supply of oil for the Navy from a British Company [in a British colony] only about twelve days steaming from home.' Charles Strachey's comment on Hopwood's letter represented Colonial Office feeling: 'If the success of this Company is important to the Navy, the Admiralty ought to assist.'[31] Eventually the Admiralty did assist – but not in Nigeria.

In September 1912 Bergheim became a victim of modern technology. He was killed in an automobile accident. With him died much of the incentive to develop oil in Nigeria. His Board of Directors continued his efforts to obtain the financial assistance he had requested from Southern Nigeria.[32] But it wasn't the same. Strachey pointed out to his colleagues that Bergheim had been 'a most plausible man and we yielded to his persuasive powers'. Now Bergheim was dead and the spell was broken. Strachey advised that:

> There is no reason *whatever* for giving them [the Nigeria Bitumen Corporation] any further financial help. The results so far have been negative, and . . . we now think we should never have done what we did – it was a gamble, and we are not going to throw away good money after bad.[33]

Sir George Fiddes none the less was very much taken with the idea of finding an oil supply under British control. He had had a long interview with Bergheim shortly before Bergheim's death. Like many before him, he had been impressed by Bergheim. Fiddes urged the Office to consider the matter once more and at least give the Company a 'sporting chance'. The Permanent Under Secretary agreed, and the Company was asked to present their case again.[34] Although the Directors of the Company were unable to tell how long it might take to find commercial quantities of oil, they assured the Colonial Office that they needed only £750 a month for one well and £1,000 a month for two. In return, the Company would increase the Government's royalties.[35] Because Southern Nigerian revenues would provide the funds requested by the Company, the Colonial Office consulted the new Governor.

Sir Walter Egerton, an enthusiastic supporter of economic development who had actively encouraged and worked with the Nigeria Bitumen Corporation, had left Nigeria. The new man, Sir Frederick Lugard, was more interested in administration than oil. He recommended, in May 1913, that no further money be lent and that the Company be asked to repay the original loan. Without Bergheim to counter such arguments the permanent officials' caution reasserted itself. Strachey was pleased, Fiddes unhappy, but they all decided they should accept Lugard's recommendation to end all financial assistance in the search for oil. They now believed no other conclusion was possible.[36]

As the effort in Nigeria was being abandoned, British politicians were finding a solution in another part of the world. The hope of oil in Nigeria could not begin to compete with the fact of already-booming fields in Persia. Winston Churchill, as First Lord of the Admiralty, told the House of Commons in 1913 that:

> We must become the owners, or at any rate, the controllers at the source, of at least a proportion of the supply of natural oil we require for the Navy.[37]

In the following year, the Admiralty bought controlling interest in the Anglo-Persian Oil Company.[38] The first search for oil in Nigeria ended in mid-1913. Fiddes had warned his colleagues that: 'If operations stop now, no one will touch it again for a long time, and we shall be left in doubt as to whether we have missed a good thing or not.'[39] His words proved prophetic. The search would not be resumed seriously for almost twenty-five years. Oil would not be found until the mid-1950s and would not flow in commercial quantities until the eve of Nigerian independence. The British government had indeed missed a 'good thing'. The Colonial Office files of 1914 provide a sad postscript to Bergheim's high hopes. The liquidation of the Company's assets was almost complete. There was only £130 left – £60 was to be split between two old employees of the company and the liquidator would take the rest.[40]

What conclusions can be drawn from examining Bergheim's and the Colonial Office's attempt to develop petroleum in Southern Nigeria? Clearly the search contributed to the realisation that government had a role to play in colonial economic development. Otherwise it would take an unconscionable time for economic progress to occur. How this role would ultimately be defined was still undetermined in 1913, but some progress, some clarification, had taken place. From the events narrated we can see that no one lived up to traditional expectations. Neither the Colonial Office staff nor Bergheim adhered rigidly to the doctrine of *laissez-faire* when the subject was colonial development, though both could have been expected to. They agreed on the need for development, and from their shared desire to exploit the oil of Southern Nigeria came an informal partnership.

Permanent officials, as workers and partners in this enterprise, were rather conservative. In this precedent-ridden office, a clerk was likely to find out how something had been done in the past before he recommended how something should be done in the future. Neither departmental tradition nor administrative structure encouraged adventurous solutions. Much of this was revealed in or implied by officials' deliberate and methodical minutes. Butler clearly described the Colonial Office approach when he wrote in 1908 that the governor ought to understand and appreciate the Colonial Office's essential function of cautious criticism just as permanent officials appreciated his of enthusiastic development.[41] The possibility of sanctioning what might later turn out to be a financial and economic disaster also gave permanent officials incentive to proceed with extreme caution.

But having made this point about the conservatism of permanent officials, we should also note and emphasise that they were flexible. Almost certainly they came to the administrative occupation of British tropical Africa committed to the idea of non-interference by government in the economy. It is to their credit that their commitment to this idea was modified by their experience. In the face of new situations and new demands they responded in a decidedly pragmatic, albeit cautious way. The most compelling reason for the permanent officials' flexible and 'unconservative' response was the persuasiveness and inspiration of Bergheim. In their partnership he was more innovative than permanent officials. As a vigorously single-minded person he acted as a catalyst. Officials used his ideas to support policy decisions, and as the basis for legislation they drafted. Had Bergheim lived longer he might have continued to capture the officials' imaginations, and insure their aid. But his successors at the Nigeria Bitumen Corporation were mere ordinary men, and in ordinary fashion permanent officials refused to assist them in the search for oil. One thing is clear – the likelihood of creative responses to colonial development schemes markedly decreased without individuals of imagination and drive such as Bergheim to lift permanent officials out of their routine.

This partnership was of course not formal or legal; none the less it was real. Until 1912 it was characterised by co-operativeness, flexibility, and hope. Neither Bergheim nor the permanent officials would have dissented from the notion that they were partners in an alliance for progress. That this partnership ended without the discovery of petroleum should not obscure its very positive nature.

However, there was a bottom line for Colonial Office officials. It was, understandably enough, the discovery of oil in commercial quantities within a reasonable length of time. Unfortunately, a considerable gap existed between what the Colonial Office and Bergheim thought was a reasonable length of time. When permanent officials concluded that the Nigeria Bitumen Corporation, after six years, was no closer to the discovery of oil than it had been when drilling began, their patience ran out. And the Company, without further financial assistance, was unable to continue the search. In short, the partnership accomplished very little in actually developing Southern Nigeria. Ironically, its major consequence was to convince officials that commercial quantities of oil did not exist in Nigeria. The significance of the partnership was that it represented a form of co-operation that could – in other circumstances – aid economic progress and development. It was an important break from officials' adherence to traditional economic dogma, and pointed the way to the future. In this sense it was an important model to officials and entrepreneurs as to what could be done, and how it should be done.

In the final analysis, no matter how good a working relationship existed between the Colonial Office and Bergheim, the essential purpose of that relationship was not accomplished. Why not? Why wasn't the Colonial Office and the government of Southern Nigeria willing to try harder? Undoubtedly, the major deterrent to a lengthier search was the success of the Persian oil fields. In Southern Nigeria, a major discovery had yet to take place. The terrain was rough and hard to open up to large-scale exploitation. Nigeria petroleum did not appear to be as close to the surface as was Persian Gulf oil. To drill deeper in Nigeria would not have been impossible, but why bother when easily accessible oil could be had in large and inexpensive quantities elsewhere. The only clear advantage to developing petroleum in Nigeria would be the absence of political and strategic complications. But the Nigeria Bitumen Corporation and the Colonial Office could not produce convincing reasons to find and exploit Southern Nigeria oil. In fact, by abandoning the search in Nigeria the Colonial Office staff and Bergheim may have unwittingly contributed to the British Government's decision to rely on oil from a politically vulnerable area. The high technological costs of what was after all only potential oil in Southern Nigeria outweighed the political risks of Persian oil. And the decision to concentrate on Persia expressed the British Government's confidence that it could handle any complication that might arise. Given its authority in world affairs at the time, this was not an unreasonable assumption. Despite all efforts by the Colonial Office and the Nigeria Bitumen Corporation, Persian oil in 1913 was the obvious solution to Britain's needs.

Conclusion

'Nigeria is a Crown Colony and we [the Colonial Office] have a right to supervise its proceedings.'—Secretary of State Lord Elgin

'The British Empire is in the hands of a lot of clerks.'—Lord Leverhulme[1]

How did Great Britain respond to the need to 'do something' with the new possessions that came under British rule consequent to the partition of Africa? Using Nigeria as a case study, this book has attempted to give an answer to this question. Under Colonial Office supervision much development – of an economic, financial, and administrative sort – was accomplished. The foundation stones of Nigeria's future were laid in these years, but this development, it should be emphasised, did not happen because Colonial Office officials possessed a political philosophy of progress, imperial or otherwise. Rather it happened because those officials were determined to maintain primacy over the affairs of the Colonial Office and the colonial empire. This factor sometimes required that they do things one might call progressive, or, on other occasions, conservative. Some examples of the former are the works that officials did on the establishment and maintenance of Crown Colony government in Nigeria, the formation and implementation of the amalgamation policy, all phases of the creation of the Lagos Railway and the Baro–Kano Railway, the attempt to find and develop petroleum in Southern Nigeria, and the successful campaign to keep Nigeria free from Treasury control during the amalgamation process. An example of their conservative side is the work Colonial Office officials did to ensure that the doctrine of financial restraint prevailed over economic development. Another example would be their work in establishing a non-interventionist approach to indirect rule as the model for local government across the colonial empire. Few African nationalists have had kind words for the principles and application of

199

indirect rule as it evolved in British tropical Africa. It has been called a backward and retrograde approach to local government which maintained in power the most conservative elements in native society. Finally one should also realise that some of the Colonial Office's most effective administrative work had little or no effect on economic or administrative development in Nigeria. For example, the campaign against Lugard's scheme of continuous administration was important to permanent officials because it threatened to remove them from the locus of decision-making for a large portion of each year.

Nigerian work was done by District Officers in the south and by Residents in the north, by Nigerian governors and high commissioners, by the Crown Agents, by the Treasury, and on occasion by other agencies of the British state. But above all there was the Colonial Office, always in charge of the Colonial Empire. This was not a simple fact of imperial life but, as has been shown, something that had to be vigorously and regularly defended against challenges from Nigerian governors and from others in London. When Sir Frederick Lugard wished to establish his scheme of continuous administration, permanent officials fought to stop him, as they did when he tried to free indirect rule from the non-interventionist senior residents in Northern Nigeria. In both cases the Colonial Office prevailed. And when Lugard returned to Nigeria in 1912 to amalgamate the northern and southern colonies, hoping to be allowed to legislate without Colonial Office review, he was diplomatically but decisively turned down. This rejection was, again, due to the efforts of the Colonial Office's permanent staff. Lugard was not alone in his attempt to break away from Colonial Office control. Sir Walter Egerton, a very modern man in his attitude to financing economic development, tried for almost a decade to get the Colonial Office to recognise that he was right in his belief that the Government of a Crown Colony must spend money if it was to increase its revenue. The Colonial Office did not accept his argument and when the opportunity presented itself officials made certain that their ideas of financing development prevailed. As Antrobus noted, a colonial administration must 'cut its coat according to the cloth of its revenues'.[2] Additionally, in the search for oil in Southern Nigeria, Egerton proposed that the Southern Nigerian Government become part-owner in the Nigeria Bitumen Corporation. The Colonial Office, however, rejected this, and instead would only permit the Southern Nigerian Government to lend the private company money. When oil in commercial quantities was not found after several years, it was the Colonial Office, against Egerton's wishes, that refused to allow the Southern Nigerian Government to lend more money to the Nigerian Bitumen Corporation. When Lugard or Egerton, or other governors, tried to do what the Colonial Office did not think appropriate, they were not allowed to. Governors and high commissioners were not well positioned to seriously challenge the Colonial Office.

As advisers to the Colonial Office in financial matters and in the construction of public works in Crown Colonies, the Crown Agents represented a more subtle challenge to the Colonial Office, the challenge of expertise. By no stretch of the imagination could permanent officials be characterised as experts in these fields, and so they had to be guided by the Crown Agents. In public works, for example, the Crown Agents had an obvious special interest: the more railway-, bridge-, road-, and canal-building projects and the more harbour-improvement schemes the Colonial Office sanctioned, the more business the Crown Agents would get. It was always advantageous for the Crown Agents to recommend construction, whether or not it was needed. No matter that, constitutionally speaking, the Crown Agents Office was a creature of the Colonial Office and under the supervision of the Secretary of State, the Crown Agents could, and did, pose a challenge to the Colonial Office's authority.

However, the Colonial Office was able to meet this challenge. Permanent officials, although not trained in finance or public works, had, from the late 1890s on, an increasing amount of experience in these very subjects (mainly because of the work done on the administrative occupation of the new colonial territories). Consequently they became more accustomed to dealing with the complexities involved, and were ready to reject public works proposals if they did not make sense, and did so on many occasions. Two such incidents occurred when the Colonial Office turned down a request for a railway route survey in Lagos Colony in 1900, and in Northern Nigeria in 1902. The Colonial Office's reasoning was sound: there was no need for a route survey in these parts of Nigeria when it had not yet been decided whether or not a railway was needed. In addition to this experience gained over time we should mention that, after 1900, the Colonial Office also had the expertise of Sir Montagu Ommanney to draw upon. He is one of the more important and least-known high Colonial Office officials of the early twentieth century. The highlighting of Ommanney's role in this book has, one hopes, made his work better known. In short, the Colonial Office's judgement in the area of colonial public works and colonial public finance in the early years of the century became especially acute.

The Treasury posed a different sort of challenge to the Colonial Office. The Treasury and the Colonial Office were great departments of state and, theoretically at least, equals, whereas the Crown Colonies and the Crown Agents Office were constitutionally inferior to the Colonial Office. However, this theoretical quality seemed to be offset in many respects by a strong tradition that the Treasury was to be considered as first among equals. In financial affairs the Treasury assumed that at the very least it had the right, no matter what department of state was involved, to advise and on occasion insist that a certain course be followed. However, no matter how true this might have been generally – if indeed it was – the Colonial Office, as had been shown here, was in no way fettered by Treasury control.

In the case of the Northern Nigerian estimates and the Treasury grants-in-aid of revenue to Northern Nigeria, the Colonial Office asked for advice and money from the Treasury for the dependency, but by and large went its own way. The formation and implementation of Northern Nigerian financial policy was something to be worked out at the Colonial Office in consultation with the colonial government. The Treasury was not a part, or at least not a major part, of this process. The Treasury also proffered advice regarding the financing of the Lagos and the Baro–Kano railways. This advice was taken when it fitted in with the needs of the Colonial Office and Nigeria. However, it was very clear from the occasions when the Colonial Office did reject Treasury advice, that the Colonial Office felt no obligation to accept it. Outside of the financial aid provided in the loan of 1900 for part of the Lagos Railway and the annual grant-in-aid to Northern Nigeria, the Treasury did not actually provide much financial assistance to the Colonial Office and Nigeria. For instance, a great deal of advice was given by the Treasury, and not taken by the Colonial Office, concerning both the 1905 and 1908 railway loans. Before the 1905 loan was successfully floated on the open market, the Treasury tried to persuade the Colonial Office that its (the Treasury's) borrowing needs were so great that Southern Nigeria should not be allowed to borrow. In this way the money could be loaned to the Treasury. In this instance, and in others, the Colonial Office simply ignored the Treasury.

As a matter of record we should realise that permanent officials were able to negotiate with the Treasury and very successfully assert the Colonial Office's position in financial matters. Another example of this can be seen in the skilful way Sir John Anderson and Sir George Fiddes, especially Fiddes, persuaded the Treasury to provide Nigeria with an annual grant-in-aid of revenue of £100,000 for five years free of Treasury control. The Colonial Office was not and did not see itself as being dominated by the Treasury. Permanent officials saw the Treasury as a hindrance occasionally but never as a major inhibition on the Colonial Office's freedom of action. The origin of permanent officials' actions was the feeling that the Colonial Office was indeed independent of Treasury control, and free, within the limitations which faced all departments, to do as it wished. This did not preclude co-operation between the two offices when the situation required it, but when this happened it was usually on Colonial Office terms. Indeed the suggestion made in the Introduction that the two poles of the Treasury–Colonial Office relationship were co-operation on the one hand and Colonial Office independence on the other are confirmed by this study.

The Colonial Office and its staff successfully resisted the challenges mentioned above and others which have been discussed in the body of this text. In all of this we should be reminded that the mainspring of action by Colonial Office officials was not any imperialist ideology. Indeed they did not work in accordance with such an ideology. They were at heart administrators whose ethos of work and method of work was that of their colleagues in the Home Civil Service – to do the best they could for their department and to remain in control of their department's work. In a sense they were administrative pragmatists who acted in accordance with the theory of the territorial imperative.

In view of the material covered by this book, it is hard to give credence to Sir John Fisher's lament to his friend Sir Francis Hopwood in 1912 – 'a permanent official is always timorous'. Hopwood had been Permanent Under Secretary at the Colonial Office and in 1912 was an Additional Civil Lord at the Admiralty. Later on in the year, Fisher wrote again to exclaim that 'Every permanent official expert wants to be safe!!'[3] Although Fisher was writing about officials at the Admiralty, his comments reflect the negative reputation permanent officials had at the time, and still have. For example, a modern (1968) assessment of the pre-1914 Colonial Office officials by Ronald Hyam characterised them as 'proud, patronising and precedent-ridden pundits' who lived in an ivory tower.[4] These comments are untrue and unfair. Permanent officials were not afraid to take chances, but at the same time they were very careful and cautious in assessing a situation. It would not be too far off the mark to say that they raised caution to the level of administrative doctrine. This is best illustrated by repeating Frederick Butler's 1908 maxim: 'If any mistake is to be made in the Colonial Office, it should be that of excessive caution, rather than the opposite.'[5]

That Fisher's evaluation of permanent officials, and Hyam's in particular, should be rejected has been made abundantly clear in this study. In its place, and in the context of permanent officials' role as examined in this book, we should be able to arrive at a more balanced evaluation and judgement. (Such evaluations and judgements are rare because permanent officials have seldom been the central focus of scholarly studies – colonial governors and Secretaries of State being more frequently studied.) There should now be little doubt that substantial accomplishments were achieved in the years 1898–1914. These developments, which took place during the administrative occupation of Nigeria and indeed define it, established the framework of later Nigerian development throughout the colonial period and beyond. Additionally there should be little doubt that the Colonial Office and its permanent officials were at the heart of the process by which this happened. In the final analysis the Colonial Office was in charge of the formation and implementation of colonial policy for Nigeria, and, by extension, in charge of Britain's Colonial Empire.

Notes and References

INTRODUCTION

1. Minute by Antrobus, 24 July 1902, on Lugard to CO, 18 August 1901, CO 446/21/29344.
2. Foreign Office to CO, 25 June 1898, CO 537/135/476.
3. Minute by Chamberlain, 21 July 1898, on Foreign Office to CO, 18 July 1898, CO 537/135/490. For the Committee's report itself, see 'Report of the Nigeria Committee', by the Earl of Selborne, 4 August 1898, CO 879/52/555.
4. A. F. Afigbo, 'The Establishment of Colonial Rule, 1900–1918', in *History of West Africa,* ed. by J. F. A. Ajayi and Michael Crowder, 2 vols (London, 1974) 2:440; John E. Flint, 'Nigeria: The Colonial Experience from 1880 to 1914', in *Colonialism in Africa,* vol. 1: *The History and Politics of Colonialism in Africa, 1870–1914,* ed. by L. H. Gann and Peter Duignan (Cambridge, 1969) p. 258.
5. A. Taylor Milne (compiler), 'Bibliography', in the *Cambridge History of the British Empire,* vol. 3: *The Empire-Commonwealth, 1870–1919,* ed. by E. A. Benians, Sir James Butler, and C. E. Carrington (Cambridge, 1967) p. 907.
6. See, for example, Richard M. Kesner, *Economic Control and Colonial Development: Crown Colony Management in the Age of Joseph Chamberlain* (Westport, Conn., 1981); Robert V. Kubicek, *The Administration of Imperialism: Joseph Chamberlain at the Colonial Office* (Durham, N.C., 1969); and Ronald Hyam, *Elgin and Churchill at the Colonial Office, 1905–1908: The Watershed of the Empire-Commonwealth* (London, 1968).
7. Robert Ardey, *The Territorial Imperative* (New York, 1966).

1 THE COLONIAL OFFICE AND NIGERIA, 1898–1914

1. It should be borne in mind throughout that clerks of the Upper Division were the administrative élite of the Home Civil Service and not 'clerks' in the American sense.
2. A. Lawrence Lowell, *The Government of England,* 2 vols (New York, 1908) 1:184.
3. 'Memorandum on the Organisation and Establishment of the Colonial

Office', by Sir Montagu Ommanney, 13 March 1903, CO 885/8/156, p. 1.

4. Sir John Anderson's testimony, 17 May 1912, 'Royal Commission on the Civil Service', *Parl. Pap.*, 1912–13 (Cd 6535) 134. (Hereafter referred to as the 'Macdonnell Commission' after its chairman Lord Macdonnell.)

5. 'Memorandum on the Colonial Office Establishment', by Frederick Graham, March 1903, CO 885/8/154, pp. 2–4.

6. Minute by Herbert, n.d. but probably April or May 1888, on Colonial Office, 15 May 1888, CO 323/374/9754.

7. Anderson's testimony, 'Macdonnell Commission', p. 141.

8. 'Memorandum on the Colonial Office Establishment', by Frederick Graham, March 1903, CO 885/8/154, p. 4.

9. 'Memorandum on the Organisation and Establishment of the Colonial Office', by Sir Montagu Ommanney, 13 March 1903, CO 885/8/156, p. 2.

10. 'Memorandum on the Colonial Office Establishment', by Frederick Graham, March 1903, CO 885/8/154, p. 4.

11. 'Memorandum on the Organisation and Establishment of the Colonial Office', by Sir Montagu Ommanney, 13 March 1903, CO 885/8/156, p. 2.

12. Treasury Lords, quoted in 'Memorandum on the Colonial Office Establishment', by Frederick Graham, March 1903, CO 885/8/154, p. 5.

13. Anderson's testimony, 'Macdonnell Commission', p. 135.

14. 'Memorandum on the Organisation and Establishment of the Colonial Office', by Sir Montagu Ommanney, 13 March 1903, CO 885/8/156, p. 3.

15. 'Memorandum on the Colonial Office Establishment', by Frederick Graham, March 1903, CO 885/8/154, p. 9.

16. Crewe to Asquith, 6 November 1910, Crewe Papers, C/40.

17. Elgin to Hopwood, 15 January 1907, Southborough Papers.

18. Crewe to Asquith, 6 November 1910, Crewe Papers, C/40.

19. R. C. Snelling and T. O. Barron, 'The Colonial Office and its Permanent Officials, 1801–1914', in *Studies in the Growth of Nineteenth Century Government,* ed. by Glllian Sutherland (London, 1972) p. 161.

20. Margaret Olivier (ed.), *Sydney Olivier: Letters and Selected Writings* (London, 1948) p. 32.

21. Sir Ralph Furse, *Aucuparius: Recollections of a Recruiting Officer* (London, 1962) p. 22. Whatever their workload, the junior clerks always seemed able to find time for office athletics: in the 1870s they found an empty attic above their office at 11 Downing Street with enough room for five courts. The rumblings and vibrations soon attracted senior staff, however, who thought the building was falling. In 'a most gentlemanlike manner' they told the junior clerks to 'go and play somewhere else'. Sir William Baillie Hamilton, 'Forty-Four Years at the Colonial Office', *Nineteenth Century and After,* LXX (1909) 602. By the 1880s they had indeed found somewhere else to play: one upper division clerk recalls playing cricket with a paper ball and a long tin map-case for a bat in the Clerks' room of the Eastern Department.

Olivier, *Sydney Olivier,* p. 34. By the turn of the century they had moved into the Secretary of State's office – 'an immense room' – where they bowled from the Great Door and used the fireplace as a wicket. Furse, *Aucuparius,* p. 31.

22. Ex-CO. [Sir Augustus Hemming] 'Apotheosis of Juvenility in the Civil Service', *Spectator,* 29 July 1905, 151.
23. Anderson's testimony, 'Macdonnell Commission', p. 138.
24. R. B. Pugh, 'The Colonial Office, 1801–1925', in the *Cambridge History of the British Empire,* vol. 3: *The Empire-Commonwealth, 1870–1919,* ed. by E. A. Benians, Sir James Butler, and C. E. Carrington (Cambridge, 1967) p. 721.
25. Robert V. Kubicek, *The Administration of Imperialism: Joseph Chamberlain at the Colonial Office* (Durham, N.C., 1969) p. 175.
26. A. F. Madden, 'Changing Attitudes and Widening Responsibilities', in the *Cambridge History of the British Empire,* vol. 3, p. 382.
27. Ronald Robinson and John Gallagher with Alice Denny, *Africa and the Victorians: The Official Mind of Imperialism* (London, 1961) p. 396.
28. Sir Harry Wilson, 'Joseph Chamberlain as I Knew Him', *United Empire,* N.S., VIII (February 1917) 105.
29. Speech of 12 December 1887, in Toronto, quoted in Kubicek, *Administration of Imperialism,* p. 9.
30. Essay on Lyttelton, *D.N.B.,* 1912–1921, 350; his son claimed he was the 'greatest all-rounder in the annals of British sports'. Olivier Lyttelton, Viscount Chandos, *The Memoirs of Lord Chandos* (London, 1962) p. xiii. Appropriately enough, he died shortly after being hit by a cricket ball.
31. Alfred Gollin, *Balfour's Burden: Arthur Balfour and Imperial Preference* (London, 1965) p. 177.
32. Edith Lyttelton, *Alfred Lyttelton: An Account of His Life* (London, 1917), and Lyttelton Papers at Churchill College Archives, Cambridge University.
33. Elgin to Crewe, 7 May 1908, Crewe Papers, C/14.
34. Chamberlain to Lady Lugard, 8 February 1906, Lugard Papers, s.62/270.
35. Ronald Hyam, *Elgin and Churchill at the Colonial Office, 1905–1908: The Watershed of the Empire-Commonwealth* (London, 1968) p. 522. Elgin's predecessor thought the opposite, at least on the issue of Lugard's continuous administration scheme. When Elgin rejected the scheme, Lyttelton wrote to Lugard, 'I am deeply distressed and annoyed at the "office" having got their way and at Lord Elgin's timidity.' Lyttelton to Lugard, Lugard Papers, s.65/107, 23 June 1906.
36. Essay on Crewe, *D.N.B.,* 1941–1950, 184.
37. Nicholas Mansergh, *The Commonwealth Experience* (New York, 1969) p. 161.
38. Crewe to Asquith, 6 November 1910, Crewe Papers, C/40.
39. Sir Lionel Earle, *Turn Over the Page* (London, 1935) p. 79.
40. See, for example, his several-hour speech in June of 1912 in which he provided for the House of Commons a detailed picture of, and future

plans for, development in the Crown Colonies. Great Britain, *Parliamentary Debates* (Commons), 5th Ser., 40 (27 June 1912).
41. Butler to Harcourt, 5 December 1915, Lewis Harcourt Papers, CO 7/1.
42. Furse, *Aucuparius,* p. 30.
43. Elgin to Hopwood, 25 December 1907, Southborough Papers. This letter to Hopwood was written regarding Churchill's activities on his East African trip, but its general truth may be accepted with the supporting evidence of Elgin to Crewe, 7 May 1908, Crewe Papers, C/14. In this letter Elgin said:
    When I accepted Churchill as my under secretary I knew I had no easy task. I resolved to give him access to all business – but to keep control (and my temper). I think I may say I succeeded. . . . But all the same I know quite well that it has affected my position *outside the office* and the strain has often been severe.
44. That Churchill laboured at the Colonial Office to obviate the constitutional obstacles in the way of his assertiveness is clear from his official biography. See Randolph S. Churchill, *Winston S. Churchill: Young Statesman, 1901–1914* (Boston, 1967) 2:222–3.
45. Sir Edward was born in 1834, and educated at Winchester and at New College, Oxford. His father was a justice of the peace. Called to the Bar (Lincoln's Inn) in 1859, Wingfield practised extensively on the Home Circuit before coming to the Colonial Office.
46. CO to Treas., 16 February 1899, CO 323/443/4690.
47. Ommanney's testimony, 10 July 1908, before the Committee of Enquiry into the Organisation of the Crown Agents' Office: Reports, Minutes of Evidence, and Appendices, December 1908, CO 885/19/226. Lord Carnarvon himself wrote in 1876, 'I am satisfied that I can make no better choice, having regard to knowledge, ability, and all the qualities which are essential for such an office.' Carnarvon to Sir Robert Herbert, 17 November 1876, CO 323/332/654.
48. Kubicek, *Administration of Imperialism,* p. 41.
49. An Appreciation, *The Times* (London) 25 August 1925, p. 13.
50. 'I didn't know a change at the CO was impending . . . but I am very glad to hear you would be ready to go there and I will put in my word gladly'. Sir Edward Grey to Hopwood, 15 December 1905, Southborough Papers.
51. Snelling and Baron, 'The Colonial Office and its Permanent Officials, 1801–1914', p. 161.
52. Elgin to Campbell-Bannerman, 11 December 1906, Campbell-Bannerman Papers, British Library Add. MSS. 52515.
53. Elgin to Campbell-Bannerman, 14 December 1906, Campbell-Bannerman Papers, British Library Add. MSS. 52515.
54. Elgin to Hopwood, 12 December 1906, Southborough Papers.
55. Buckle to Hopwood, 17 December 1908 (but Buckle must have meant 1907 because on 17 December 1908 Hopwood had been Permanent Under Secretary almost a year) Southborough Papers.
56. Elgin to Crewe, 7 May 1908, Crewe Papers C/14.
57. Anderson was born in 1858, the eldest son of an Aberdeen mission superintendent. He graduated from the University of Aberdeen in 1877

with first-class honours in mathematics. Like Wingfield and Hopwood he studied law, but never practised.

58. Elgin to Campbell-Bannerman, 11 December 1906, Campbell-Bannerman Papers, British Library Add. MSS. 52515.

59. Snelling and Baron, 'The Colonial Office and its Permanent Officials, 1801–1914', p. 161.

60. Information contained in this table comes from a variety of sources: in alphabetical order they are – Burke's *Genealogical and Heraldic History of the Peerage, Baronage, and Knightage; Colonial Office List,* 1898–1914; Debrett's *Peerage, Baronetage, Knightage, and Companionage; Dictionary of National Biography* (twentieth century supplements); John Foster (compiler), *Alumni Oxonienses: The Members of the University of Oxford, 1715–1886: Their Parentage, Birthplace and Year of their Degrees,* 3 vols (Oxford and London, 1885); John Foster, *Oxford Men, 1880–1892: With A Record of Schools and Degrees* (Oxford and London, 1893); *The Historical Register of the University of Oxford: Being a Supplement to the Oxford University Calendar with an Alphabetical Record of University Honours and Distinctions Completed to the End of Trinity Term, 1900* (Oxford, 1900); J. A. Venn, *Alumni Cantabrigienses: A Biographical List of All Known Students, Graduates and Holders of Office at the Univerisity of Cambridge, from the Earliest Times to 1900: Part II; from 1752 to 1900,* 6 vols (Cambridge, 1940); *The Times* (London); *Who's Who; Who Was Who.*

61. G. Kitson Clark, *The Making of Victorian England* (London, 1962) p. 51. W. L. Burn gives substantially the same definition in his *The Age of Equipoise: A Study of the Mid-Victorian Generation* (New York, 1965) p. 253.

62. Clark, *Victorian England,* pp. 119–22.

63. Strachey's father was Sir John Strachey, brother to Sir Edward Strachey, Bart., and uncle to Sir Edward's son, the first Lord Strachie. Hamilton's mother was sister to the first Duke of Abercorn; Malcolm's to the fourth Duke of Wellington.

64. Burn, *Age of Equipoise,* p. 254.

65. Joseph Foster (compiler), *Alumni Oxonienses: The Members of the University of Oxford, 1715–1886: Their Parentage, Birthplace and Year of Birth, With a Record of their Degrees,* II (Oxford and London, 1885) 459.

66. Edward C. Mack, *Public Schools and British Opinion since 1860: The Relationship between Contemporary Ideas and the Evolution of an English Institution* (Westport, Conn., 1971) p. 108.

67. By Erving Goffman in Ian Weinberg, *The English Public Schools: The Sociology of Elite Education* (New York, 1967) p. 8.

68. Geoffrey Best, *Mid-Victorian Britain, 1851–1875* (London, 1971) p. 254.

69. Charles Strachey to Giles Lytton Strachey, 8 May 1929, Strachey Papers, British Library, uncatalogued in 1979 when examined.

70. See Best, pp. 245–56; Burn, *Age of Equipoise,* pp. 253–67; Clark, *Victorian England,* pp. 253–74; G. M. Young, *Victorian England: Portrait of an Age* (London, 1960) pp. 96–9.

71. The 'old-established public school was an educational engine designed to produce a common approach to life for the *élite* of society'. T. W. Bamford, *Rise of the Public Schools: A Study of Boys' Public Boarding Schools from 1837 to the Present Day* (London, 1967) p. 187.

72. Arthur Ponsonby, MP, *The Decline of Aristocracy* (London, 1912) p. 199.

73. 'Report of Her Majesty's Commissioners appointed to inquire into the Revenues and Management of certain Colleges and Schools and the studies pursued and Instruction given therein', *Parl. Pap.* 1864, XX (vol. 1) 56, quoted in Clark, *Victorian England*, p. 271.

74. Minute by Antrobus, 4 December 1901, on acting high commissioner Wallace to CO (287) 10 July 1901, CO 446/15/28410.

75. Minute by Ezechiel, 10 October 1901, ibid.

76. Major Barbara, Act I, p. 461, in *The Complete Plays of Bernard Shaw* (London, 1931).

77. Clark, *Victorian England*, p. 264.

78. D. A. Winstanley, *Later Victorian Cambridge* (Cambridge, 1947) p. 210.

79. One might ask in what fields could these men get an honours degree at, for example, Oxford? How limited were the choices? A look at Oxford's offerings betwen 1850 and 1900 answers this question. In 1850 young men could only take degrees in classics and mathematics. By 1876, when Antrobus graduated, one could be examined in, in addition to classics and mathematics, natural science, jurisprudence, modern history, theology, and civil law. To these subjects two others, oriental languages and literature and English literature, had been added by 1900. *The Historical Register of the University of Oxford*, pp. 192–3.

80. L. N. Helsby, 'Recruitment to the Civil Service', *Political Quarterly*, XXV (1954) 324–5.

81. Lowell, *The Government of England*, 1:156–65. This of course did not happen, unless one wishes to count Sidney Webb.

82. See 'Report of Her Majesty's Civil Service Commissioners; with Appendices: Twenty-Second, 1878', *Parl. Pap.*, 1878, XXVII, v; 'Report of Her Majesty's Civil Service Commissioners; with Appendices, 1895', *Parl. Pap.*, 1895, XXVI (C. 7888), v–vi; and 'Report of His Majesty's Civil Service Commissioners; with Appendices, 1909', *Parl. Pap.*, 1910, Cd. 5751, iii–iv.

83. The source of this information is 'Report of Her Majesty's Civil Service Commissioners; with Appendices: Twenty-sixth, 1882', *Parl. Pap.*, 1882, XII, 190. It is interesting to note that the exception to the nine who took the Latin and Greek examinations as well as the exception to the nine who did not take the German examination, was Sidney Webb. He was also the only one of eleven first division clerks who entered the Colonial Office between 1877 and 1889 not to have a university education.

84. For Oliver, see 'Report of Her Majesty's Civil Service Commissioners; with Appendices: Twenty-seventh, 1883', *Parl. Pap.*, 1883, XXIII, 196. For Keith, see 'Report of His Majesty's Civil Service Commissioners; with Appendices: Forty-sixth, 1902', *Parl. Pap.*, 1902, XXII (Cd. 1203)

v. For Antrobus, see 'Report of Her Majesty's Civil Service Commissioners; with Appendices: Twenty-second, 1878', *Parl. Pap.*, 1878, XXVII, 177. For Anderson, see 'Report of His Majesty's Civil Service Commissioners; with Appendices: Fiftieth, 1906', *Parl. Pap.*, 1906, XXVI (Cd. 3108) v.

85. See 'Report and Papers Relating to the Re-organisation of the Civil Service', *Parl. Pap.*, 1854–5, XX (C. 1870) 77.
86. Ibid, p. 76.
87. Elgin to Crewe, 7 May 1908, Crewe Papers, C/14.
88. A Former Colleague Writes, *The Times* (London) 7 January 1931, p. 7.
89. The other was Sir Charles Lucas, who was first to Antrobus's second. 'Reports of her Majesty's Civil Service Commissioners; with Appendices: Twenty-second, 1878', *Parl. Pap.*, 1878, XXVII, 177.
90. Elgin to Crewe, 7 May 1908, Crewe Papers, C/14.
91. Fiddes's Obituary, *The Times* (London), 24 December 1936, p. 14.
92. Olivier to G. B. Shaw, 1889, B.M. Add. MSS. 50553, quoted in Blakeley, *The Colonial Office, 1868–1892* (Durham, N.C., 1972) p. 91.
93. Furse, *Aucuparius,* pp. 24–5.
94. Hamilton, 'Forty-Four Years', 607–8.
95. Minute by Hamilton, 20 December 1901, on Director General of Military Intelligence to CO, 12 December 1901, CO 446/19/44044.
96. *Colonial Office List,* 1907, 540.
97. W. A. Baillie Hamilton, *Mr. Montenello: A Romance of the Civil Service,* 3 vols (Edinburgh and London, 1885) 1:25.
98. A Correspondent Writes, *The Times* (London) 18 October 1932, p. 9.
99. Minute by Mercer, 12 September 1899, on Lugard to CO, 24 August 1899, CO 446/8/22878.
100. A Correspondent Writes, *The Times* (London) 18 October 1932, p. 9.
101. Olivier's Obituary, *The Times* (London) 16 February 1943, p. 6.
102. Essay on Olivier, *D.N.B.*, 1941–1950, 641.
103. *Who Was Who,* 1941–1950, 867.
104. Minute by Lucas, 5 August 1902, J. Chamberlain Papers, 14/3, quoted in Kubicek, *Administration of Imperialism,* p. 19.
105. Furse, *Aucuparius,* p. 69.
106. C. R. Sanders, *The Strachey Family: Their Writings and Literary Associations* (Durham, N.C., 1953) p. 209.
107. Ibid, pp. 12–13.
108. One of the grandchildren, William, was truly eccentric. During his five years in India he became convinced that he should order his life by Calcutta time, and did so for the rest of his life – in England. His days became nights and vice-versa. Sanders, *Strachey Family,* p. 211. In the 1850s and 1860s he was a précis writer for the Colonial Office – the 'mysterious and secretive individual' in the 'highly paid sinecure' that Sir William Baillie Hamilton mentioned but refused to name, in his article on the Colonial Office. Hamilton, 'Forty-Four Years', 60.
109. Strachey's Obituary, *The Times* (London) 17 March 1942, p. 6.
110. See Lord Salter's Essay on Anderson, *D.N.B.*, 1951–1960, 23.
111. Grindle's Obituary, *The Times* (London) 7 February 1934, p. 17.
112. Furse, *Aucuparius,* p. 27.

113. Harding's Obituary, *The Times* (London) 22 May 1953, p. 10.
114. Sir Cosmo Parkinson, *The Colonial Office from Within, 1909–1945* (London, [1947]) p. 21.
115. Sydney Olivier and Sidney Webb entered the Colonial Service in the early 1880s. Webb, after a decade in the Colonial Office, decided that the world of the permanent civil servant that he had worked so hard to enter was not for him. He would return to the Colonial Office as Secretary of State in 1929.
116. H. E. Dale, *The Higher Civil Service of Great Britain* (Oxford, 1941) p. 76.
117. Anthony H. M. Kirk-Greene, 'On Governorship and Governors in British Africa', in *African Proconsuls: European Governors in Africa,* ed. by L. H. Gann and Peter Duignan (New York, 1978) p. 224.
118. Sir Charles Bruce, *The Broad Stone of Empire: Problems of Crown Colony Administration,* 2 vols (London, 1910) 1:218–21.
119. Minute by Hamilton, 19 December 1898, on CO 885/7/123, quoted in Kubicek, *Administration of Imperialism,* p. 47.
120. Kubicek, *Administration of imperialism,* p. 45.
121. Bell's Obituary, *The Times* (London) 5 August 1952, p. 4; and Essay on Girouard, *D.N.B.,* 1951–1960, 342.
122. R. B. Joyce, 'Sir William MacGregor – A Colonial Governor', *Historical Studies: Australia and New Zealand,* XI (1963) 18.
123. R. B. Joyce, *Sir William MacGregor* (Melbourne, 1971) p. 7.
124. Margery Perham, *Lugard: The Years of Adventure, 1858–1898* (London, 1956) p. 7.
125. Essay on McCallum, *D.N.B.,* 1931–1940, 342; and see Perham, *Lugard: The Years of Adventure, 1858–1898,* 1:63.
126. Director, Sudan Railways, 1896; President, Egyptian Railways and Telegraph Administration, 1898; Director of Railways, South African Field Force, 1899; and Commissioner of Railways Transvaal and Orange River Colony, 1902.
127. See Lugard to CO, 20 May 1906, CO 446/54/21112.
128. The pattern of diverse backgrounds – social and educational – of these seven Nigerian governors conforms to the findings of Anthony H. M. Kirk-Greene in his wide-ranging study of colonial governors in British Africa. See his 'On Governorship and Governors in British Africa', p. 249.
129. Minute by Butler, 30 June 1902, on Moor to CO (238) 28 May 1902, CO 520/14/25230.
130. Minute by Butler, 14 March 1903, on Moor to CO (38) 19 January 1903, CO 520/18/6334.
131. See Egerton to CO (753) 23 November 1910, CO 520/96/37931.
132. Minute by Fiddes, 28 December 1910, ibid.
133. Minute by Harcourt, 29 December 1910, ibid.
134. Minute by Fiddes, 4 March 1912, on Bell to CO (conf.) 19 December 1911, CO 446/101/1527:11/12. See minutes by John Anderson, Malcolm, Fiddes, and Sir John Anderson on the same file; and see Bell to Harcourt, 4 January 1912, Lewis Harcourt Papers, CO 5/2.
135. 'I have had,' Fiddes said, 'Two other talks with him [Girouard] – to

clear the air and try to convince him that the "permanent officials" . . . are not abnormally obstructive. His tone has been quite pleasant and friendly so far.' Fiddes to Harcourt, 9 December 1910, Lewis Harcourt Papers, CO 6/1.

136. Lugard to Edward Lugard, 3 June 1900, Lugard Papers, s.62/8c.
137. Lugard to Lady Lugard, 13 April 1905, Lugard Papers, quoted in Margery Perham, *Lugard: The Years of Authority, 1898–1945* (London, 1960) p. 194.
138. Minute by Butler, 25 April 1900, on Lugard to CO, 28 February 1900, CO 446/9/12020.
139. Minute by Butler, 9 December 1902, on Lugard to CO (conf.) 4 November 1902, CO 446/25/48672.
140. Minute by Ezechiel, 1 May 1900, on Lugard to CO (61) 28 February 1900, CO 446/9/12029.
141. Perham, *Lugard: The Years of Authority, 1898–1945,* p. 626.
142. Minute by Hamilton, 23 May 1903, on Lugard to CO (conf.) 16 April 1903, CO 446/31/18364.
143. Minutes by Antrobus, 25 May 1903, and Chamberlain, 26 May 1903, ibid.
144. Bruce, *The Broad Stone of Empire,* 1:200. Confidential Memorandum: Administration at Home and Abroad by Lugard, 1907, Lugard Papers, s.65/247.
145. Lugard to Edward Lugard, 29 July 1900, Lugard Papers, s.62/8c. In an earlier and stronger outburst, again to his brother, Lugard said that 'These damned officials make me vomit.' 7 February 1898, ibid, s.59/3. In spite of these comments Lugard would not have been averse to being the top permanent official in the Colonial Office. On one occasion he rather circuitously nominated himself for the position of permanent under secretary. In 1906 he wrote to Lord Elgin that:

> several people have told me that my name, among others, has been mentioned in relation to Sir M. Ommanney's post, which shortly becomes vacant. . . . I have never in my life asked for any post, and it is with some reluctance that I have said as much as I have done. If you cannot utilise me in the direct service of the state I shall hope to contribute in some way. – ibid, s.65/280–1.

146. Minute by Butler, 30 December 1902, on Lugard to CO, 17 November 1902, CO 446/25/52539.
147. Much of the material presented here concerns case studies of conflicts between the Colonial Office and the colonial governors. A state of conflict between the two was not necessarily the natural state of affairs, far from it; none the less it was a very real part of their relationship. Furthermore it is probably not correct to assert, as does Anthony H. M. Kirk-Greene, that 'in every case the balance of power depended upon the determination and character of both the secretary of state and the colonial governors'. A truer assessment, made by Kirk-Greene in the same article, is that 'Given the relative permanence of the colonial office staff and given the power of precedent, the governor was likely to come off second best in any of those rare conflicts between Government House and Whitehall.' One might add that these conflicts very likely

occurred more frequently than he suggests. Anthony H. M. Kirk-Greene, 'On Governorship and Governors in British Africa', p. 230.
148. Lowell, *The Government of England,* 1:81–2.
149. See Richard M. Kesner, 'The Financial Management of the British Empire, 1895–1903: Studies in Treasury–Colonial Office Relations' (Ph.D. diss., Stanford University, 1977) p. 91, where he says 'the Colonial Office decision making process is very similar to that of the Treasury'.
150. Lowell, *The Government of England,* 1:184–5.
151. Sir Reginald Welby to the Royal Commission on Civil Establishments (RCCE) 3 December 1887, attached to 'Royal Commission on Civil Establishments – Second Report', *Parl. Pap.,* 1888 (C. 5545) 444.
152. H. Calcraft to RCCE, 24 February 1888, ibid, 482.
153. Richard Ebden to RCCE, 11 December 1886, ibid, 459.
154. See 'Report of Her Majesty's Civil Service Commissioners; with Appendices: Twenty-Second, 1878', *Parl. Pap.,* 1878, XXVII, v; 'Report of Her Majesty's Civil Service Commissioners; with Appendices, 1895', *Parl. Pap.,* 1895, XXVI (C. 7888) v, vi; and 'Report of His Majesty's Civil Service Commissioners; with Appendices, 1909', *Parl. Pap.,* 1910, CD. 5751, iii–iv.
155. Lowell, *The Government of England,* 1:165.
156. Henry Taylor, *The Statesman* (New York, 1958) p. 32.
157. 'Editorial Notes', *Colonial Office Journal,* 2 (1908) 10, 12.

2 CROWN COLONY GOVERNMENT IN NIGERIA, 1897–1914

1. Sir Charles Bruce, *The Broad Stone of Empire: Problems of Crown Colony Administration,* 2 vols (London, 1910) 1:226.
2. Minute by Strachey, 10 December 1909, on Colonial Office, December 1909, CO 520/520/40542.
3. Bruce, *The Broad Stone of Empire,* 1:226–7.
4. 'Memorandum on British Possessions in West Africa', by H. J. Read, 12 May 1897, CO 879/49/534.
5. Ibid, p. 48.
6. Ibid, p. 33.
7. G. Uzoigue, 'The Niger Committee of 1898; Lord Selborne's Report', *Journal of the Historical Society of Nigeria,* 4 (1968) 472.
8. See Foreign Office to CO (secret) 18 July 1898, CO 537/135/490.
9. 'Report of the Niger Committee', by the Earl of Selborne, 4 August 1898, CO 879/52/550, pp. 284–5.
10. Ibid, p. 285.
11. Ibid.
12. See McCallum to CO, 14 August 1898, CO 879/52-550; and Moor to CO, 18 August 1898, CO 446/3/18809.
13. Minutes by Mercer, 13 October 1899, and Antrobus, 21 October 1899, on Foreign Office to CO, 10 October 1899, CO 446/5/27494.

14. Minute by Antrobus, 19 November 1899, and marginal minute by Chamberlain, n.d. but probably 23 November 1899, on Lugard to CO, 2 November 1899, CO 446/8/30397.
15. 'Memorandum on the Development of Northern Nigeria', by Lugard, and minutes on it by Mercer, 11 November 1899, and Antrobus, 19 November 1899, ibid.
16. Minute by Antrobus, 30 June 1898, on Foreign Office to CO (secret) 25 June 1898, CO 537/135/476.
17. Minute by Antrobus, 19 November 1899, on Lugard to CO, 2 November 1899, CO 446/8/30397.
18. Minute by Antrobus, 21 October 1899, on Foreign Office to CO, 10 October 1899, CO 446/5/27494.
19. Minute by Antrobus, 8 February 1899, on Lugard to CO (secret) 8 February 1899, CO 537/11/519.
20. Minutes by Antrobus, 13 November 1898 and 6 April 1899, Wingfield, 28 November 1899, Selborne, 10 April 1899, and Chamberlain, 10 April 1899, on Colonial Office, 13 November 1898, CO 446/3/25517.
21. When the Niger Committee met, Lugard had not yet been appointed High Commissioner. But even before it was set up, Antrobus had recommended Lugard for the job. 'If Col. Lugard is to be the first Gov. or Commr. for the Niger Territories (and I think that he will be quite the best man that we could get for the purpose), I would suggest that he should be directed to come and consult with us.' Minute by Antrobus, 11 July 1898, on Foreign Office to CO (secret), 25 June 1898, CO 537/135/476. The actual offer was made to Lugard when he was a house guest of Chamberlain's in late October 1899. Margery Perham, *Lugard: The Years of Authority, 1898–1945* (London, 1960) pp. 5–7.
22. For the full story of the conquest, see Obaro Ikime, *The Fall of Nigeria; The British Conquest* (London, 1977).
23. Moor to CO, 9 September 1899, CO 444/2/27400.
24. Minutes by Strachey, 11 October 1899, Mercer, 16 October 1899, and Chamberlain, 9 November, 1899, ibid.
25. Goldie to CO, 17 November 1899, CO 444/4/31980.
26. Lugard to CO, 20 November 1899, CO 444/4/43469.
27. Minute by Antrobus, 9 May 1900, on Moor to CO (79) 23 March 1900, CO 520/1/11979.
28. Minute by Mercer, 8 June 1900, on Moor to CO, 5 June 1900, CO 520/6/17764.
29. Minutes by Antrobus, 24 June 1900, and Chamberlain, 26 June 1900, ibid.
30. Minute by Baillie Hamilton, 25 August 1900, on Acting Governor Gallway to CO (201) 19 July 1900, CO 520/2/27049.
31. Minute by Antrobus, 29 September 1900, on Acting High Commissioner Gallway to CO (128) 3 August 1900, CO 520/2/28599.
32. Minutes by Strachey, 22 July 1901, Baillie Hamilton, 24 July 1901, Antrobus, 26 July 1901, and Chamberlain, 29 July 1901, on Moor to CO, 25 June 1901, CO 520/8/24954.
33. Minute by Butler, 3 August 1901, on Acting Governor Probyn to CO (200) 6 July 1901, CO 520/8/26747.

34. Minutes by Butler, 31 March 1902, and Chamberlain, 9 April 1902, on Moor to CO (tel. 22) 30 March 1902, CO 520/13/12454.
35. See Egerton's 'Memorandum', 7 October 1909, attached to Egerton to CO, 8 October 1909, CO 520/82/35419.
36. Minute by Churchill, 30 January 1906, on Acting High Commissioner Thorburn to CO (conf.) 9 December 1905, CO 520/32/353:05/06.
37. Minute by Butler, 9 August 1908, on Egerton to CO, 22 June 1908, CO 520/52/24798. Butler noted this in a minute that was strongly reminiscent of the 1864 Russian Foreign Minister's circular to the Great Powers explaining Russia's need to expand in central Asia. Butler's explanation and justification of British pacification and occupation policies in Southern Nigeria was that: .

> It is difficult to stop when once we have started. The natives on the fringe of the new area controlled expect to be protected against their neighbours outside the pale. If they are not protected, or if their neighbours are not required to submit to law and order, they are unable to believe that the halt in the advance is due to anything but fear or weakness. When they once come to believe that, a very large portion of the work is spoiled.

Hopwood put it differently when he said that they had to allow the pacification patrols to continue, especially against unpacified tribes that were raiding the peaceful ones, because 'we took from the raided the means of defence against the raiders'. Minute by Hopwood, 29 July 1907, on Egerton to CO, 10 July 1907, CO 520/56/24251. The Russian Foreign Minister Gorchakov explained how Russian expansion had been forced upon the nations:

> The position of Russia in Central Asia is that of all civilised states which come into contact with half-savage wandering tribes possessing no fixed social organization.
>
> It invariably happens in such cases that the interests of security on the frontier, and of commercial relations, compel the more civilised state to exercise a certain ascendancy over neighbours whose turbulence and nomad instincts render them difficult to live with.
>
> In order to cut short these perpetual disorders we established strong places in the midst of a hostile population, and thus we obtained an ascendancy which shortly but surely reduced them to a more or less willing submission. But beyond this line there are other tribes which soon provoked the same dangers, the same repression. The state then finds itself on the horns of a dilemma. It must abandon the incessant struggle and deliver its frontier over to disorder, which renders property, security and civilisation impossible; or it must plunge into the depths of savage countries, where the difficulties and sacrifices to which it is exposed increase with each step in advance. Such has been the lot of all countries placed in the same conditions. The United States in America, France in Algiers, Holland in her colonies, England in India, – all have been invariably drawn into a course wherein ambition plays a smaller part than imperious necessity, and where the greatest difficulty is in knowing where to stop.

Excerpts from Prince Gorchakov's memorandum, dated St Petersburg, 21 November 1864, quoted in W. K. Fraser-Tyler's *Afghanistan* (London, 1967) pp. 333–7.

38. See John E. Flint, 'Frederick Lugard: The Making of an Autocrat', in *African Proconsuls: European Governors in africa,* ed. by L. H. Gann and Peter Duignan (New York, 1978) pp. 290–312.

39. Minute by Butler, 17 December 1901, on Director-General of Military Intelligence to CO, 12 December 1901, CO 446/19/44044.

40. Minute by Antrobus, 9 February 1899, on Lugard to CO, 8 February 1899, CO 537/11/519.

41. Antrobus, prior to Lugard's going out to Northern Nigeria, said that 'I am afraid . . . that strong pressure will be put on Col. Lugard by the military element to undertake expeditions which are not really necessary, and it will help him to resist the pressure if we say something about it.' Minute by Antrobus, 27 October 1899, on Foreign Office to CO, 10 October 1899, CO 446/5/27494.

42. Minute by Butler, 21 November 1901, on Acting High Commissioner Wallace to CO, 13 August 1901, CO 446/16/34435.

43. Minute by Antrobus, 9 February 1899, on Lugard to CO, 8 February 1899, CO 537/11/519.

44. Minute by Antrobus, 3 April 1903, on Treas. to CO, 2 April 1903, CO 446/35/12433.

45. Minute by Butler, 16 December 1902, on Lugard to CO (tel. 124) 12 December 1902, CO 446/26/51465.

46. Minute by Antrobus, 1 March 1901, on Lugard to CO (tel.) 17 February 1901, CO 446/14/6744.

47. Minute by Antrobus, 25 February 1902, on Director-General of Military Intelligence to CO, 15 February 1902, CO 445/28/7121.

48. Reginald Popham-Lobb to his mother, 27 April 1902, Lugard Papers, s.64, 23.

49. Perham, *Lugard: The Years of Authority,* p. 96.

50. Perham, *Lugard: The Years of Authority,* p. 99; and minute by Antrobus, 24 December 1902, on J. A. Hutton to CO (tel.) 24 December 1902, CO 446/29/52870.

51. Minute by Ommanney, 27 December 1902, on Lugard to CO (tel. 127) 23 December 1902, CO 446/26/52960.

52. Minute by Ommanney, 17 December 1902, on Lugard to CO (tel. 124) 12 December 1902, CO 446/26/51465.

53. Minute by Butler, 16 December 1902, on Lugard to CO (tel. 124) 12 December 1902, CO 446/26/51465. For Lugard's despatch in which the vague references to his forthcoming campaign appeared, see Lugard to CO (conf.) 12 December 1902, CO 446/26/2674. On it note Antrobus's minute of 21 January 1902: 'there were only incidental allusions to Sokoto and Kano in the five despatches to which he refers . . . and there is no foundation for the suggestion that we ought to have taken up those references and replied to them'.

54. Minute by Ommanney, 27 December 1902, on Lugard to CO (tel. 127) 23 December 1902, CO 446/26/52960.

55. Minute by Antrobus, 11 March 1903, on Lugard to CO (conf.) 23 January 1903, CO 446/30/8286.
56. Minute by Antrobus, 1 January 1903, on Chamberlain to CO, 28 December 1902, CO 446/29/53142.
57. See final draft of telegram attached to Lugard to CO (tel.) 4 January 1903, CO 446/30/863. It was sent on the 8th.
58. Lugard to CO, 12 December 1902, 446/26/2674.
59. Minute by Ommanney, 26 May 1903, on Lugard to CO (conf.) 17 April 1903, CO 446/31/18355.
60. Excerpted from Lugard's 1902 Annual Report and quoted in Perham, *Lugard: The Years of Authority*, p. 92.
61. Minute by Chamberlain, 26 May 1903, on Lugard to CO (tel.) 19 January 1906, CO 446/52/2224. The reader wishing to learn more of this story from a general, as opposed to the Colonial Office, perspective presented here, should read D. J. M. Muffet's *Concerning Brave Captains* (London, 1964). He also argues that Lugard was guilty of rather precipitately jumping the gun in his attack on Kano.
62. Minutes by Churchill, 23 January 1906, and Elgin, 27 January 1906, on Lugard to CO (tel.) 19 January 1906, CO 446/52/2224.
63. Lugard to Lady Lugard, 28 January 1906, Lugard Papers, quoted in Perham, *Lugard: The Years of Authority*, pp. 250–1.
64. Minutes by Olivier, 30 January 1906, and Elgin, n.d., on Lugard to CO (tel. 11) 29 January 1906, CO 446/52/3443.
65. See Acting High Commissioner Wallace to CO, 31 March 1908, CO 446/72/15260; and Ikime, *The Fall of Nigeria*, p. 176.
66. Minute by Butler, 16 December 1902, on Lugard to CO (tel. 124) 12 December 1902, CO 446/26/51465.
67. Minute by Ommanney, 17 July 1906, on Lugard to CO, 9 July 1906, CO 446/59/24992.
68. Minute by Fiddes, 4 December 1911, on Bell to CO (799) 31 October 1911, CO 446/100/38057.
69. See her article, 'Indirect Rule in Northern Nigeria, 1906–1911', in *Essays in Imperial Government*, ed. by Kenneth Robinson and Frederick Madden (Oxford, 1963).
70. Michael Crowder, *West Africa Under Colonial Rule* (London, 1968) p. 169.
71. Quoted in Perham, *Lugard: The Years of Authority*, p. 140.
72. Ibid, p. 149.
73. See Minute by Antrobus, 13 November 1899, on Treas. to CO, 2 November 1899, CO 446/6/30313; and another Minute by Antrobus, 22 July 1905, on Lugard to CO (197a) 26 April 1905, CO 446/45/18383.
74. A. H. M. Kirk-Greene (ed.), *The Principles of Native Administration in Nigeria: Selected Documents, 1900–1947* (London, 1965) p. 43.
75. Ibid, p. 6.
76. Perham, *Lugard: The Years of Authority*, p. 149.
77. Minute by Antrobus, 13 November 1899, on Treasury to CO, 2 November 1899, CO 446/6/30313.
78. Minute by Olivier, 21 September 1905, on Lugard to CO, 23 August 1908, CO 446/50/30774.

79. Perham, *Lugard: The Years of Authority,* p. 473.
80. Ibid, p. 476.
81. Kirk-Greene, *Principles of Native Administration,* pp. 10–11.
82. C. L. Temple, *Native Races and Their Rulers* (Cape Town, 1918) pp. 67–8.
83. Ibid, p. 64.
84. Bull, 'Indirect Rule', p. 67.
85. Perham, *Lugard: The Years of Authority,* pp. 70–72.
86. That the Native Treasury system was quickly copied by other Residents can be seen in the Northern Nigerian Governor's annual report to the Colonial Office for 1910–11. The Governor informed the Secretary of State that a Native Treasury had been established, or was in the process of being established, in every Northern Nigerian state. See *Colonial Reports – Annual: Northern Nigeria,* 1910–11, pp. 3–4. That the Residents realised their power would be greatly enhanced by being in control of the Native Treasury is made clear by Mary Bull in 'Indirect Rule', pp. 67–8.
87. Minute by Harding, 24 May 1912, on Acting Governor Goldsmith to CO, 27 April 1912, CO 446/104/15541.
88. Minute by Strachey, 5 February 1913, on Lugard to CO (742) 27 November 1912, CO 446/107/39706.
89. Minute by Harding, 4 July 1912, on Acting Governor Temple to CO (374) 8 June 1912, CO 446/105/20249. See also Harding's minute of 9 May 1913, on D. Neasham to CO, 6 May 1913, CO 446/114/15506, in which he commented on a Church Missionary Society accusation, false as it turned out, that the government of Northern Nigeria had adopted a pro-Islamic policy. 'The statement,' wrote Harding,

> that 'gov't. subscribes to the building and repairing of mosques' is an illustration of what we may expect if Sir F. Lugard's proposals to incorporate the revenue and expenditure of the Native Governments in the Protectorate Estimates and Accounts are allowed. I pointed out this danger in my minute . . . [of 4 July 1912]. . . . [T]he Native Gov'ts. spend various sums on upkeep and repairs of mosques – and it is quite proper that they should – but it is only while Native Expenditure is kept quite separate from Protectorate Expenditure that the S. of S. or the Prot. Gov't. can deny such a statement as that made by the CMS.

90. Minute by Harding, 17 January 1913, on Lugard to CO (742) 27 November 1912, CO 446/107/39706.
91. Minute by Strachey, 5 February 1913, ibid.
92. Lugard to CO (conf.) 23 March 1913, CO 446/111/13658, and Strachey's minute on it of 16 June 1913.
93. Minute by Fiddes, 6 February 1913, on Lugard to CO (742) 27 November 1912, CO 446/107/39706.
94. Lugard to CO (conf.), 23 March 1912, CO 446/111/13658.
95. Minute by Harding, 27 May 1913, ibid.
96. Minutes by Strachey, 14 June 1913, and Sir John Anderson, 14 June 1913, ibid.

97. Minute by Sir John Anderson, 14 June 1913, ibid. Also see Harding's draft despatch to Lugard attached to this file.
98. Perham, *Lugard: The Years of Authority,* p. 480.
99. Strachey to Harding, 12 January 1914, attached to Lugard to CO (319) 24 December 1913, CO 583/7/1314:13/14.
100. Minutes by Fiddes, 23 April 1914, Sir John Anderson, 23 April 1914, and Harcourt, 23 April 1914, on Lugard to CO (conf.) 22 March 1914, CO 583/12/13496.
101. For the details of this story after 1914, see Perham, *Lugard: The Years of Authority,* pp. 482–8.
102. Minute by Strachey, 5 February 1913, on Lugard to CO (742) 27 November 1912, CO 446/107/39706.
103. Flint, 'The Making of an Autocrat', p. 309.
104. Minutes by Antrobus, 25 August 1898 and 22 July 1900, and Ezechiel, 26 March 1900, on Moor to CO, 18 August 1898, CO 446/3/18809.
105. 'Amalgamation of Southern Nigeria and Lagos', by Antrobus, 8 June 1904, and see Ommanney's minute of 10 June 1904, on Colonial Office, CO 520/27/21004.
106. See Egerton's amalgamation despatch, 29 January 1905, CO 520/29/5453.
107. Minutes by Ommanney, 14 July 1905, and Antrobus, 8 July 1905, ibid.
108. I. F. Nicolson, *The Administration of Nigeria, 1900–1960: Men, Methods, and Myths* (Oxford, 1969) p. 103.
109. Minute by Antrobus, 1 January 1906, on Egerton to CO (conf.) 29 January 1905, CO 520/29/5453.
110. The details of the various schemes to amalgamate Southern and Northern Nigeria may conveniently be found in A. H. M. Kirk-Greene's *Lugard and the Amalgamation of Nigeria: A Documentary Record* (London, 1968). His forty-four-page Introduction is an excellent general account of how Lugard's amalgamation plan was shaped and implemented. One noteworthy aspect is Kirk-Greene's pioneering treatment of the Nigerian reaction, mainly through the Lagos press, to amalgamation.
111. Minute by Antrobus, 26 October 1902, on Lugard to CO (438) 28 August 1902, CO 446/24/40550.
112. See 'Administration of Tropical Africa', by Lugard, CO 879/88/789, pp. 5–6.
113. See Antrobus's minute of 3 August 1906, on Lugard to CO (conf.) 20 May 1906, CO 446/54/21112. See also the final draft of the letter – by Antrobus on verbal directions – to Girouard offering him the High Commissionership, dated 22 December 1906 and attached to this file. When it became clear that amalgamation would not take place for another two years (at least), it was decided that Girouard would be allowed another tour of duty to continue his work on the Baro–Kano Railway. Minutes by Antrobus, 27 December 1907, and Elgin, 27 November 1907, on Girouard to CO (conf.) 24 October 1907, CO 446/65/41063.
114. Minute by Fiddes, 21 September 1909, on House of Commons, Question by Mr. L. Harris, 20 September 1909, CO 520/86/31372.

115. Minute by Fiddes, 27 January 1911, on Bell to CO (conf.) 19 December 1910, CO 446/92/1637:10/11.
116. 'Amalgamation of Northern and Southern Nigeria: Financial Questions', by Strachey, 30 November 1911, and minutes on it by Fiddes, 13 December 1911, and Harcourt, 17 December 1911, Colonial Office, CO 520/110/38852. Strachey brought the memorandum up to date with a short minute on 11 December 1911. In explaining why he wrote it, Strachey said that he had begun a memorandum on the general subject of amalgamation, but before getting very far with it 'I came to the conclusion that the Financial side of the question was so important that it was not of much use discussing the matter generally . . . before some conclusions could be arrived at with regard to the financial outlook.' Minute by Strachey, 1 December 1911, on Bell to CO (conf.) 30 August 1911, CO 446/99/31917.
117. Minute by Sir John Anderson, 3 June 1912, on Lugard to CO (conf. 2) 12 May 1912, CO 520/121/15142. The letter was sent to the Treasury 27 June 1912.
118. Treasury to CO, 23 July 1912, CO 520/119/23230; and see Minute by Strachey, 7 April 1913, on Treas. to CO, 12 October 1912, CO 520/119/32362.
119. Robert V. Kubicek, *The Administration of Imperialism: Joseph Chamberlain at the Colonial Office* (Durham, N.C., 1969) pp. 142–4, 149–50.
120. 'Amalgamation of Northern and Southern Nigeria: Financial Questions', by Strachey, 30 November 1911, Colonial Office, CO 520/110/38852.
121. Sir John Anderson to Lugard (private and personal) 17 August 1911, Lugard Papers, s.73/3.
122. Harcourt to Lugard (private and personal) 12 September 1911, ibid, s. 73/5.
123. Lugard to Sir John Anderson 22 December 1911, ibid, s.73/20.
124. Great Britain *Parliamentary Debates* (Commons) 5th ser., 40 (27 June 1912): 512–13.
125. For the plan in its entirety, see Lugard to CO (conf.) 9 May 1912, CO 583/3/16460.
126. John E. Flint, 'Nigeria: The Colonial Experience from 1880 to 1914', in *Colonialism in Africa*, vol. 2: *The History and Politics of Colonialism in Africa, 1870–1914*, ed. by L. H. Gann and Peter Duignan (Cambridge, 1969) p. 258.
127. Minutes by Strachey, 21 June 1913, and Fiddes, 27 June 1913, on Lugard to CO (conf.) 9 May 1913, CO 583/3/16460.
128. Minute by Sir John Anderson, 15 November 1913, on Lugard to CO (conf.) 25 October 1913, CO 583/5/39208.
129. Flint, 'Nigeria: The Colonial Experience', p. 255.
130. Minute by Harding, 16 June 1913, on Lugard to CO (conf.) 9 May 1913, CO 583/3/16460.
131. Permanent officials believed that the person most immediately relevant to colonial administration was the Officer Acting as Governor, whether Governor or Acting Governor. See Antrobus's minute of 17 March

1899, on Foreign Office to CO, 14 March 1899, CO 537/135/523, where he said, 'I think that our representative on the spot is the officer who should primarily be kept informed of everything, and that a Governor or Commissioner on leave should only be informed of such things as it is necessary for him to know while in England.'

132. This was submitted on Lugard to CO, 11 August 1905, CO 446/50/25244. Strachey exhaustively minuted it. Afterwards his minutes (called 'Colonial Office Comments') and the memorandum were printed in the CO 879 series as CO 879/88/789. I have used this to quote excerpts from the memorandum and Strachey's minutes.

As early as 1901 Lugard had already shown his desire to keep his hand in – whether in or out of his colony. In that year, while on leave from Northern Nigeria and in transit to England, he continued to write despatches from the ship. Butler thought this 'tiresome' and suggested that Lugard be told that once he left Northern Nigeria he was no longer in charge. Minute by Butler, 13 May 1901, on Lugard to CO, 9 April 1901, CO 446/15/14958. The hint was given but did not, as was evident over the next sixteen years, have its intended effect.

133. 'Administration of Tropical Africa', by Lugard, 11 July 1905, CO 879/88/789, p. 10.
134. Ibid, p. 12.
135. Minute by Ommanney, 31 January 1905, on Lugard to CO, 11 July 1905, CO 446/50/25244.
136. Minute by Strachey, 25 July 1905, on Lugard to CO, 11 July 1905, CO 879/88/789.
137. Minute by Olivier, 25 July 1905, on Lugard to CO, 11 July 1905, CO 446/50/25244.
138. Lugard to Lyttelton, 16 July 1905, Lyttelton Papers, Churchill College Archives, Cambridge University.
139. Perham, *Lugard: The Years of Authority, 1898–1945*, p. 234.
140. Minute by Lyttelton, 25 September 1905, on Lugard to CO, 11 July 1905, CO 446/50/25244.
141. *The Times* (London) 5 December 1905, p. 14.
142. Minute by Antrobus, 28 January 1906, on Sir Charles Bruce to CO, 8 December 1905, CO 446/50/43564.
143. Reginald Popham-Lobb to Lady Lugard, 1 February 1906, Lugard Papers, s.65/144–45. Popham-Lobb was Lady Lugard's informant at the CO during these critical weeks, and is the source of the information that Antrobus, supported by Ommanney and Churchill, led the fight against the scheme. He had served in Northern Nigeria as Lugard's Private Secretary and then in the Political Department from 1900 to 1905. On 1 January 1906 he was attached to the Colonial Office as a (temporary) Junior Clerk. See *Colonial Office List,* 1907, 562. In letters to Lady Lugard he referred to her husband as the 'Chief'. His loyalty to Lugard seemed to have overshadowed that which one might have expected him to feel for the Colonial Office. However, when Lady Lugard used Popham-Lobb's confidential information to persuade Lyttelton to influence Elgin in favour of the scheme she got a sharp response. Her informant, Lyttelton said, was 'committing a very serious breach of

confidence in letting anyone outside the office know of these things'. He could not make use of information obtained in this way. Lyttelton to Lady Lugard, 7 February 1906, Lugard Papers, s.65/102–13.

144. Minute by Lugard, 28 January 1906, on Sir Charles Bruce to CO, 8 December 1905, CO 446/50/43564.
145. Minute by Churchill, 30 January 1906, on Lugard to CO, 11 July 1905, CO 446/50/25244.
146. Minute by Ommanney, 30 January 1906, on Sir Charles Bruce to CO, 8 December 1905, CO 446/50/43564.
147. Minute by Ommanney, 31 January 1906, on Lugard to CO, 11 July 1905, CO 446/50/25244.
148. The final draft of the despatch rejecting Lugard's scheme is attached to Sir Charles Bruce to CO, 8 December 1905, CO 446/50/43564. For Antrobus's private note see Antrobus to Lugard, 9 March 1906, Lugard Papers, s.65/174.
149. Perham, *Lugard: The Years of Authority, 1898–1945*, p. 280.
150. Crewe to Hopwood, 22 July 1910, Southborough Papers.
151. Hopwood to Crewe, 15 August 1910, Crewe Papers, C/47.
152. Harcourt to Lugard (private and personal) 12 September 1911, Lugard Papers, s.73/5.
153. Lugard to Sir John Anderson, 10 October 1911, Lugard Papers, s.73/7.
154. Sir John Anderson to Lugard, 9 November 1911, Lugard Papers, s.73/14–15; Lugard to Sir John Anderson, 22 December 1911, Lugard Papers, s.73/20; and see also Perham, *Lugard: The Years of Authority, 1898–1945*, pp. 365–6.
155. Sir John Kirk to Lady Lugard, 5 February 1905, Lugard Papers, s.65/157.
156. Minutes by Strachey, 21 June 1913, and Fiddes, 27 June 1913, on Lugard to CO (conf.) 9 May 1913, CO 583/3/16460.
157. Minute by Harding, 3 March 1913, on Lugard to CO (tel.) 3 March 1913, CO 583/2/7407.
158. Minute by Baynes, 12 September 1913, on Lugard to CO (conf. A) 8 September 1913, CO 583/5/31369.
159. Minutes by Sir John Anderson, 16 January 1914, and Harcourt, 16 January 1914, on Lugard to CO (342) 2 December 1913, CO 446/114/44579.
160. See officials' minutes on Lugard to CO (conf.) 9 May 1913, CO 583/3/16464.
161. Minute by Harding, 4 September 1913, on Lugard to CO (258) 11 August 1913, CO 446/113/28138.
162. Minute by Harcourt, 30 August 1913, on Lugard to CO (conf.) 9 May 1913, CO 583/3/16464.
163. Minutes by Harding, 24 February 1914, Fiddes, 24 February 1914, Sir John Anderson, 25 February 1914, and Harcourt, 25 February 1913, on Lugard to CO (personal and confidential) 4 February 1914, CO 583/10/6863.
164. Perham, *Lugard: The Years of Authority*, pp. 633–4.
165. See Antrobus's draft of Elgin to Lugard, sent 9 March 1906, and

attached to Sir Charles Bruce to CO, 8 December 1905, CO 446/50/43564.
166. Minute by Antrobus, 28 January 1906, on Sir Charles Bruce to CO, 8 December 1905, CO 446/50/43564.

3 PUBLIC EXPENDITURE AND DEVELOPMENT IN SOUTHERN NIGERIA, 1900–12

1. Great Britain, *Parliamentary Debates* (Commons) 4th ser., 36 (22 August 1895): 640–44.
2. Earl Grey, *The Colonial Policy of Lord John Russell's Administration*, 2 vols (reprint edn: New York, 1970) 2:281.
3. Ronald Robinson and John Gallagher with Alice Denny, *Africa and the Victorians: The Official Mind of Imperialism* (London, 1961) p. 427.
4. Robert V. Kubicek, *The Administration of Imperialism: Joseph Chamberlain at the Colonial Office* (Durham, N.C., 1969) p. 175.
5. Minute by R. L. Antrobus, 16 November 1905, on Sir Frederick Lugard to Colonial Office (CO) 11 November 1905, CO 446/51/40319.
6. These dates refer to the Colonial Development Act of 1929, and the Colonial Development and Welfare Act of 1940.
7. Four such historians and their works are as follows: R. E. Dumett, 'Joseph Chamberlain, Imperial Finance, and Railway Policy in British West Africa in the late Nineteenth Century', *English Historical Review*, 90 (1975); Ronald Hyam, *Elgin and Churchill at the Colonial Office, 1905–1908: The Watershed of the Empire-Commonwealth* (London, 1968); Richard Kesner, *Economic Control and Colonial Development: Crown Colony Financial Management in the Age of Joseph Chamberlain* (Westport, Conn., 1981); and Kubicek, *Administration of Imperialism*.
8. Another facet of this general topic has to do with financing railways to advance development in Nigeria. The financial side of the Nigerian railway question concerns how money was raised, not spent: the reverse is true in this chapter. Here I am interested in showing the processes by which budgetary decisions were made about how to spend money for development. Within this context I have also been able to focus on the attitudes and assumptions on which permanent officials based their policy recommendations. For analyses of the Colonial Office and the formation and implementation of a railway policy in Nigeria, see Chapters 5 and 6 in this book.
9. See S. B. Saul, 'The Economic Significance of "Constructive Imperialism', *Journal of Economic History*, 17 (1957) 188; Hyam, *Elgin and Churchill at the Colonial Office*, p. 469; Anthony Hopkins, *An Economic History of West Africa* (New York, 1973) p. 190; Bernard Porter, *The Lion's Share: A Short History of British Imperialism, 1850–1970* (London and New York, 1975) p. 190; and Ronald Robinson, 'Sir Andrew Cohen: Proconsul of African Nationalism 1909–1968', in *African Proconsuls: European Governors in Africa*, ed. by L. H. Gann and Peter Duignan (New York, 1978) p. 356.

10. John E. Flint, 'Nigeria: The Colonial Experience from 1880 to 1914', in L. H. Gann and Peter Duignan (eds), *Colonialism in Africa, 1870–1960*, 5 vols (Cambridge, 1969) 1:243.
11. Minute by Antrobus, 4 April 1907, on Sir Walter Egerton to CO, 5 January 1907, CO 520/43/2743.
12. Minute by Antrobus, 24 May 1904, on Acting Governor Moseley to CO (120) 17 March 1904, CO 147/170/12726; and minute by Antrobus, 16 November 1905, on Lugard to CO, 11 November 1905, CO 446/51/40319.
13. Minute by Charles Strachey, 22 March 1905; on Egerton to CO (55) 18 February 1905, CO 520/29/7694.
14. Kesner, 'Treasury–Colonial Office Relations', p. 63.
15. Minute by Antrobus, 29 April 1901, on Sir Ralph Moor to CO, 5 March 1901, CO 520/17/11616.
16. Minute by Frederick Butler, 12 December 1908, on Egerton to CO (763) 20 November 1908, CO 520/67/45278.
17. See Harry Gailey, *Sir Donald Cameron: Colonial Governor* (Stanford, 1974) p. 13; and T. N. Tamuno, *The Evolution of the Nigerian State: The Southern Phase, 1898–1914* (London, 1972) p. 248.
18. Frank Swettenham, *British Malaya* (London, 1920) p. 300.
19. Egerton to CO (763) 20 November 1908, CO 520/67/45278.
20. Egerton, Address to the Legislative Council of the Protectorate of Southern Nigeria, n.d., *Government Gazette of the Protectorate of Southern Nigeria*, 26 December 1906, Old Calabar.
21. Egerton, Address to the Southern Nigeria Legislative Council (hereafter cited as SNLC) 27 September 1909, *Southern Nigeria Government Gazette* (hereafter cited as SNGG) 6 October 1909, p. 1380.
22. Minute by Strachey, 22 March 1905, on Egerton to CO (55) 18 February 1905, CO 520/29/6794.
23. In 1907, with the amalgamation of Lagos Colony and Southern Nigeria completed, the fiscal year and calendar year became the same. From this point we can talk about estimates for 1907, 1908, etc.
24. Minutes by Strachey, 30 March 1907, Antrobus, 4 April 1907, and draft despatch by Robinson, 19 April 1907, on Egerton to CO (3) 5 January 1907, CO 520/43/2743.
25. Egerton, Address to the Legislative Council of the protectorate of Southern Nigeria, n.d., *Government Gazette of the Protectorate of Southern Nigeria*, 26 December 1906, J. P. Smartt, Acting Financial Commissioner, *Southern Nigeria: Financial Report for the Year Ended 31 December 1907*, 14 July 1908, p. 17.
26. Minute by Strachey, 17 June 1907, on Acting Governor Thorburn to CO (271) 21 May 1907, CO 520/46/20334.
27. Smartt, *Southern Nigeria: Financial Report for . . . 1907*, 14 July 1908, p. 21.
28. Minutes by John Anderson, 1 February 1908, and Antrobus, 1 February 1908, on Egerton to CO (669) 29 November 1907, CO 520/50/44370.
29. *Colonial Reports – Annual: Southern Nigeria*, 1908, p. 5.
30. Egerton to CO (669) 29 November 1907, CO 520/50/44370.
31. Egerton to CO (669) 6 October 1908, CO 520/66/38979.

32. Ibid.
33. Minutes by John Anderson, 17 September 1908, Butler, 18 September 1908, and Strachey, 24 September 1908, on Egerton to CO (559) 23 August 1908, CO 520/64/33251.
34. Egerton, Address to the SNLC, 29 September 1909, SNGG, 6 October 1909, p. 1380.
35. Egerton, Address to the SNLC, 29 September 1908, SNGG, 28 October 1908, p. 1544.
36. Minutes by John Anderson, 1 December 1908, and Butler, 1 December 1908, and Antrobus, 26 December 1908, on Egerton to CO (669) 6 October 1908, CO 520/66/38979.
37. Minute by John Anderson, 17 September 1908, on Egerton to CO (559) 23 August 1908, CO 520/64/33251.
38. Ibid.
39. Minute by John Anderson, 3 December 1909, on Egerton to CO, 16 October 1909, CO 520/82/36310.
40. Egerton to CO, 16 October 1909, CO 520/82/36310.
41. Egerton, Address to the SNLC, 29 September 1909, SNGG, 6 October 1909, p. 1381.
42. Minute by Butler, 18 September 1908, on Egerton to CO (559) 23 August 1908, CO 520/64/33251.
43. Minute by R. Geikie, 21 August 1909, on Crown Agents to CO, 18 August 1909, CO 520/85/27719.
44. Minute by Butler, 12 December 1908, on Egerton to CO (763) 20 November 1908, CO 520/67/45278.
45. Minutes by John Anderson, 3 December 1909, Strachey, 16 December 1909, and Lord Crewe (Secretary of State) 21 December 1909, on Egerton to CO (555) 16 October 1909, CO 520/82/36310. Also see Crewe's despatch of 31 January 1910 to Egerton which is attached to this file.
46. See minutes by John Anderson, 23 July 1910, G. V. Fiddes, 29 July 1910, and Lord Crewe, 29 July 1910, on Egerton to CO (346) 6 June 1910, CO 620/94/19336.
47. *Colonial Reports – Annual: Southern Nigeria*, 1910, p. 5.
48. Egerton, Address to the SNLC, 18 October 1910, SNGG, 9 November 1910, p. 1784.
49. Minutes by John Anderson, 13 December 1910, and Fiddes, 30 December 1910, on Acting Governor Thorburn to CO (704) 26 October 1910, CO 520/95/35394.
50. Egerton to CO (683) 15 November 1911, CO 520/107/38994.
51. Minute by John Anderson, 9 December 1911, ibid.
52. Minutes by John Anderson, 9 December 1911, Strachey, 11 December 1911, Fiddes, 13 December 1911, Sir John Anderson, 14 December 1911, and Lewis Harcourt (Secretary of State) 17 December 1911, ibid.
53. Italics mine. Egerton to CO (tel.) 24 December 1911, CO 520/108/41275.
54. Minute by John Anderson, 9 December 1911, on Egerton to CO (683) 15 November 1911, CO 520/107/38994. Anderson states twice in this minute that 1908 was a deficit year. It was not. See *Colonial Reports – Annual:*

Southern Nigeria, 1908, p. 6; and Anderson's memorandum attached to Egerton to CO (tel.) 17 May 1911, CO 520/103/16257.
55. Minutes by John Anderson, 27 December 1910, and Fiddes, 29 December 1910, on Egerton to CO (tel.) 24 December 1911, CO 520/108/41275.
56. Source: Statistical Statement relative to the Revenue, Expenditure, and Trade of Southern Nigeria from 1900 to 1910, prepared by John Anderson, 17 May 1911, and attached to file on Gov. Egerton to CO (tel.) 17 May 1911, CO 520/103/16257; and *Colonial Reports – Annual: Southern Nigeria,* 1907–1912.
57. Minutes by John Anderson, 13 February 1912, and Fiddes, 16 February 1912, on Egerton to CO (26) 15 January 1912, CO 520/113/3629.
58. Source: *Colonial Reports – Annual: Southern Nigeria,* 1906–1912.
59. Malcolm's draft, dated 5 March 1912, is attached to the file of Egerton to CO (26) 15 January 1912, CO 520/113/3639.
60. Quoted in Alan McPhee, *The Economic Revolution in British West Africa* (1926, reprint edn, London, 1971) p. 214.
61. Sir Edward Bridges, 'Treasury Control', *The Stamp Memorial Lecture* (London, 1950) p. 6.
62. Robinson, 'Sir Andrew Cohen', p. 356; Hopkins, *Economic History of West Africa,* p. 190.

4 BUDGETARY CONFLICT OVER REVENUE ESTIMATES IN NORTHERN NIGERIA, 1899–1913

1. A few recent works that contribute to the debate are: R. E. Dumett, 'Joseph Chamberlain, Imperial Finance, and Railway Policy in British West Africa in the Late Nineteenth Century', *English Historical Review,* 90 (1975); and Richard M. Kesner, *Economic Control and Colonial Development: Crown Colony Financial Management in the Age of Joseph Chamberlain* (Westport, Conn., 1981).
2. Ann M. Burton, 'Treasury Control and Colonial Policy in the Late Nineteenth Century', *Public Administration,* XLIV (1966) 171, 173.
3. See S. B. Saul, 'The Economic Significance of "Constructive Imperialism" ', *Journal of Economic History,* 17 (1957) 188; Ronald Hyam, *Elgin and Churchill at the Colonial Office, 1905–1908: The Watershed of the Empire-Commonwealth* (London, 1968) p. 469; Anthony Hopkins, *An Economic History of West Africa* (New York, 1973) p. 190; Bernard Porter, *The Lion's Share: A Short History of British Imperialism, 1850–1970* (London and New York, 1975) p. 190; and Ronald Robinson, 'Sir Andrew Cohen: Proconsul of African Nationalism, 1906–1968', in *African Proconsuls: European Governors in Africa,* ed. by L. H. Gann and Peter Duignan (New York, 1978) p. 356.
4. Although this chapter examines only Northern Nigeria, it does so with the understanding that Northern Nigeria was representative of a larger class of colonies in receipt of Treasury grants. These other colonies were in West Africa, East Africa, Central Africa, the Caribbean, the Far East,

228 *Notes and References*

and the South Atlantic. A total of fifteen British dependencies were Treasury-aided in 1904. See Appendix D (Treasury Control over Colonial Finance) in 'Treasury Control', prepared by Treasury Clerk Roland Wilkins, August 1914, Treasury (T) 168/28.

5. The Northern Nigerian figure for 1901/2 is arrived at by taking the amount of the Southern Nigerian contribution, £34,000 (see minutes by Antrobus, 20 March 1901, on Sir Ralph Moor to Colonial Office (307) 7 December 1900, Colonial Office (CO) 520/3/847/:00/01), from the gross figure of £38,424 given for local revenue in the 'Statistical Abstract for the Several British Self-Governing Dominions, Colonies, Possessions, and Protectorates in Each Year from 1900 to 1914', *Parl. Pap.*, 1916 (Cd. 8329) XXXII, 16. (Hereafter referred to as 'Statistical Abstract'.) The figures for 1905/6 and 1910/11 are from *Colonial Reports – Annual: Northern Nigeria*, 1912, p. 8.

6. 'Statistical Abstract', 16–17.

7. Treasury Minute of 12 April 1868, copy attached to 'Treasury Control', memorandum by Roland Wilkins, Aug. 1904, T 168/28/pp. 541–74.

8. Sir Reginald Welby, 23 November 1886, Q.'s 2, 8, and 12, 'Royal Commission on Civil Establishments – First Reports', *Parl. Pap.*, 1887 (C. 5226) XIX, pp. 2–3.

9. Burton, 'Treasury Control and Colonial Policy', 187–90.

10. Minutes by Robert Lowe, 19 January 1870, and C. A. Hamilton, 14 July 1869, on T 1/7030A/11191, quoted in ibid.

11. Burton, 'Treasury Control and Colonial Policy', 191.

12. Robert Meade, 25 January 1888, Q. 12,377, 'Royal Commission on Civil Establishments – Second Report', *Parl. Pap.*, 1888 (C. 5545) XXVII, 77.

13. Welby, 9 December 1887, Q.'s 10.623; 10,627; 10,629; and 10,639; ibid.

14. When Lord Salisbury made his celebrated attack on the Treasury in the House of Lords in January 1900, Treasury clerk, Roland Wilkins, Private Secretary to the Financial Secretary, was directed 'to collect material in defence of the system of Treasury control'. The discussion petered out before the arguments and documents Wilkins put together could be used. Wilkins placed the material on permanent record in 1904. Its title is 'Treasury Control' and it is a short memorandum with several appendices. See T 168/28 pp. 541–74.

15. Minute by Antrobus, 27 August 1899, on Moor to CO (91) 16 June 1899, CO 444/1/17740.

16. Sir William Baillie Hamilton, 'Forty-Four Years at the Colonial Office', *The Nineteenth Century*, 70 (1909) 610–11.

17. Appendix 1, by George Goschen, 21 May 1887, attached to Roland Wilkins's memorandum, 'Treasury Control', August 1904, T 168/28, p. 566.

18. Welby, 9 December 1887, Q. 10,788, 'Royal Commission on Civil Establishments – Second Report', *Parl. Pap.*, 1888 (C. 5545) XXVII, 11.

19. Minutes by Wingfield, 20 April 1899, and Mercer, 2 February 1899, on Sir Frederick Lugard to CO, 2 February 1899, CO 446/7/2655.

20. Specifically, Antrobus reduced the amount to be spent on field administrative staff (i.e. district officers) from £18,000 to under £8,000, the Medical Department from £12,900 to £6,000, telegraph construction from £7,200 to £5,000, the Public Works Department from £38,000 to £8,600; and then approximately another £8,000 was removed from several other heads of the budget. See minutes by Antrobus, 16 April 1899, Wingfield, 20 April 1899, and Chamberlain, 24 April 1899, ibid.
21. Minutes by Antrobus, 28 April 1899, Wingfield, 28 April 1899, and Chamberlain, 29 April 1899, on Lugard to CO, 26 April 1899, CO 446/7/10589. See also Antrobus's explanation (of the decision taken) to Lugard, 2 May 1899, which is also attached to this file. The figures on which Chamberlain based his calculations were provided by Antrobus and attached to CO 446/7/2655.
22. Minutes by Mercer, 12 June 1899, Antrobus, 19 June 1899, Wingfield, 19 June 1899, and Chamberlain, 19 June 1899, on Lugard to CO, 10 May 1899, CO 446/7/12010.
23. Minutes by Mercer, 12 June 1899, Wingfield, 19 June 1899, ibid. Draft of CO letter of 27 June 1899 to Treasury is attached to this file.
24. Minute by Heath, 21 July 1899, on 'Form of Supplementary Estimates', 22 July 1899, T 1/9480A/12217.
25. Minutes by Antrobus, 31 August 1899, and Wingfield, 31 August 1899, on Manchester Chamber of Commerce, to CO, 18 August 1899, CO 446/6/22522. For the Treasury letter, see Treasury to CO, 1 September 1899, CO 446/6/23505. See also minute by Heath, 24 August 1899, on CO to Treasury, 17 August 1899, T 1/9480A/13711.
26. Minute by Antrobus, 9 October 1899, on Treasury to CO, 26 September 1899, CO 446/6/25949.
27. This aspect of the agreement was formally put to the Treasury in a letter of 11 October 1899; and the Treasury agreed to it on 18 October 1899. See CO to Treasury, 4 November 1899, T 1/9480B/17447.
28. See Antrobus's minutes of 9 and 10 October 1899, on Treasury to CO, 26 September 1899, CO 446/6/25040; and see Treasury to CO, 17 November 1899, CO 446/6/32021.
29. This was echoed by the Permanent Secretary Sir Francis Mowatt, who wrote in a marginal minute 'You certainly have.' See minutes by Heath, n.d., and Mowatt, 13 November 1899, on CO to Treasury, 6 Nov. 1899, T 1/9480B/17447. See also Treasury to CO, 15 November 1899, attached to this file.
30. See draft of Treasury to CO, 15 November 1899, ibid.
31. Minute by Heath, 8 February 1900, on CO to Treasury, 20 January 1900, T 1/9616A/1343.
32. See minutes on Lugard to CO (tel.) 13 January 1901, CO 446/14/1633; and see draft of CO to Treasury, sent 17 January 1901, attached to Lugard to CO, 19 January 1901, CO 446/14/6116; and see Treasury to CO, 27 July 1901, CO 446/19/26157.
33. Minutes by Butler, 11 October 1902, Antrobus, 28 October 1902, Ommanney, 28 October 1902, and Chamberlain, 30 October 1902, on Lugard to CO (438) 28 August 1902, CO 446/24/40550.

34. Minute by Antrobus, 22 February 1903, on Lugard to CO, 21 November 1902, CO 446/25/52540.
35. Minute by Chalmers, 17 January 1902, on CO to Treasury, 13 January 1902, T 1/9893A/153.
36. Minute by W. Hayes Fisher, Financial Secretary, 26 March 1903, on CO to Treasury, 5 March 1903, T 1/9937/4148; and see copy of Treasury to CO, 2 April 1903, attached to this file.
37. Minutes by Antrobus, 3 April 1903, and Ommanney, 3 April 1903, on Treasury to CO, 2 April 1903, CO 446/35/12433.
38. Minute by Murray, 29 January 1904, on CO to Treasury, 15 January 1904, T 1/10152B/15179/960.
39. Minutes by M. G. Ramsay, 25 February 1908, E. G. Herman, 27 February 1908, and Murray, 27 February 1908, on CO to Treasury, 10 February 1908, T 1/10887A/17956/2729.
40. Minute by Ramsay, 11 February 1909, on CO to Treasury, 1 February 1909, T 1/11060/16148/2616.
41. Treasury to CO, 3 February 1909, CO 446/86/6702.
42. *Colonial Reports – Annual: Northern Nigeria,* 1904–5 to 1910–11.
43. The revenue figures come from *Colonial Reports – Annual: Northern Nigeria,* 1911, p. 7; the expenditure figures come from 'Statistical Abstract', *Parl. Pap.* 1916 (Cd. 8329) XXXII, 18–19.
44. Minute by Strachey, n.d., on Treasury to CO, 16 March 1911, CO 446/102/8573.
45. Minute by Fiddes, 27 January 1911, on Hesketh Bell to CO (conf.) 19 December 1910, CO 446/92/1637:10/11.
46. 'Report of the Niger Committee', by the Earl of Selborne, 4 August 1898, CO 879/52/550, p. 284.
47. For example, see Treasury to CO, 3 February 1904, CO 446/42/3854, and Treasury to CO, 8 August 1907, CO 446/68/28160.
48. Minutes by Fiddes, 27 January 1911, and Harcourt, 28 January 1911, on Hesketh Bell to CO (conf.) 19 December 1910, CO 446/92/1637:10/11.
49. Treasury to CO, 16 March 1902, CO 446/102/8573.
50. 'Amalgamation of Northern and Southern Nigeria: Financial Questions', by Charles Strachey, 30 November 1911, Colonial Office, CO 520/110/38852. See permanent officials' minutes and Harcourt's (of 17 December 1911) attached to this file.
51. Minutes by Fiddes, 13 December 1911, Anderson, 14 December 1911, Emmott, 15 December 1911, and Harcourt, 17 December 1911, ibid.
52. The £156,000 is calculated on the following basis. Northern Nigeria was given £95,000 for the period 1 April to 31 December 1912 (see *Colonial Reports – Annual: Northern Nigeria,* 1912, p. 5) and £136,000 for calendar year 1913 (see *Colonial Reports – Annual: Nigeria,* 1914, p. 4). Since we know that the Imperial Treasury began its payments of £100,000 a year to Northern Nigeria on 1 April 1913, and also that those payments were made on the basis of £25,000 a quarter, we can say that Northern Nigeria received £75,000 between 1 April and 31 December 1913. If we then subtract the £75,000 from £136,000, we get £61,000, which represents the amount paid by the Imperial Treasury for the last

quarter of fiscal year 1912/13 (1 January to 31 March 1913). Finally, adding £95,000 to the £61,000, we get £156,000, the grant given to Northern Nigeria for 1912/13.

53. Minutes by Fiddes, 3 June 1912, and Anderson, 3 June 1912, on Lugard to CO (conf.) 12 May 1912, CO 520/121/15142.
54. CO to Treasury, 27 June 1912, T 1/1477/22165/12/13064. See minute by Behrens, 6 July 1912, attached.
55. See Strachey to Behrens, 30 July 1912, and CO to Treasury, 12 August 1912, and minutes by Behrens, 17 September 1912, and Hewby, 2 August and 10 October 1912, all in T 1/1477/22165/12/16607.
56. For the Treasury's acceptance and approval, see Treasury to CO, 12 October 1912, CO 520/119/32362.

5 THE CREATION OF THE LAGOS RAILWAY, 1895–1911

1. R. E. Dumett, 'Joseph Chamberlain, Imperial Finance and Railway Policy in British West Africa in the Late Nineteenth Century', *English Historical Review*, 90 (1975) 287–321; Ronald Hyam, *Elgin and Churchill at the Colonial Office, 1905–1908: The Watershed of the Empire-Commonwealth* (London, 1968); Richard M. Kesner, 'Builders of Empire: The Role of the Crown Agents in Imperial Development, 1880–1914', *Journal of Imperial and Commonwealth History*, 5 (1977) 310–30; and Robert Kubicek, *The Administration of Imperialism: Joseph Chamberlain at the Colonial Office* (Durham, N.C. 1969).
2. I use the concept of exploitation in the old imperial sense – i.e., as a 'description of progress, not a criticism of it'. A. P. Thornton, *Imperialism in the Twentieth Century* (Minneapolis, Minn., 1977) p. 54.
3. Olufemi Omosini, 'Railway Projects and British Attitude towards the Development of West Africa, 1872–1903', *Journal of the Historical Society of Nigeria*, 5 (1971) 501–4.
4. See minute by Ommanney, 31 July 1893, on Western Syndicate to CO, 19 July 1893, CO 147/92, quoted in C. W. Newbury, *British Policy Towards West Africa: Select Documents, 1875–1914* (Oxford, 1971) p. 479.
5. Great Britain, H.C.Deb., 36 (22 August 1895) 640–44.
6. Crown Agents (Ommanney) to CO, 31 October 1895, CO 879/40/464, quoted in Newbury, *West Africa: Select Documents*, p. 488.
7. Ibid, note 1, p. 487.
8. Minute by Grindle, 21 January 1898, on Crown Agents to CO, 19 January 1898, CO 147/137/1415. The 'necessary link' phrase comes from Crown Agents (Ommanney) to CO, 31 October 1895, CO 879/40/464, quoted in Newbury, *West Africa: Select Documents*, p. 488.
9. Minute by Mercer, 10 June 1898, on Crown Agents to CO, 4 June 1898, CO 147/137/12541.
10. See minutes by Chamberlain and others on Foreign Office to CO, 25 June 1898, CO 537/135/476; and see Foreign Office to CO, 18 July 1898, CO 537/135/490.

11. The Earl of Selborne, 'Report of the Niger Committee', 4 August 1898, CO 879/52/550, p. 287.
12. Crown Agents (Ommanney) to CO, 25 July 1898, CO 147/137/16772.
13. Minute by Antrobus, 28 November 1898, on Crown Agents to CO, 24 November 1898, CO 147/138/26400.
14. Minutes by Ezechiel, 22 June 1899, Mercer, 12 July 1899, Wingfield, 22 July 1899, and Chamberlain, 24 July 1899, on Crown Agents to CO, 20 June 1899, CO 147/146/15785.
15. See Dumett, 'Chamberlain, Imperial Finance and Railway Policy', 308–10; Kesner, 'Builders of Empire', 311–12; and Kubicek, *Administration of Imperialism,* 62–5.
16. Minute by Antrobus, 19 November 1899, on Lugard to CO, 2 November 1899, CO 446/8/30397. Antrobus repeated this is mid-1900 – see his memorandum of 23 May 1900 attached to Acting High Commissioner Gallway to CO (92) 2 April 1900, CO 520/1/12773.
17. See Consulting Engineers to Crown Agents, 30 June 1900, attached to Crown Agents to CO, 13 July 1900, *Parl. Papers,* Nigeria – Correspondence *re* Railway Construction, Cd. 2787, 1906.
18. Consulting Engineers to Crown Agents, 6 December 1900 attached to Crown Agents to CO, 19 December 1900, ibid.
19. MacGregor to CO, 9 August 1900, C.P. 879/67/647, quoted in Newbury, *West Africa: Select Documents,* p. 502.
20. Minute by Ommanney, 7 May 1901, on MacGregor to CO (84) 23 March 1901, CO 147/154/14911.
21. Lugard to CO (90) 9 April 1901, CO 446/15/14957.
22. Minute by Ezechiel, 27 June 1901, on Moor to CO (110) 25 April 1901, CO 520/7/18330.
23. Minutes by Ezechiel, 3 August 1901, Hamilton, 17 August 1901, Ommanney, 20 August 1901, and Chamberlain, 22 August 1901, on Crown Agents to CO, 29 July 1901, CO 147/158/26276; and for the Treasury's approval see its letter to the CO on 10 September 1901, *Parl. Pap.,* Nigeria – Correspondence *re* Railway Construction, Cd. 2787, 1906.
24. Consulting Engineers (Shelford and Son) to CO, 27 March 1902, attached to Crown Agents to CO, 26 April 1902, CO 147/163/16292.
25. Minute by Ezechiel, 15 May 1902, ibid.
26. Minute by Ezechiel, 27 June 1901, on Moor to CO (110) 25 April 1901, CO 520/7/18330.
27. Minute by Strachey, 2 September 1902, on Crown Agents to CO, 26 April 1902, CO 147/163/16292.
28. Minutes by Ezechiel, 15 May 1902, and Ommanney, 21 August 1902, ibid.
29. Minute by Strachey, 16 May 1902, on Lugard to CO, 1 March 1902, CO 446/22/14549.
30. Minutes by Ezechiel, 15 May and 2 September 1902, Strachey, 16 May 1902, Antrobus, 25 June 1902, and Ommanney, 21 August 1902, on Crown Agents to CO, 26 April 1902, CO 147/163/16292.
31. See Crown Agents to CO, 17 November 1902, and CO to Crown Agents,

28 November 1902, *Parl. Pap.*, Nigeria – Correspondence *re* Railway Construction, Cd. 2787, 1906.

32. See William Gee to Secretary of Northern Nigerian Administration, January 1902, and Consulting Engineers to Crown Agents, 4 November 1902, attached to Crown Agents to CO, 15 November 1902, ibid.

33. Minutes by Ezechiel, 10 February 1904, Antrobus, 20 February 1904, Ommanney, 20 February 1904, and Lyttelton, 28 February 1904, on MacGregor to CO (17) 10 January 1904, CO 147/169/3074.

34. Treasury to CO, 26 March 1904, CO 147/173/10864.

35. Minutes by Olivier, 15 October 1906, and Ommanney, 24 October 1906, on Egerton to CO (conf.) 14 September 1906, CO 520/37/38243.

36. See minutes on Egerton to CO (tel.) 1 December 1906, CO 520/38/44537.

37. Minute by Butler, 14 July 1906, on Niger Company to CO, 9 July 1906, CO 446/58/25192.

38. Minute by Butler, 2 June 1907, on Egerton to CO (188) 18 April 1907, CO 520/45/16670.

39. Sir Percy Girouard, 'Report on Transport Policy of Nigeria', attached to Girouard to CO, 30 May 1907, CO 446/63/23179.

40. Minutes by Churchill, 2 June 1907, and Elgin, 8 June 1907, on Egerton to CO (188) 18 April 1907, CO 520/45/16670.

41. Minute by Butler, 31 July 1907, on Crown Agents to CO, 29 July 1907, CO 520/52/27112.

42. Minute by Strachey, 22 August 1907, on Crown Agents to CO, ibid. See also attached to this file, Egerton to Elgin, 2 September 1907.

43. Minute by Butler, 4 September 1907, ibid.

44. Egerton to CO, 11 October 1906, *Parl. Pap.*, Nigeria – Further Correspondence *re* Railway Construction, Cd. 4523, 1909.

45. See minutes on Egerton to CO (188) 18 April 1907, CO 520/45/16670.

46. Minute by Elgin, 30 September 1907, on Crown Agents to CO, 24 September 1907, CO 520/52/34138.

47. Minute by Antrobus, 28 January 1908, on Egerton to CO (718) 21 December 1907, CO 520/50/1086:07/08.

48. Minute by Butler, 12 March 1908, on Crown Agents to CO, 10 March 1908, CO 520/69/8765.

49. Minute by Antrobus, 18 March 1908, ibid.

50. Minutes by Strachey, 23 March 1908, Antrobus, 24 March 1908, and Elgin, 30 March 1908, on Crown Agents to CO, 20 March 1908, CO 520/69/9902.

51. Minutes by Strachey, 2 August 1907, and Elgin, 22 August 1907, on Crown Agents to CO, 29 July 1907, CO 520/52/27112.

52. See Egerton to Elgin, 2 September 1907, ibid.

53. Minutes by Butler, 4 September 1907, Antrobus, 4 September 1907, and Elgin, 6 September 1907, and also Elgin's reply to Egerton, 6 September 1907, ibid.

54. Minutes by Butler, 26 September 1907, Elgin, 30 September and 1 October 1907, on Crown Agents to CO, 24 September 1907, CO 520/52/34138.

55. CO to Egerton, 22 October 1907; CO to Crown Agents, 25 October

1907; and Crown Agents to CO, 8 November 1907, *Parl. Pap.*, Nigeria – Further Correspondence *re* Railway Construction, Cd. 4523, 1909.

56. Minute by Ommanney, 15 June 1903, on MacGregor to CO (conf.) 4 March 1903, CO 147/165/13757.
57. Minute by Chamberlain, 25 June 1902, on Crown Agents to CO, 26 April 1902, CO 147/163/16292.
58. Minute by Herbert, 20 November 1899, on Lugard to CO, 2 November 1899, CO 446/8/30397.
59. Minute by Antrobus, 1 June 1903, on Manchester Chamber of Commerce to CO, 18 May 1903, CO 147/168/18489.
60. Minute by Ommanney, 2 June 1903, ibid.
61. Minutes by Antrobus, 7 August 1903, Ommanney, 12 August 1903, and Chamberlain, 13 August and 22 August 1903, on Manchester Chamber of Commerce to CO, 26 June 1903, CO 147/168/23850.
62. Richard M. Kesner, 'Builders of Empire', 322.
63. Minutes by Ezechiel, 10 February 1904, and Ommanney, marginal minute – n.d. but probably 20 February 1904, on MacGregor to CO (17) 10 January 1904, CO 147/169/3074.
64. Great Britain, *Parliamentary Debates* (Lords), 4th ser., 135 (10 June 1904): 1333.
65. This description of the departmental system, or method, draws upon my examination of two Colonial Office record series in the Public Record Office – CO 147 (Lagos) and CO 520 (Southern Nigeria) – for the years 1896 to 1913. Kesner's article, 'Builders of Empire', 320–23, discusses how the Colonial Office and the Treasury affected the development of this method. For an official paper critical of the departmental system, see *Parl. Pap.*, Private Enterprise in British Tropical Africa, Cmnd. 2016, 1924.
66. And the Crown Agents did generally have such a reputation. However, there is an intriguing but undocumented charge that the Crown Agents were guilty of great dishonesty and that an alliance between Ommanney and the Consulting Engineers promoted 'a lucrative private business involving a staggering loss of funds by the West African colonies through a conventional system of patronage and graft'. See Kenneth Dike Nworah, 'The Liverpool "Sect" and British West African Policy, 1895–1915', *African Affairs,* 70 (1971) 364. However, Nworah's accusation leaves one dissatisfied. If he had firm evidence of this dishonesty why did he not use it in this article; if he did not, why should he make such statements? The Earl of Portsmouth in 1904 also suggested the possibility of dishonest behaviour in the Crown Agents' work, because of family relationships between permanent officials at the Colonial Office, employees of the Crown Agents, the Consulting Engineers, and the Crown Agents' solicitor. He noted that Ommanney's son-in-law was Mr Shelford of Shelford and Son (the Consulting Engineers), and that Ommanney's nephew was a member of the firm which acted as solicitors for the Crown Agents. He could have mentioned also that Antrobus had a brother who was a senior employee of the Crown Agents. See speech of the Earl of Portsmouth to House of Lords, H.L. Deb., 135 (10 June

1904): 1333. No one paid much attention to Portsmouth's allegations. However, by 1908, more allegations concerning the Crown Agents' work had been made. An interdepartmental committee was set up in 1908 to investigate these allegations. The committee was made up primarily of permanent officials and members of the Government who concluded that the Crown Agents' work 'appears to be on the whole well done and . . . clear from all suspicion of corruption'. See *Parl. Pap.*, Crown Agents' Office – Report from Committee of Enquiry and Minutes, Cd. 4473, 1909, iv. In short, the Crown Agents were exonerated. But this was not an independent assessment. To this day no historian has directly addressed the question of corruption in the Crown Agents during the crucial years before the First World War. Such an assessment would be helpful to historians working in the field.

67. See minute by Antrobus, 19 December 1904, on Egerton to CO (conf.) 26 November 1904, CO 147/172/42359.
68. Minute by Ommanney, 19 December 1904, on Egerton to CO (352) 28 October 1904, CO 147/171/39173.
69. These proposals are discussed in Richard M. Kesner, 'The Financial Management of the British Empire, 1895–1903: Studies in Treasury–Colonial Office Relations' (Ph.D. diss., Stanford University, 1977) pp. 151–7, and in Kubicek, *Administration of Imperialism*, pp. 75–6.
70. Kesner, 'Financial Management of the British Empire', pp. 157–64, and Kubicek, *Administration of Imperialism*, pp. 79–83.
71. Dumett, 'Chamberlain, Imperial Finance and Railway Policy', 306.
72. Ibid.
73. Crown Agents (Ommanney) to CO, 11 December 1895, CO 879/40/464, quoted in Newbury, *West Africa: Select Documents*, p. 387.
74. This analysis owes much to R. E. Dumett with whom I am in full agreement regarding the role and importance of the Crown Agents in this process. See Dumett, 'Chamberlain, Imperial Finance and Railway Policy', 309.
75. For a general appreciation of the evolution of the Crown Agents before the mid-1890s, see Brian L. Blakeley, *The Colonial Office: 1868–1892* (Durham, N.C., 1972) pp. 94–106.
76. Kesner, 'Financial Management of the British Empire', pp. 165–8, and Kubicek, *Administration of Imperialism*, pp. 80–85.
77. Kesner, 'Builders of Empire', 318.
78. Dumett, 'Chamberlain, Imperial Finance and Railway Policy', 313.
79. Crown Agents (Ommanney) to CO, 16 August 1899, CO 147/146, quoted in Newbury, *West Africa: Select Documents*, pp. 394–5.
80. Minutes by Antrobus, 22 June 1900, Ommanney, 22 June 1900, and Chamberlain, 22 June 1900, on Crown Agents to CO, 21 June 1900, CO 147/152/19706.
81. Treasury to CO, 30 June 1900, CO 147/152/20818.
82. Minute by Ezechiel, 10 February 1904, on MacGregor to CO (17) 10 January 1904, CO 147/169/3074.
83. Dumett, 'Chamberlain, Imperial Finance and Railway Policy', 318.
84. Minutes by Ezechiel, 10 February 1904, Antrobus, 20 February 1904, Ommanney, 20 February 1904, and Lyttelton, 28 February 1904, on

MacGregor to CO (17) CO 147/169/3074, and see draft of CO to Treasury, 15 March 1904, attached to this file.
85. Minutes by Ommanney, 25 April 1904, and Lyttelton, 5 May 1904, on Treasury to CO, 26 March 1904, CO 147/173/10864.
86. Minutes by Ommanney, 18 May and 8 June 1904, ibid.
87. Crown Agents to CO, 3 August 1904, CO 879/79/695, quoted in Newbury, *West Africa: Select Documents,* pp. 401–2.

6 THE CREATION OF THE BARO–KANO RAILWAY, 1897–1911

1. 'Memorandum on British Possessions', by H. J. Read, 12 May 1897, CO 879/49/534, p. 40.
2. CO to Treasury, 28 February 1907, T 1/10675/15732/4017.
3. Minute by Olivier, 14 December 1906, on Egerton to CO (conf.) 14 September 1906, CO 520/37/38714.
4. Minute by Ommanney, 19 March 1903, on Crown Agents to CO, 12 February 1903, CO 446/34/5822.
5. Letter dated 22 December 1906, attached to Lugard to CO (conf.) 20 May 1906, CO 446/54/2112.
6. Girouard to CO (246) 30 May 1907, CO 446/63/23179.
7. Ronald Hyam, *Elgin and Churchill at the Colonial Office, 1905–1908: The Watershed of the Empire-Commonwealth* (London, 1968) p. 488.
8. Egerton, Address to the Southern Nigerian Legislative Council, 15 August 1906, *Southern Nigeria Government Gazette,* 12 September 1906.
9. Minutes by Antrobus, 26 September 1908, and Crewe, 1 October 1908, on Egerton to CO (conf.) 27 July 1908, CO 520/63/29951.
10. See Consulting Engineers' report on these surveys attached to Crown Agents to CO, 19 April 1905, CO 446/47/12976.
11. It was in this way that the twenty-mile tramway was built. See minutes on Lugard to CO (431) 25 August 1902, CO 446/24/40503.
12. Lugard to CO, 23 August 1903, CO 446/36/32307.
13. Minute by Antrobus, 16 September 1903, ibid.
14. Minute by Ommanney, 14 August 1906, on Colonial Office, 14 July 1906, CO 446/58/26478.
15. Consulting Engineers to Crown Agents, 28 February 1905, *Parl. Pap.,* Nigeria – Correspondence *re* Railway Construction, Cd. 2787, 1906.
16. See Girouard's 'Memorandum on Northern Nigerian Railways', attached to CO to Treasury, 28 February 1907, T 1/10675/15732/4017.
17. Minute by Butler, 19 September 1907, on Crown Agents to CO, 18 September 1907, CO 446/67/33410.
18. A good account of this work is found in *Colonial Reports – Annual: Northern Nigeria,* 'Report for 1910–1911', Appendix II, pp. 39–41.
19. Private Enterprise in British Tropical Africa, pp. 6–7, Cmnd. 2016, 1924.
20. See minute by Ommanney, 10 November 1905, on Crown Agents to CO, 19 April 1905, CO 446/47/12976.

21. For a discussion of this, see CO to Treasury, 28 February 1907, T 1/10675/15732/4017, and also see Sir Percy Girouard's attached 'Memorandum on Northern Nigerian Railways'.
22. Ibid.
23. Private note of Elgin to Asquith, 28 February 1907, ibid.
24. Minute by Murray, 3 March 1907, ibid.
25. See the copy of Walter Runciman to Churchill, 11 March 1907, attached to this file, ibid.
26. Private note of Asquith to Elgin, 14 MArch 1907, ibid.
27. Treasury to CO, 30 March 1907, CO 446/68/11468.
28. Minutes by Churchill, 8 April 1907, ibid., and also see letter Strachey drafted, attached to this file, which was sent to the Treasury 16 May 1907.
29. Minutes by Ramsay, 3 June 1907, and Chalmers, 4 June 1907, on CO to Treasury, 16 May 1907, T 1/10675/15732/9390.
30. Girouard's memorandum, 'Report on Transport Policy of Nigeria', was attached to Girouard to CO (246) 30 May 1907, CO 446/63/23179. See also Strachey's minute of 1 July 1907 also on the despatch.
31. Minute by Ramsay, 16 July 1907, on CO to Treasury, 10 July 1907, T 1/10675/15732/12892.
32. Churchill to Runciman, 12 July 1907, attached to the file on CO to Treasury, 26 July 1907, T 1/10675/15732/14031.
33. Minute by Chalmers, n.d. but probably mid- or late July 1907, ibid.
34. Minute by Blain, 2 August 1907, on CO on Treasury, 1 August 1907, T 1/10675/15732/14423.
35. Treasury to CO, 1 August 1907, CO 446/68/27466.
36. Runciman to Churchill, n.d. but probably 1 August 1907, copy attached to file on CO to Treasury, 26 July 1907, T 1/10675/15732/14031.
37. Treasury to CO, 8 August 1907, CO 446/68/28160.
38. See minute by Strachey, 8 August 1907, a copy of which was sent with CO to Treasury, 1 August 1907, T 1/10675/15732/14423.
39. Minute by Churchill, 12 August 1907, on Treasury to CO, 8 August 1907, CO 446/68/28160.
40. 'Memorandum: Conference held in the Chancellor of the Exchequer's room at the House of Commons on Monday 12 August 1907 at 4.15 p.m.', prepared by Robert Chalmers, 14 August 1907, CO to Treasury, 1 August 1907, T 1/10675/15732/14423.
41. Minute by Churchill, 20 August 1907, on Treasury to CO, 8 August 1907, CO 446/68/28160.
42. Minutes by Butler, 15 August 1907, and Elgin, 21 August 1907, ibid.
43. See Blain's minute of 5 September 1907, on CO to Treasury, 22 August 1907, T 1/10675/15732. A copy of the Treasury reply to this letter, in draft, is attached to this file and dated 12 September 1907.
44. Minutes by Butler, 18 September 1907, and Elgin, 19 September 1907, on Treasury to CO, 12 September 1907, CO 446/68/32673.
45. Minute by Strchey, 14 October 1907, on Crown Agents to CO, 24 September 1907, CO 520/52/34138.
46. Minute by Butler, 16 January 1908, on Egerton to CO (656) 23 November 1907, CO 520/50/43450.

47. Minutes by Butler, 16 January 1908, Hopwood, 22 January 1908, Churchill, 5 February 1908, and Elgin, 6 February 1908, ibid.
48. Minute by Butler, 13 February 1908, on Crown Agents to CO, 11 February 1908, CO 520/69/5174. Draft of CO to Treasury, 26 February 1908, is attached.
49. Minutes by Butler, 31 March 1908, Hopwood, 1 April 1908, and Elgin, 4 April 1908, on Treasury to CO, 23 March 1908, CO 520/72/10372.
50. CO to Treasury, 10 April 1908, *Parl. Pap.*, Nigeria – Further Correspondence *re* Railway Construction, Cd. 4523, 1909.
51. See Crown Agents to CO, 8 May 1908, CO 520/69/16505.
52. Confidential Cabinet Memorandum by Joseph Chamberlain, 'The Suez Canal Shares', 15 November 1895, enclosed in letter from Chamberlain to Salisbury, 26 November 1896, Salisbury Papers, Box A/92 (Colonial Office, Private, 1895–1900) Christ Church, Oxford, quoted in R. E. Dumett, 'Joseph Chamberlain, Imperial Finance, and Railway Policy in British West Africa in the Late Nineteenth Century', *English Historical Review*, 90 (1975) 302.
53. John Gallagher and Ronald Robinson, 'The Imperialism of Free Trade', *Economic History Review*, 2nd ser. 6 (1953) 5.
54. Michael Crowder has called the railways the major legacy of the economic policies of the colonial powers. See his *West Africa Under Colonial Rule* (London, 1968) p. 273. Olufemi Omosini has said that railways had the greatest impact of any single innovation in transport brought into West Africa from Europe. See his 'Railway Projects and British Attitude towards the Development of West Africa, 1872–1903', *Journal of the Historical Society of Nigeria*, 5 (1971) 504.

7 THE SEARCH FOR PETROLEUM IN SOUTHERN NIGERIA, 1906–14

1. Sydney Brooks, 'Great Britain, the Empire, and Oil', *Nineteenth Century*, LXXIV (1918) 687.
2. John Holt to Reginald Antrobus, 6 December 1899, attached to Frederick Lugard to CO, 22 November 1899, CO 446/8/32810.
3. Antrobus to Holt, 28 June 1909, Holt Papers, Box 12, File 1, Rhodes House, Oxford.
4. Bergheim's Obituary, *The Times* (London) 11 September 1912, p. 9.
5. Alfred Fischendorf, *Great Britain and Mexico in the Era of Porfirio Diaz* (Durham, N.C., 1916) p. 168.
6. Sydney Olivier to G. B. Shaw, 1899, G. B. Shaw Papers, British Library, Add. MSS. 50543.
7. J. S. Bergheim to CO, 1 August 1906, CO 520/40/28382.
8. J. S. Bergheim to CO, 19 November 1907, CO 520/55/40763.
9. For a full discussion of the options open to the office and the reasoning behind the decision taken, see Butler's long minute of 10 September 1906, on Imperial Institute to CO, 7 September 1906, CO 520/39/33228.

See also additional minutes on this by Olivier, 18 September 1906, and Elgin, 28 September 1906.

10. Bergheim to CO, 1 August 1906, CO 502/40/28382.
11. Minute by Antrobus, 28 September 1906, on Imperial Institute to CO, 7 September 1906, CO 520/39/33228.
12. Documentation for the preceding paragraphs comes from Bergheim's letter of 8 November 1906 (which he wrote as Chairman of the Nigeria Bitumen Corporation), and minutes of various permanent officials in which they recorded the happenings of the next few weeks. See minutes by Butler, 12 November and 21 November 1906, Olivier, 22 November 1906, Antrobus, 22 November 1906, and Elgin, 24 November 1906, on Nigeria Bitumen Corporation to CO, 8 November 1906, CO 520/40/41401.
13. Minute by Olivier, n.d., on Nigeria Bitumen Corporation to CO, 12 November 1906, CO 520/40/41864.
14. Minutes by Antrobus, 22 November 1906, and Elgin, 24 November 1906, on Nigeria Bitumen Corporation to CO, 8 November 1906, CO 520/40/41401.
15. Minute by Butler, 21 December 1906, on Nigeria Bitumen Corporation to CO, 19 December 1906, CO 520/40/46886.
16. Ibid. See Butler's minute of 21 December 1906 and 1 January 1907, and Antrobus's of 2 January 1907.
17. See Ordinance Number 12 of 1907 – 'The Mining Regulation (Oil) Ordinance 1907', CO 588/2.
18. Minute by Antrobus, 7 March 1907, on Nigeria Bitumen Corporation to CO, 5 March 1907, CO 520/54/8347.
19. Minute by Antrobus, 11 December 1907, on Bergheim to CO, 19 November 1907, CO 520/55/40763.
20. Minute by Butler, 22 January 1908, on Egerton to CO (725) 27 December 1907, CO 520/50/2042:07/08.
21. Bergheim to CO, 19 November 1907, CO 520/55/40763.
22. Minute by Butler, 22 January 1908, and Sir Francis Hopwood, 24 January 1908, on Egerton to CO (725) 27 December 1907, CO 520/50/2042:07/08.
23. Documentation for this story is found in Butler's fifteen-page minute of 6 July 1908, on Egerton to CO (conf.) 9 June 1908, CO 520/61/23066.
24. Ibid.
25. Egerton to CO (conf.) 4 October 1908, CO 520/66/39022.
26. Minute by Butler, 17 November 1908, on Bergheim to CO, 16 November 1908, CO 520/73/42020.
27. Minute by Strachey, 25 September 1909, on Nigeria Bitumen Corporation to CO, 24 September 1909, CO 520/87/31740.
28. For the entire letter, see Bergheim to Lugard, 12 July 1912, attached to Nigeria Bitumen Corporation to CO, 28 October 1912, CO 520/120/34245.
29. Nigeria Bitumen Corporation to CO, 11 November 1912, CO 520/120/35742.
30. Bergheim to Lugard, 12 July 1912, attached to Nigeria Bitumen Corporation to CO, 28 October 1912, CO 520/120/34245.

31. Hopwood to J. E. B. Seely, Parliamentary Under Secretary at the Colonial Office, 7 October 1912, attached to Nigeria Bitumen Corporation to CO, 22 October 1912, CO 520/120/33433.
32. Nigeria Bitumen Corporation to CO, 28 October 1912, CO 520/120/34245.
33. Minute by Strachey, 16 October 1912, on Nigeria Bitumen Corporation to CO, 22 October 1912, CO 520/120/33433.
34. Ibid. See also Fiddes's minute of 1 November 1912, and Sir John Anderson's of 1 November 1912 on Nigeria Bitumen Corporation to CO, 28 October 1912, CO 520/120/34245.
35. Nigeria Bitumen Corporation to CO, 11 November 1912, CO 520/120/35742.
36. See minutes by Strachey, 12 June 1913, and Fiddes, 13 June 1913, on Lugard to CO, 30 May 1913, CO 520/124/19732.
37. Quoted in P. H. Frankel, *Essentials of Petroleum: A Key to Oil Economics* (London, 1969) p. 110.
38. D. J. Payton-Smith, *Oil: A Study of War-time Policy and Administration* (London, 1971) p. 11.
39. Minute by Fiddes, 1 Novembr 1912, on Nigeria Bitumen Corporation to CO, 28 October 1912, CO 520/120/34245.
40. R. H. Young (Liquidator) to Crown Agents, 13 May 1914, attached to Crown Agents to CO, 15 May 1914, CO 583/22/17893.
41. Minute by Butler, 12 December 1908, on Egerton to CO (763) 20 November 1908, CO 520/67/45278.

CONCLUSION

1. See Lord Elgin's minute of 6 September 1907, on Crown Agents to CO, 29 July 1907, CO 520/52/27112. Lord Leverhulme is quoted in *The Mirrors of Downing Street: Some Reflections* (New York and London, 1921) p. 157.
2. Minute by Antrobus, 16 November 1905, on Lugard to CO, 11 November 1905, CO 446/51/40319.
3. See Fisher to Hopwood, 30 January 1912 and 16 June 1912, Southborough Papers.
4. Ronald Hyam, *Elgin and Churchill at the Colonial Office, 1905–1908: The Watershed of the Empire-Commonwealth* (London, 1968) p. 484.
5. Minute by Butler, 12 December 1908, on Egerton to CO (763) 20 November 1908, CO 520/67/45278.

Bibliography

PRIMARY AUTHORITIES

A. Colonial Office and Treasury Records: Despatches, Letters, and Minutes

CO 147: Lagos, 1898–1906
CO 444: Niger Coast Protectorate, 1899
CO 446: Northern Nigeria, 1898–1913
CO 520: Southern Nigeria, 1900–1913
CO 537: Supplementary Correspondence [West Africa]
CO 554: Africa, West, 1911–14
CO 583: Nigeria, 1912–14
CO 879: Confidential Prints: Africa
T 1: Treasury Board Papers

B. Reports and Memoranda

Antrobus, Reginald. 'Amalgamation of Southern Nigeria and Lagos'. 8 June 1904. CO 520/27/21004.
Colonial Reports – Annual: Northern Nigeria. 1900–1912.
Colonial Reports – Annual: Southern Nigeria. 1906–1912.
'Committee of Enquiry into the Organisation of the Crown Agents' Office: Reports, Minutes of Evidence, and Appendices'. December 1908. CO 885/19/226.
Girouard, Sir Percy. 'Report on Transport Policy in Nigeria'. 30 May 1907. CO 446/63/23179.
Government Gazette of the Protectorate of Southern Nigeria. 1900–1906.
Graham, Frederick. 'Memorandum on the Colonial Office Establishment'. March 1903. CO 885/8/154.
Lugard, Sir Frederick. 'Memorandum on the Development of Northern Nigeria'. 2 November 1899. CO 446/8/30397.
—— 'Administration of Tropical Africa'. 11 July 1905. CO 879/88/789.
—— 'Confidential Memorandum: Administration at Home and Abroad'. 1907. Lugard Papers, s.65/247.
Ommanney, Sir Montagu. 'Memorandum on the Organisation and Establishment of the Colonial Office'. 13 March 1903. CO 885/8/156.
Read, H. J. 'Memorandum on British Possessions in West Africa'. 12 May 1897. CO 879/49/534.

Selborne, Earl of. 'Report of the Niger Committee'. 4 August 1898. CO 879/52/550.
Smartt, J. P. *Southern Nigeria: Financial Report for the Year Ended 31 December 1907.* Lagos, 1908.
Southern Nigeria Government Gazette. 1907–1913.
Strachey, Charles. 'Amalgamation of Northern and Southern Nigeria: Financial Questions'. 30 November 1911. CO 520/110/38852.
Wilkins, Roland. 'Treasury Control'. August 1904. T 168/28. (See Appendix D, 'Treasury Control over Colonial Finance'.)

C. Parliamentary Papers

Anderson, Sir John. Testimony before the 'Royal Commission on the Civil Service'. 17 May 1912. *Parl. Pap.*, 1912–13, XV. C. 6535.
'Nigeria – Correspondence *re* Railway Construction', *Parl. Pap.*, 1906, Cd. 2787.
'Nigeria – Further Correspondence *re* Railway Construction'. *Parl. Pap.*, 1909, Cd. 4523.
'Private Enterprise in British Tropical Africa'. *Parl. Pap.*, 1924, Cmnd. 2016.
'Report and Papers Relating to the Re-organization of the Civil Service'. *Parl. Pap.*, 1854–55, XX, C. 1870. See letter from Sir James Stephen, 12 April 1854.
'Report of Her Majesty's Civil Service Commissioners; with Appendices: Twenty-second, 1878'. *Parl. Pap.*, 1878, XXVIII.
'Report of Her Majesty's Civil Service Commissioners; with Appendices: Twenty-sixth, 1882'. *Parl. Pap.*, 1882, XII.
'Report of Her Majesty's Civil Service Commissioners; with Appendices: Twenty-seventh, 1883'. *Parl. Pap.*, 1883, XXIII.
'Report of Her Majesty's Civil Service Commissioners; with Appendices: Thirty-ninth, 1895'. XXVI.
'Report of His Majesty's Civil Service Commissioners; with Appendices: Forty-sixth, 1902.' *Parl. Pap.*, 1902, XXII, Cd. 1203.
'Report of His Majesty's Civil Service Commissioners; with Appendices: Fiftieth, 1906'. *Parl. Pap.*, 1906, XXVI Cd. 3108.
'Report of His Majesty's Civil Service Commissioners; with Appendices: Fifty-fifth, 1911'. *Parl. Pap.*, 1911, XIII, Cd. 5751.
'Royal Commission on Civil Establishments – Second Report'. *Parl. Pap.*, 1888, C. 5545. See letters from Sir Reginald Welby, 3 December 1887, H. Calcraft, 24 February 1888, and Richard Ebden, 11 December 1886.
Swettenham, Sir Frank. Testimony before the 'Committee of Enquiry into the Organisation of the Crown Agents' Office'. 24 June 1908. *Parl. Pap.*, 1909, XVI.

D. Private Manuscript Collections

Campbell-Bannerman Papers (Elgin's correspondence with Campbell-Bannerman). British Library, London.

Chamberlain Papers. University of Birmingham Library, Birmingham.
Crewe Papers. University Library, Cambridge University.
Lewis Harcourt Papers. Bodleian Library, Oxford University.
John Holt Papers. Rhodes House Library, Oxford University.
Lugard Papers. Rhodes House Library, Oxford University.
Alfred Lyttelton Papers. Churchill College Archives, Cambridge University.
Southborough (Sir Francis Hopwood) Papers. In the possession of the 3rd
   Baron Southborough.

E. Biographical Data Sources

Burke's *Genealogical and Heraldic History of the Peerage, Baronage, and
   Knightage.*
Colonial Offict List.
Debrett's *Peerage, Baronetage, Knightage, and Companionage.*
Dictionary of National Biography.
Foster, John (compiler), *Alumni Oxonienses: The Members of the University
   of Oxford, 1715–1886: Their Parentage, Birthplace and Year of Birth, with
   Record of their Degrees.* 2 vols. Oxford and London, 1885.
—— *Oxford Men, 1880–1892: With A Record of Schools and Degrees.*
   Oxford and London, 1893.
*The Historical Register of the University of Oxford: Being a Supplement to the
   Oxford University Calendar with an Alphabetical Record of University
   Honours and Distinctions Completed to the End of Trinity Term, 1900.*
   Oxford, 1900.
The Times (London).
Venn, J. A. *Alumni Cantabrigienses: A Biographical List of All Known
   Students, Graduates, and Holders of Office at the University of Cambridge,
   from the Earliest Times to 1900: Part II; from 1752–1900.* 6 vols.
   Cambridge, 1940.
Who's Who.
Who Was Who.

SECONDARY AUTHORITIES

Note: The most important sources for this present book are the Colonial
   Office and Treasury records mentioned above. This bibliography of
   secondary sources includes those books, articles, lectures, and theses cited
   in the text.

A. Books

Adeleye, R. A. *Power and Diplomacy in Northern Nigeria, 1804–1906: The
   Sokoto Caliphate and its Enemies.* London, 1971.
Bamford, T. W. *Rise of the Public Schools: A Study of Boys' Public Boarding
   Schools in England and Wales from 1837 to the Present Day.* London, 1967.

244 *Bibliography*

Best, Geoffrey. *The History of British Society: Mid-Victorian Britain, 1851–75.* London, 1971.
Blakeley, Brian. *The Colonial Office, 1868–1892.* Durham, N.C., 1972.
Bruce, Sir Charles. *The Broad Stone of Empire: Problems of Crown Colony Administration,* 2 vols. London, 1910.
Burn, W. L. *The Age of Equipoise: A Study of the Mid-Victorian Generation.* New York, 1965.
Churchill, Randolph S. *Winston S. Churchill: Young Statesman, 1901–1914,* vol. 2. Boston, 1967.
Clark, G. Kitson. *The Making of Victorian England.* London, 1962.
Clarke, M. L. *Classical Education in Britain: 1500–1900.* Cambridge, 1959.
Crowder, Michael. *West Africa Under Colonial Rule.* London, 1968.
Dale, H. E. *The Higher Civil Service of Great Britain.* Oxford, 1941.
Earle, Sir Lionel. *Turn Over the Page.* London, 1935.
Frankel, P. H. *Essentials of Petroleum: A Key to Oil Economics.* London, 1969.
Fruse, Sir Ralph. *Aucuparius: Recollections of A Recruiting Officer.* London, 1962.
Gailey, Harry. *Sir Donald Cameron: Colonial Governor.* Stanford, 1974.
Gardner, Brian. *The Public Schools: An Historical Survey.* London, 1973.
Gollin, Alfred. *Balfour's Burden: Arthur Balfour and Imperial Preference.* London, 1965.
Grey, Earl. *The Colonial Policy of Lord John Russell's Administration.* Rpt of 1853 edn. New York, 1970.
Hamilton, Sir W. A. Baillie. *Mr. Montenello: A Romance of the Civil Service.* 3 vols. Edinburgh and London, 1885.
Hopkins, A. G. *An Economic History of West Africa.* London, 1973.
Hyam, Ronald, *Elgin and Churchill at the Colonial Office, 1905–1908: The Watershed of the Empire-Commonwealth.* London, 1968.
Ikime, Obaro. *The Fall of Nigeria: The British Conquest.* London, 1977.
Joyce, R. B. *Sir William MacGregor.* Melbourne, 1971.
Kesner, Richard M. *Economic Control and Colonial Development: Crown Colony Financial Management in the Age of Joseph Chamberlain.* Westport, Conn., 1981.
Kirk-Greene, A. H. M. (ed.). *The Principles of Native Administration in Nigeria: Selected Documents.* London, 1965.
Kubicek, Robert. *The Administration of Imperialism: Joseph Chamberlain at the Colonial Office.* Durham, N.C., 1969.
Lowell, A. Lawrence. *The Government of England.* 2 vols. New York, 1908.
Lyttelton, Edith. *Alfred Lyttelton: An Account of His LIfe.* London, 1917.
Lyttelton, Oliver, Viscount Chandos. *The Memoirs of Lord Chandos.* London, 1962.
Mack, Edward C. *Public Schools and British Opinion since 1860: The Relationship between Contemporary Ideas and the Evolution of an English Institution.* Rpt of 1941 edn. Westport, Conn., 1971.
McPhee, Allan. *The Economic Revolution in British West Africa.* Rpt of 1926 edn. London, 1971.
Mansergh, Nicholas. *The Commonwealth Experience.* New York, 1969.

Newbury, C. W. *British Policy towards West Africa: Selected Documents, 1875–1914.* Oxford, 1971.
Nicolson, I. F. *The Administration of Nigeria, 1900–1960: Men, Methods, and Myths.* Oxford, 1969.
Olivier, Margaret (ed.) *Sydney Olivier: Letters and Selected Writings.* London, 1948.
Parkinson, Sir Cosmo. *The Colonial Office from Within: 1909–1945.* London, 1947.
Payton-Smith, D. J. *Oil: A Study of War-time Policy and Administration.* London, 1971.
Perham, Margery. *Lugard: The Years of Adventure, 1858–1898.* London, 1956.
—— *Lugard: The Years of Authority, 1898–1945.* London, 1960.
Ponsonby, Arthur. *The Decline of Aristocracy.* London, 1912.
Porter, Bernard. *The Lion's Share: A Short History of British Imperialism.* London and New York, 1955.
Robinson, Ronald, and John Gallagher, with Alice Denny. *Africa and the Victorians: The Official Mind of Imperialism.* London, 1961.
Sanders, C. R. *The Strachey Family: Their Writings and Literary Associations.* Durham, N.C., 1953.
Swettenham, Frank. *British Malaya.* London, 1920.
Tamuno, T. N. *The Evolution of the Nigerian State: The Southern Phase, 1898–1914. London, 1972.*
Temple, C. L. *Native Races and Their Rulers.* Cape Town, 1918.
Weinberg, Ian. *The English Public Schools: The Sociology of Elite Education.* New York, 1967.
Winstanley, D. A. *Later Victorian Cambridge.* Cambridge, 1947.
Young, G. M. *Victorian England: Portrait of An age.* 2 edn. London, 1960.

B. Articles and Lectures

Afigbo, A. F. 'The Establishment of Colonial Rule, 1900–1918'. In *History of West Africa,* ed. by J. F. A. Ajayi and Michael Crowder. Vol. 2. London, 1974.
Bridges, Sir Edward. *Treasury Control.* The Stamp Memorial Lecture. London, 1950.
Brooks, Sydney. 'Great Britain, the Empire, and Oil'. *Nineteenth Century,* LXXIV (1918) 689–701.
Bull, Mary. 'Indirect Rule in Northern Nigeria, 1906–1911'. In *Essays in Imperial Government,* ed. by Kenneth Robinson and Frederick Madden. Oxford, 1963.
Burton, Ann. 'Treasury Control and Colonial Policy in the Late Nineteenth Century'. *Public Administration,* XLIV (1966) 169–92.
Dumett, R. E. 'Joseph Chamberlain, Imperial Finance and Railway Policy in British West Africa in the Late Nineteenth Century'. *English Historical Review,* XC (1975) 287–321.
'Editorial Notes'. *Colonial Office Journal,* 2 (1908) 10–12.

Flint, John E. 'Frederick Lugard: The Making of an Autocrat'. In *African Proconsuls: European Governors in Africa*, ed. by L. H. Gann and Peter Duignan. New York, 1978.
——— 'Nigeria: The Colonial Experience from 1880 to 1914'. In *The History and Politics of Colonialism: 1870–1914.* Vol. 1 of *Colonialism in Africa, 1870–1960*, ed. by L. H. Gann and Peter Duignan. Cambridge, 1969.
Gallagher, John, and Robinson, Ronald. 'The Imperialism of Free Trade'. *Economic History Review*, Second Series, 6 (1953) 1–15.
Hamilton, Sir W. A. Baillie. 'Forty-Four Years at the Colonial Office'. *Nineteenth Century and After*, LXV (1909) 599–613.
Helsby, L. N. 'Recruitment to the Civil Service'. *Political Quarterly*, XXV (1954) 324–35.
Joyce, R. B. 'Sir William MacGregor – A Colonial Governor'. *Historical Studies: Australia and New Zealand*, XI (1963) 18–31.
Hopkins, A. G. 'The Creation of a Colonial Monetary System: The Origins of the West African Currency Board'. *African Historical Studies*, III, no. 1 (1970) 101–32.
Kesner, Richard M. 'Builders of Empire: The Role of the Crown Agents in Imperial Development, 1880–1914'. *Journal of Imperial and Commonwealth History*, 5 (1977) 310–30.
Kirk-Greene, Anthony H. M. (compiler). 'Introduction'. *Lugard and the Amalgamation of Nigeria: A Documentary Report*. London, 1968.
——— 'On Governorship and Governors in British Africa'. In *African Proconsuls: European Governors in Africa*, ed. by L. H. Gann and Peter Duignan. New York, 1978.
Madden, Frederick. 'Changing Attitudes and Widening Responsibilities, 1895–1914'. In *The Empire-Commonwealth, 1870–1919.* Vol. 1 of *The Cambridge History of the British Empire*, ed. by E. A. Benians, Sir James Butler, and C. E. Carrington. Cambridge, 1967.
Milne, A. Taylor (compiler). 'Bibliography'. *The Empire-Commonwealth: 1870–1919.* Vol. III of *The Cambridge History of the British Empire*, ed. by E. A. Benians, Sir James Butler, and C. E. Carrington. Cambridge, 1967.
Nworah, Kenneth Dike. 'The Liverpool "Sect" and British West African Policy, 1895–1915'. *African Affairs*, LXX (1971) 349–64.
Omosini, Olufemi. 'Railway Projects and British Attitude toward the Development of West Africa, 1872–1903'. *Journal of the Historical Society of Nigeria*, V, (1971) 491–507.
Pugh, R. B. 'The Colonial Office, 1801–1925', *The Empire-Commonwealth: 1870–1919.* Vol. III of *The Cambridge History of the British Empire*, ed. by E. A. Benians, Sir James Butler, and C. E. Carrington. Cambridge, 1967.
Robinson, Ronald. 'Sir Andrew Cohen: Proconsul of African Nationalism'. In *African Proconsuls: European Governors in Africa*, ed by L. H. Gann and Peter Duignan. New York, 1978.
Saul, S. B. 'The Economic Significance of "Constructive Imperialism" '. *Journal of Economic History*, XVIII (1957) 173–92.
Snelling, R. C. and T. O. Barron. 'The Colonial Office and its Permanent Officials, 1801–1914'. *Studies in the Growth of Nineteenth-Century Government*, ed. by Gillian Sutherland. London, 1972.

Wilson, Sir Harry. 'Joseph Chamberlain as I Knew Him'. *United Empire: The Royal Colonial Institute Journal*, New Series, VIII (1917) 102–11.
Uzoigwe, G. N. 'The Niger Committee of 1898: Lord Selborne's Report'. *Journal of the Historical Society of Nigeria*, 4 (1968) 467–76.

C. Theses

Carland, John M. 'Colonial Office Staff and Nigeria, 1898–1914'. Ph.D. diss., University of Toronto, 1977.
Kesner, Richard M. 'The Financial Management of the British Empire, 1895–1903: Studies in Treasury–Colonial Office Relations'. Ph.D. diss., Stanford University, 1977.

Index